Listening to God:
Inspirational Stories
for My Grandchildren

Rabbi Shlomo Riskin

LISTENINGtoGOD

INSPIRATIONAL STORIES FOR MY GRANDCHILDREN

Maggid Books

Listening to God: Inspirational Stories for My Grandchildren

First Edition, 2010
Maggid Books
An imprint of Koren Publishers Jerusalem Ltd.

POB 8531, New Milford, CT 06676-8531, USA
POB 2455, London W1A 5WY, England
& POB 4044, Jerusalem 91040, Israel

www.korenpub.com

Published in cooperation with Ohr Torah
Stone Colleges & Graduate Programs

ISBN 978 159 264 292 2, *hardcover*

A CIP catalogue record for this title is
available from the British Library

Printed in USA

This book is lovingly dedicated to our beloved grandchildren

Yosef, Mevaseret, Naomi and Akiva Jacobs
Avishai, Amiel and Elai HaKohanim Feder
Eden Barkai, Yaal David and Saar Ari HaKohanim Riskin
Shalev Hod Harel, Maayan Ivri, Nehora Yafit,
Shoham Ahava and Carmi Rut HaKohanim Riskin

for whom these stories were originally written and who are the lights of our lives and the continuity of our beings.

As is true of everything else in my life, they would never be were it not for my beloved life partner, Vicky.

Ohr Torah Stone Partner-Donors

Ohr Torah Stone Institutions, which have revolutionized Israeli society as well as Jewish education worldwide, would not have been possible without our Partner-Donors, who have shared the dreams and made them a reality through their material largesse, planning and direction. Space allows us to mention only those who have given names to schools and campuses, but we are eternally grateful to each and every one of our contributors.

Irving Stone *z"l* Morry & Judy Weiss	Ohr Torah Stone Institutions
Robert M. Beren	Israel Henry Beren Academic Center Robert M. Beren College Ethel and Adolph Beren Educators Institute
Zalman Bernstein *z"l*	Beit Yaakov Leib Institute for Jewish Experience
Belda & Marcel Lindenbaum	Midreshet Lindenbaum Women's College and Graduate School
Stanley & Raine Silverstein	Chana and Yaakov Tilles Women's College Campus
Gwendolyn Straus *z"l* Moshael & Daniel Straus	Joseph and Gwendolyn Straus Rabbinical Seminary, Yeshivat Torat Yosef
Rabbi Joseph & Stera Gutnick	Kiryat Shoshana Rabbinical Village
Bernard Goldberg	Monica Dennis Goldberg Women's Advocates Institute
Ron Perelman	Claudia Cohen Women Educators' Institute

Warren & Jane Weiss	Diane Hope Weiss Advanced Talmud Institute for Women
Fred & Susan Ehrman	Neveh Shmuel High School Neveh Channah High School
Marvin & Miriam Belsky	Ann Belsky Moranis Institute for Arts and Drama
Roger & Susan Hertog	Susan and Roger Hertog Center for Jewish-Christian Understanding

May every one of our Donor-Partners continue to have much *naḥat* from the student-leaders educated in our institutions.

Tribute to Jerome Stern

The publication of this book was made possible by the generosity of Jerome Stern, a beloved friend and supporter for almost five decades. His involvement with me and my dreams began in the early days of Lincoln Square Synagogue, where he served as Vice President and attended services and Torah lectures every week together with his growing family. It continued as he became a trustee of the original Ohr Torah Schools in Riverdale and Queens, and extended to his unwavering support of our municipality of Efrat (he was present at the laying of the cornerstone in February 1981) and of the Ohr Torah Stone Institutions that developed in its wake.

Jerome is a regal patrician with a common touch, a throw-back to the aristocratic medieval patrons of the arts and artists, of religion and religionists, of Israel and its institutions. I am deeply grateful to have benefited from his warm friendship, guidance and personal concern, his overwhelming hospitality in Westhampton – which has extended to my children and grandchildren whom he continues to influence deeply – and to the very special relationship of our families, which I hope will continue to develop through the generations.

≈

Jerome is a dedicated son of very special parents. His father, David S. Stern, was a Hungarian yeshiva student who became a successful businessman in America. He was most patriotic toward his adopted country and was a passionate Zionist who truly loved Israel; he always remained faithful to the Jewish traditions. Most of all, however, he was a loving and devoted husband and father. Jerome's mother, Henriette Abraham Stern, was an outspoken individualist who, much ahead of her time, believed in the importance of a sound mind in a sound body. She taught all of her children and grandchildren the regimen of regular exercise, healthful diet and moderation in every aspect of life. She was blessed with a generous spirit and an honest tongue; the only one she held in reverential awe was the Lord God Himself. Their example continues to influence their grandchildren and great-grandchildren.

The words in this volume are offered as a tribute to the memory of David S. and Henriette Stern.

Contents

PART IX:

COMING HOME 1983–PRESENT

God is My Partner in Building Torah

Embattled in My New Home

Acknowledgements

First and foremost, I must thank a good friend and a leading resident of Efrat, Toby Klein Greenwald, who originally suggested the writing of this book and who initially taped, transcribed and edited its first draft. My very intelligent, unflappable and charming administrative aide, Micky Mirvis, was greatly involved in the organization of the text from its origin to its present state, with the help of Sue Epstein and Deena Angstreich who did much of the typing. And of course the final product would never have been produced without the guidance and shepherding of my beloved friend Matthew Miller, Publisher of Koren Publishers Jerusalem, and Rachel Meghnagi who edited the manuscript with expertise and elegance.

Finally my vocation as chancellor of Ohr Torah Stone Institutions, for whose twenty-fifth anniversary celebration this book has been completed, would certainly not have been as fortuitous had it not been for the tireless and productive expertise of my beloved brother-in-law, Dr. Roy Stern, Israeli Chairman of the Board; Yinon Aḥiman, CEO extraordinaire; and David Katz, International Director of Development without peer.

Author's Note

Somewhat of a Disclaimer

INSPIRED BY MATTHEW &
BENNETT LINDENBAUM

There are some stories that actually happened but are not true, and there are some stories that are true but did not actually happen.

There are stories that actually happened but are not true, because they are not significant, because they never left a lasting mark and so they are lost in the sands of time as though they never happened. And there are stories that may not have actually happened exactly as reported, either because the author has changed the names and places so as not to reveal unwelcome details or because the author may remember the story as having occurred in a certain way, different from the way it actually happened. But he, and others, were greatly affected by the story as he remembered it, and as he retold it.

Memory, after all, often creates a life and a story of its own. And so the stories in this book are true; they happened, not necessarily exactly as described, but rather in the way that the author remembers them.

Introduction

Life as a Series of Divine Messages

Many ask the question, "Where is God? How can I find Him?" The wonderful answer attributed to the famed Rebbe Menaḥem Mendel of Kotzk is, "God is to be found wherever you let Him in."

I truly believe that the Kotzker Rebbe is correct. The Bible teaches us that at least since the great Divine Revelation at Sinai, the Almighty continues to communicate: "A great voice that never ceases" (Deuteronomy 5:19, *Targum* there). The Hebrew word for divine speech is *Middaber* (Numbers 7:89), which is a reflexive form meaning that God is constantly "speaking to Himself," as it were, constantly emitting divine messages. And from a kabbalistic perspective, the Eternal and Infinite One (*Ein Sof*) is always emanating rays of splendorous light, ready to be accepted by anyone who is properly prepared to receive the divine emanation (Kabbala).

From this point of view, the most important challenge before each of us is sensitizing our hearts, minds and souls to be able to accept the divine emanations – from wherever they may be coming. We learn from Moses that God can sometimes communicate to us from a lowly, prickly thorn bush, and we learn from Balaam that God can even communicate to us from the mouth of a donkey. Rabbeinu Tzaddok, the famed Pri Tzaddik of Lublin, records how he learned one of the most important lessons of his life from a Gentile Polish peasant, who asked his help to gather the hay that had fallen to the ground when his wagon collapsed. "I can't," said the Pri Tzaddik. "You mean you won't," said the peasant farmer. "If you wanted to, you would be able to." What an important lesson he felt that God had taught him through the mouth of a Polish peasant!

And the God-messages can often come from individuals who play the role of God-messengers, or God's angels, even unbeknownst to them. When the biblical Joseph went in search of his brothers, and could not find them – an anonymous person pointed out to Joseph the direction toward which his siblings had gone, to Dotan. Rashi suggests that this unnamed individual was the angel Gabriel, literally a "man of God" (*gavri-el*). The Ramban (Nahmanides) adds that he was only a mortal, flesh-and-blood human being, through whose help Joseph met up with his brothers, landed up in Egypt and fulfilled God's will and prophecy – the Israelite enslavement and subsequent redemption. The world is filled with God-messages and God-messengers who are there to communicate with and direct us. Our challenge is to accept their teaching and hear their words.

I agree with Harry Potter's Professor Dumbledore that it is the decisions we make, rather than the intellectual gifts with which we are endowed, that are ultimately the measure of the human being and the life that one lives. These decisions express a partnership: God's messages and the individual's ability to correctly perceive and utilize them. I have always believed that God has sent me messages through special individuals, special moments, special experiences. It is these divine messages that I have attempted to record in this book. If my grandchildren, and other people's grandchildren, will be inspired by these stories to see God in their lives as well – and, even more importantly, to look for Him in every nook and cranny, then I shall have been more than rewarded for my efforts. And, of course, wherever I have been found wanting, it was not because of the lack of divine messages, but rather because of my inability to receive, perceive and utilize them properly.

Shlomo Riskin

Part I

Childhood Models 1940–56

Chapter One

My Grandmother – The First Angel in My Life

I had amazing grandparents, on both sides, and they had a strong impact on my early life.

My maternal grandmother was Ḥaya Beila bat Rav Shlomo HaKohen and Mindel, but everyone called her Baltcha, a diminutive of Beila. She was, indeed, a diminutive woman, this matriarch of the family, and gentle, but very strong-minded and deeply respected by my grandfather and all of their progeny. They had seven children, but, as was typical for that generation, not one of them was observant.

It was the first half of the twentieth century in America. There were few day schools and therefore, despite her piety, none of her children had the opportunity to study Torah properly, a Torah that they identified with the old world they had left behind and wanted to trade in for America. But she prayed three times a day and she was very learned. I grew up thinking that all European women were learned, indeed, even knew Gemara (Talmud)! I grew close to her in a very special way.

We lived in the Bedford Stuyvesant section of Brooklyn, in a small one-bedroom apartment at 103 Hart Street, between Tompkins and Marcy. Today it looks like a burnt-out war zone. The neighborhood has degenerated into street gangs and racial "warfare." My parents were quite poor, but they sent me to a Jewish day school because it was much better than the local public schools. I was the oldest son of the youngest of my grandmother's seven children.

My grandmother lived two blocks away at 128 Vernon Avenue, corner of Tompkins, in a house that my uncle had purchased for her. He was the one uncle who was very successful in business – Uncle Dave. My grandmother lived in that house from the time that she joined my grandfather in America until perhaps ten years before her death, at age ninety.

Grandma saw a unique opportunity when I started attending yeshiva day school. She offered to supply the meat for the house if my mother would keep a kosher home. So my mother became the only one of the seven children to keep a kosher home. My grandmother took me to yeshiva every morning herself, and picked me up from there every afternoon.

When I was eight, my grandfather had a massive stroke, and was moved to a convalescent home. Because I was really the light of her life, the family felt strongly that I should at least spend Friday evening with my grandmother, thinking that perhaps that would get her out of the doldrums over my grandfather's illness and she would eat something, as she was almost on a food strike.

From ages eight to sixteen I spent every Friday evening and every festival evening with her. As the only grandchild who attended a yeshiva, and as her only progeny involved in the Jewish religion, I naturally became the *naches*, the joy of Grandma's existence. Friday evening was our special time together: I would arrive about half an hour before candle-lighting, help her remove the Yiddish newspapers from the scrubbed linoleum floor, and gaze intently as she would *bentsh licht*, bless the candles, for at least twenty minutes. Her face framed by the flames, her eyes shut tight, I watched Grandma speaking to God, happily mentioning the successes and tearfully mentioning the problems of each family member in turn. I once thought of writing a book about her; I would call it, "God Was My Psychiatrist." She spoke to Him, she remonstrated with Him, she cried to Him, she argued with Him, she thanked Him. She seemed to be talking to a very beloved and respected friend for twenty minutes every Friday evening just before sunset.

Then we would sit and pray together, sitting on opposite sides of the candelabrum. We went through *Kabbalat Shabbat* and *Ma'ariv*, the welcoming of Shabbat and the evening prayers. And then we ate together and sang *zemirot* (Shabbat songs) together between each portion, which she would bring to the table with a flourish, declaring, "In honor of the holy Sabbath" ("*likhvod Shabbos Kodesh*"). During the delectable meal ("*Shloimele, tayere,* dear one, take my *kneidl.* I don't need to get fat, and you need the strength to study Torah," this eighty-pound woman would say to me in Yiddish), she would reminisce about life in the *shtetl* Lubien, and, after a while, its streets and inhabitants became more real to me than those of Bedford-Stuyvesant. My great-grandfather Shlomo HaKohen, her father, was a Dayan, a rabbinical judge, in the small town of Lubien. According to the family story he lived to be 115.

After dinner we would study the biblical portion of the week with *Yiddish Teitsch,* a marvelous translation-commentary, replete with miracle stories and moral lessons culled from midrashic literature. I treasured those personal Friday evenings even more than the gala family gatherings, when I was merely one of many – and one of the younger ones at that.

I went back to Lubien much later, in 1994. There I found an elderly woman, Helene Michallak, who knew the whole family because her father had been the mayor of Lubien. She didn't tell me that my great-grandfather lived to be 115, but she said, "Oh, Rabina Kowalski. Rabina Kowalski was a very, very old man. Even the Gentiles in the area came to him for a blessing for long life." He had three consecutive wives, as he had been widowed twice. My grandmother was the eldest daughter from the first wife and there were three other daughters who came after her; in the absence of sons, my great-grandfather taught Baltcha. First he taught her *Ḥumash* (Pentateuch), then the commentaries on the *Ḥumash,* then Mishna. He saw she had an open mind and so he began to teach her Gemara as well. She always smiled when she told me the secret, the special privilege she had to study with him. She said it with *hislayves,* with enthusiasm – the fact that she had learned that which only men learned in those days. As a result, my first Gemara teacher was Grandma Baltcha.

My great-grandfather Shlomo dealt in oats and hay, *huber* and *hey* in Yiddish. He never took a salary for his communal position as the Dayan in Lubien. At that time there were three hundred families in the town, half of which were Jewish. There was a rabbi, Rav Petrovski, and the "*Rabbiner* over the *rabbiner*" who was my great-grandfather (according to Helene Michallak), the Dayan.

My great-grandfather was apparently a great scholar; there were always four young men from neighboring towns who would work and learn with him. And as my grandmother would tell me, they would wake up at twelve o'clock at night for *tikkun ḥatzot* (midnight prayer), after which they would study until daybreak. Just before sunrise they went to the *mikveh,* the ritual bath, after which they would *daven* (pray), reciting the *Amida* precisely at sunrise. Then they would labor with the hay and oats, more or less till midday. Apparently their compensation for the work was the learning. Among the young men was a gentleman named Ḥayyim Valter from Wloclawek, a city much larger than Lubien. He was from a wealthy family of very good pedigree, a direct descendant of the son-in-law of the Sefat Emet, and a devoted Gerer Hasid. My grandmother also studied with my great-grandfather in the afternoons when he had finished working and learning with his students, but she was always anxious to study more. So she would lie in wait after *tikkun ḥatzot,* not far from where my grandfather would study with the young men, and she would listen to the Torah, hoping she would not be noticed.

She saw that when the young men studied, they put their *tefillin* (phylacteries) on a sheet spread out on the ground. She felt this was disrespectful to the holy objects, so she strung out a clothesline and she would hang the *tefillin* up on it every night. Apparently Ḥayyim Valter noticed her and he fell in love. He had been engaged to a very wealthy young woman, who also lived in the big city of Wloclawek, whom he had met only once. As my grandmother would blushingly tell it (at age eighty plus), he loved her sensitivity to the *tefillin* and he loved her interest in learning Torah. She was also a very beautiful young girl. He told his father he wanted to marry Rav Shlomo Kowalski's eldest daughter, and – despite a considerable financial loss – the previous engagement was broken. My grandmother always told me that she really believed that whatever good fortune she had in life was because of her sensitivity to the *tefillin* and her love of Torah. And she did have a very profound love relationship with my grandfather all their lives.

When my grandfather was in the convalescent home after his stroke, I remember my grandmother saying to my mother that she wanted to buy a dress. My mother was a little bit surprised; Grandma was hardly eating and she wanted to buy a new dress? That wasn't like her at all. I tagged along and saw my grandmother pick out a flaming red dress. My mother said to my grandmother: "Mama, *ès past nisht,* it's not appropriate. How can you wear a dress like this?" With the tears rolling down her cheeks, my grandmother said, "*Mayn Ḥam,*" (she always called Ḥayyim, her husband, 'Ḥam'). "*Mayn Ḥam* always liked me in red. Maybe he'll see me in the dress and he'll wake up from the slumber he is in." I do not remember either of my grandparents speaking a harsh word – not to each other nor to anyone else. And until my grandfather became ill, I cannot remember seeing them apart from each other. I learned from my grandmother how important it is to teach women Torah. Indeed, she probably inspired my own dedication to women's learning – Ohr Torah Stone's women's *yeshivat hesder* and school for women-advocates in the religious courts. I learned from my grandmother how important it is to love and respect the person you marry. I also learned from her much more. She was undoubtedly the most dominant influence in my early life.

Chapter Two

Grandma and "The Goy"

More than a decade of Thanksgivings ago, my eldest daughter, Batya, announced her plans for aliya, immigration to Israel, and her intention to join the Israeli army. Since I did not know when next she would be in America for a protracted visit, and especially since the rest of the family was already planning its move to Efrat, Israel, I took my first-born on a ride back to Bedford-Stuyvesant, the Brooklyn neighborhood where her father had been born and raised.

Batya was named after my maternal grandmother. I wanted my daughter to walk through the house of her namesake, to catch the remnant of the sounds and the smells, the tastes and the tunes that had made the Jewish tradition alive and meaningful for me during my formative years.

But Thomas Wolfe was right: you can't go home again. Today the neighborhood most resembles a battleground, and grandmother's house, reduced to rubble, has become a playground for a local public school. So, no sounds, no smells, no tastes or tunes: just a vignette, here offered as a memorial to Grandma and her world, in the spirit of the Talmudic dictum: "The righteous require no monuments: their deeds are their most enduring monuments."

We thought of Grandma's house as the family home. My grandmother lived on the first floor, my aunt lived on the third floor, and on the second floor there was an apartment for family members or cousins who were just starting out in life and needed a place to live.

There was one room on that second floor that was occupied by an individual whose name I never knew. Everybody called him *"der goy"* (the Gentile). My grandmother also called him *"der goy."* I can picture him: short with very long ears and a vacant smile. When I was a child I thought at first he was a deaf-mute because he was at every important family or religious function, but he never spoke. Each Friday afternoon when I would arrive at my grandmother's house, I would meet "the goy" carrying his rent-envelope with a modest sum for his one room on the second floor, with bathroom (but no kitchen) privileges. He would always smile at me warmly, but he never spoke to me.

All my grandmother's seven children were married. Everyone had children and some even had grandchildren. The whole family would gather at my grandmother's home for Purim *se'uda,* for the Pesaḥ *seder,* and on at least one day of Ḥol HaMo'ed –the intermediary days – during Sukkot and Pesaḥ. We all got together for major birthdays. Whenever we had these very large family gatherings, *"der goy"* always sat in a place of honor, to the left of my grandfather (my grandmother always sat to her husband's right), and, after my grandfather's stroke, next to my grandmother. But obviously he never joined in the prayers or the family gossip. In fact, at these family gatherings he never spoke at all.

I eventually realized that he only spoke Polish because I heard him sometimes speaking to my grandmother or grandfather in this dialect. I understood that he was a Polish man who had needed a place to live. He put whatever payment he gave them in an envelope once a week. But I couldn't quite figure out why he was invited to all religious and family celebrations and why he had such an honored place. Perhaps he was the prophet Elijah, in masquerade, or a *gilgul,* a reincarnation of Balaam, the Gentile prophet of the Bible. I do remember, at one particular *seder,* watching him very intently as we opened the door for Elijah.

Anyway, I was about eleven and a half, and the neighborhood was becoming increasingly dangerous. One Sunday afternoon, when I was with my grandmother in the living room, my Uncle Dave sat my grandmother down and said that the neighborhood was impossible, that certainly she had to move and that he would arrange to move my grandmother, my aunt and my uncle to a much better site in a nicer area of Brooklyn. I heard him suggest Bensonhurst, on Bay Ridge Parkway. He had even located an apartment with an efficiency room because he knew my grandmother would always insist on cooking for herself. So she would have a room with a kitchenette, and my aunt and uncle would be able to live in much better accommodations while seeing to it that grandma would not be alone.

My grandmother thanked him very much, but said, "You have to give me a little time. I have to think about it." My uncle was a bit taken aback. "What do you have to think about?" he asked her. "The neighborhood is terrible, especially with old people being mugged left and right. What do you have to think about?" She said again, "I appreciate it, but you have to give me a little time."

After my uncle left, she explained herself to me: "Shloimele, of course I would like to move and it's important for your aunt and uncle to move, but what will happen to the Gentile? He's been living with us for forty years. He doesn't speak English. We'll have to find a place for the goy and then I can move. Come to me Friday after school." We were always dismissed from school early on Fridays, so that Friday I went straight to my grandmother's house.

We started combing the neighborhood, searching for "To Let" signs. There we were, an odd couple if ever there was one, a woman in her eighties and her grandson who was not quite twelve, looking for a room for "*der goy*." We climbed up high flights of stairs in houses, some of whose owners hardly seemed reputable. I was the translator because my grandmother didn't speak English. "I have to take care of the goy," she told me. "After all, I am a *tzitizen* (citizen). I love America; I love President Rosenfeld [*sic*]. I know my rights and I also know my obligations. America is a free country, but Judaism teaches that we must watch over each other. The goy is all alone. He only has me to help him."

We did it for four Fridays – an old Jewish woman and her young American grandson. It was the winter. It was cold, sometimes even icy, and difficult. But we continued seeking a home for "*der goy*." For me this was a lesson in what Judaism is really about. And I think it was that experience more than anything else that made me realize that her lifestyle and life values were exactly the kind of life I wanted to live myself.

Chapter Three

West Point and Kosher Muscle

I was about eight years old when a kosher-style Chinese restaurant opened up near our house. The area was changing rapidly, but there still were Jews living in the neighborhood, and at that time, Jews loved Chinese food.

My parents were keen to go out to eat and this restaurant was the rage of the neighborhood. I was anxious to join them, but first I felt I'd better call my grandmother, my religio-legal authority. "Can I eat in the new restaurant?" I asked. My grandmother said, "*Mayn kind*, my child, if it's kosher-style, you can't eat. You can only eat if it's really kosher and it has rabbinic supervision." I asked her why it was so important that Jews have to eat kosher. She said to me, "Well you want to be big and strong. If you want to be big and strong, you have to eat only kosher food." I was nonathletic and rather short and round. I very, very much wanted to be big and strong. I even used to do exercises that she taught me, to stretch my limbs. To the best of my knowledge, from that telephone call on, I never ate anything that was not kosher. I strongly internalized the message: if I wanted to be strong, I'd have to eat kosher.

Time went by; I was a student in Yeshiva University and made the varsity debating team. The first debate on the schedule was with West Point Military Academy. It was exciting for me; it was really my first real trip away from home. Two friends and I (interestingly, both of them now live in Israel) were on the debating team, so we made the trip together to West Point.

It was on a Sunday and apparently there was a whole scheduled program. It began with a tour of the magnificent campus, continued with a local football game, and ended with a special steak-and-fries Sunday dinner. I had never seen such a thick steak in my life, nor such generous portions. The "powers that were" in West Point had been coached in advance, so the three Orthodox Jewish debaters, forbidden from eating the non-kosher beef, were given instead two whole cucumbers and tomatoes on paper plates with plastic utensils.

Then came the debate in front of the entire military academy. Debate etiquette insists that the visitors shake hands with the home team, so the three of us shook hands with our three opponents. My nose reached, perhaps, to the navel of my opponent. I can still feel the way my bones crunched when I extended my trembling hand and he took my hand in his. And I must admit that what went through my mind at that moment was, "Grandma, you lied to me! I ate the cucumbers and tomatoes, he ate the T-bone steak, and he's much bigger and stronger than me. What happened?" Apparently, *kashrut* wasn't working for me in the way my grandmother had told me it would.

In the end, we won the debate. But even if we hadn't, I understood as a result of that experience that *kashrut* laws may not make you big and strong, but they can teach you to say "no" to something you would like to have but shouldn't – either because it's not yours, or because it's not really good for you, ethically, morally or Jewishly. Yes, from that perspective *kashrut* does make you big and strong. It gives you bigness of soul and strength of character.

Grandma was right, after all.

Chapter Four

Elijah the Prophet on Willoughby Avenue

The Talmud (in the ninth chapter of *Massekhet* [Tractate] *Berakhot*) speaks about the interpretations of dreams. The rabbinical sages explain that the way you interpret the dream is ultimately the way it turns out to be (*hakol holekh aḥar hapeh*). We all understand that there are self-defeating prophecies, and self-affirming prophecies. If you give a positive interpretation, then very often a positive interpretation emerges in life; if you give a negative interpretation, if a person goes around feeling he's doomed, he may well, God forbid, become doomed.

I consider myself a rationalist, a student of Rav Soloveitchik and of the Rambam (Maimonides). But let me tell you a story. I must have been nine or ten years old. I was going to an Orthodox day school and loved it. And although I learned about the Jewish holidays, since there was no school in the summer time, we didn't learn about Tisha B'Av (the ninth day of the Hebrew month of Av, when we fast and lament the destruction of both Holy Temples). I imagine now, thinking back, there were certain things my grandmother didn't tell me; for instance, she did not tell me about Tisha B'Av because she knew my mother would not be happy about me fasting at my very young age. There has to be a certain kind of balance in these situations. My mother considered herself a "modern" woman, and she was not an Orthodox Jewish woman for most of her life. (Toward the end of her life she moved here to Efrat and she did become more observant.) But I think that when I was young, she was even a little anti-religious.

When I had been married for a few months I developed terrible kidney stones. I was in pain, and, of course, my mother came to our new apartment to see what she could do to help.

I loved Yiddish (I still do), and Vicky, my wife, who also did not come from an observant background, wanted to learn the language that gave me such pleasure. She knew how much I loved it and she felt some kind of a tie to it as well. So, since I didn't feel well, and we were home together that Sunday, the radio was tuned to WEVD, *which was then broadcast in Yiddish. I especially loved Yiddish music, which always had the effect of calming me, and since I was in pain, listening to a Yiddish radio station was the logical thing for us to do.*

My mother walked into the apartment and she stood as if shell-shocked. I said, "Mom, what's wrong?" She stood there and she said, "I just don't believe it. You know, when I was a little girl I went to public school. I would never bring any of my Christian or even my 'Yankee' American friends home with me because – now it's almost difficult for me to admit it – I was ashamed. WEVD, *the Yiddish radio station, was always on in my parents' house, and I was embarrassed at the European Yiddishism it represented. I wanted more than anything else to be American! But I certainly never dreamt then that I would have a son and daughter-in-law who would be listening to* WEVD.*" My mother, like most first generation Jews in America, associated religion with old-worldism. I represented the beginning of the generation of "return to tradition" that took place, thank God, mainly due to the day-school movement and the youth groups (Bnei Akiva, Agudah Pirchei) that were beginning to spring up. And so my involvement with Judaism, with the active encouragement of my grandmother, nevertheless had the potential of creating delicate parent-child tensions that my wise grandmother tried to avoid. Hence she probably never told me about the restrictions of the Nine Days leading up to Tisha B'Av, when eating meat is forbidden, nor about the fast of Tisha B'Av, because she felt that these were the kinds of observances that my mother would have objected to. They would have caused a minor revolution in the way my mother prepared meals for my father and for the rest of the family during the Nine Days period, and certainly my fasting would not have gone down too well.*

By that time I was *davening* in a small Hasidic *shtiebl* down the block from where I lived. The Rebbe, Rav Gottesman, knew I was serious. When he informed me of the approaching fast day called Tisha B'Av in commemoration of the destruction of both Holy Temples, I decided I was not going to eat. I wasn't going to tell my parents, and I wasn't going to say anything to my grandmother because I felt that if she hadn't said anything to me, she had somehow decided that it wasn't time yet for me to know about it.

I was only nine or ten at the time and I wanted to do something that was "Tisha B'av-*ish*." I was already studying Gemara at the Yeshiva of Brooklyn, with the older boys of twelve and thirteen, and that year my class had studied the tractate dealing with damages, mostly against one's animals, called *Bava Kamma*.

The Yeshiva of Brooklyn was housed in a large and mostly deserted synagogue on the corner of Throop and Willoughby. After praying in the *shtiebl* on the morning of Tisha B'Av, I took a walk to the Yeshiva and decided I would spend the day reviewing some of the Gemara that I had learned that last year.

I was sitting and studying the tractate of *Bava Kamma* when a tall, stately man walked in. I can still picture him. He was wearing a black frock coat (*kaputa*), with a black *kippa* – a yarmulke, not a hat – and the *kaputa* was torn on the right side, which is a sign of mourning for anyone or anything other than the loss of a parent (when we make the tear on the left side). He sat next to me and put his arm around me. He had a beard and *pe'ot* (sidelocks), which was a rarity in our neighborhood at the time.

He said to me, "You know, you're not supposed to study regular Torah on Tisha B'Av, because Torah brings joy to a person's life. This is a day of mourning; let's study something else," and he took out the Tractate *Gittin* and he started studying with me. For the first time I heard the story of Kamtza and Bar Kamtza, which is a story illustrating how the Second Temple was destroyed because of baseless hatred between Jews. We must have spent three or four hours learning that whole passage. The time passed very rapidly. Not only were the stories of the Destruction riveting, but he taught them as if he himself had actually been there. The priestly service of the Temple, the very stones of the altar, that entire historical period, came alive – it was magical.

Then he kissed me on the forehead and recited the *Birkat Kohanim* (priestly blessing) over me. He then said, "With God's help, you'll be a rabbi in Israel," and he quickly left the synagogue.

I went back to my grandmother. She was at home, fasting. She was lying down, actually, and I told her the story. My grandmother's reaction was very odd. First of all, she started spitting in my eye. I couldn't imagine what was happening, and then she explained that it was in order to ward off the "Evil Eye." I was surprised because usually my grandmother was very rational. And then she said to me, with tears of joy in her eyes, "I believe you met Eliyahu HaNavi" – Elijah the Prophet – "and you are going to be a rabbi." Did I really meet Elijah, or didn't I? Was it only a dream, or merely a meeting with a very kind Talmud scholar? Whichever it was, that event and my grandmother's interpretation of it left an indelible impression on me, and had a significant influence on my development. And just as I had never seen the tall, stately gentleman with the torn *kaputa* before that Tisha B'Av, nor did I ever see him in the neighborhood afterwards.

Chapter Five

From Budapest with Love (A Letter to My Communist-Atheist Grandfather)

I had strong familial influences in addition to my grandmother. My paternal grandfather was an avid, intellectual, idealistic Communist, who wrote a regular column for the Yiddish Communist newspaper, *Freiheit*. Here is the letter I wrote to him, after visiting a Budapest camp that transferred Russian Jews to Israel after the Communist regime fell and the Iron Curtain collapsed.

Dear Grandpa Shmuel,

When we used to publicly debate in Murray Bershad's *shvitz* on Myrtle Avenue, relaxing over schmaltz herring, baked potatoes, and wine with seltzer, after a goodly amount of time in the steam-room where we sweated, poured buckets of cold water over each other and took massages with leafy brooms, did you have any idea that your grandson would end up a rabbi? You, the passionate Communist standing up for everyone's rights – and I, not even bar-mitzvahed, trying to match your Marx with my Moses, not so much a debate, but a chance to slug it out with words and feel very much like a grown-up. Your anti-religious views forced me to begin clarifying my thoughts, about God, Judaism, Torah. We didn't pray together, but we certainly sweated together when I'd join you on Saturday night for a session on philosophy and politics. You didn't agree with my Yeshiva ideology, but I could feel you were proud of my ability to analyze and debate, to speak with passion and commitment. And I was proud of you, a public speaker and writer, a Yiddish Communist intellectual who took his pre-adolescent grandson seriously and treated him very much like an adult. Before I knew it, you had me reading Marx, Engels and Lenin.

Because you hadn't stepped inside a synagogue since your own bar mitzva, attending Sabbath services when I turned thirteen proved a moral dilemma for you. On the Saturday night before my bar mitzva you told me that you would come to my party that next Saturday night, but that you wouldn't be in shul [synagogue] for my *Haftara* reading. You explained that you had taken an oath at your bar mitzva never to go into a shul again. I remember thinking, "But who did you make the oath to?" I was devastated; after all, you had even helped me with the Yiddish of the *pilpul* I had prepared with one of my yeshiva teachers, a Talmudic discourse of Reb Ḥayyim of Brisk on the Talmudic portion dealing with one who speaks out between putting on the *tefillin* of the hand and the *tefillin* of the head. How could you not come to hear me? Maybe you believed that religion was the opiate of the masses, which you quoted again and again, but I was your close grandson! I didn't say any of this to you, but I felt it in my heart, and I was bitterly disappointed. But then when you walked into the shul right before my *Haftara* reading to be followed with my *pilpul*, you made my bar mitzva day. No matter that you were carrying a brown paper bag in which were two books, the Communist Manifesto and the Constitution of the Soviet Union as my bar mitzva gifts! I even appreciated your intellectual honesty when you left shul before *Musaf* [additional prayer]. That is how you assuaged your conscience. I was proud of you – especially since I realized that you were also proud of me... but I received much more from you than books on Communism.

What I really received was the spirit of a man who sought answers to difficult problems and worked to share with others; an idealist who truly wished to redeem the world. If anyone in the family understands my move to Israel it should be you, even though as a Communist you had no room for a Jewish homeland. "Petty and parochial Nationalism," you called it, as you were swept along by the gods of a new world order in which all the workers would unite, and greed and God would be banished forever. You taught me to read Shalom Aleichem in the original because you wanted me to feel for the Jewish poor and to develop a distinctly Jewish sense of humor. Perhaps you also realized that if I ever seriously tackled Jewish study, Yiddish would be invaluable. And so the words you taught me on your knee, ironically enough, made it possible for me to study Torah with one of the great Talmudists of the century, Rav J.B. Soloveitchik, and set me on the path of a life dedicated to Torah and Israel. And you read, with me, passages from Isaiah, in Hebrew, which railed against the insensitivity of the religious establishment toward the widow, the orphan, the poor. You even studied portions of the Talmud with me, which insisted on the rights of the worker (*Bava Metzia, "HaSokher et HaUmanim"; "HaSokher et HaPo'alim"*). You may have been a heretic, an *apikores*, but you were far from an ignoramus, an *am ha'aretz*. You may have been an atheist, but strangely enough you still saw yourself as a proud Jew. And that pride I also received from you.

One of my profound memories goes back to the Saturday night right before you suffered your first heart attack. Reports of Communist purges had arrived, including the atrocities against the Jewish doctors, and even you, a staunch Stalinist who kept the Soviet premier's picture on the kitchen wall alongside that of

FDR, suddenly began to feel that the world you had adopted was experiencing an earthquake. All your life you had been a fervent believer, not just in theory through the articles you wrote for the *Freiheit*, the Yiddish Communist daily, but in practice. You practiced Communism in the way that a religious Jew practices Judaism: on a daily basis. The moment the woodwork and carpentry shop that you set up did well, you began to share profits among the workers. (Grandma Lena didn't speak to you for six months afterwards.) You truly believed, and now you felt you had been betrayed.

We were lying down after hours of steam that Saturday night. You were uncharacteristically quiet, preoccupied, and you began reminiscing about the Sabbath in your parents' home during the pre-revolution days, the Sabbath you rejected in favor of faith in a new world order (in which "God doesn't exist and Lenin is His prophet"). You wondered aloud to me, your religious grandson, with a catch in your throat, if perhaps you'd given up too much too soon.

Why am I writing this letter to you fifty years after you've died? I've just returned from a trip to Budapest, where I met with people involved in the drama of the Soviet Jewish exodus. The Keren Hayesod delegation I was traveling with visited a former Russian army camp transformed into a little Ellis Island, with room for a thousand people with beds and kitchens and medical facilities. As I walked through the vast hall, I found myself facing a man who reminded me of you, Grandpa Shmuel. A life-long Communist, he was now leaving his dreams behind. He explained that Communism had failed because it ignored individual human rights, and had miscalculated the tremendous power of nationalism. "People cannot sacrifice for a universal ideal that does not take into account individual human rights. And to ask for this sacrifice when the heads of government themselves were leading hedonistic and corrupt lifestyles was intolerable and unforgivable." I could hear you saying those words, Grandpa! While the man spoke, it struck me that if not for your idealism, I, too, may have been sitting in Budapest, waiting for my name to be called. I grew up in America, became religious, went to yeshiva, and came to Israel only because in your youth, you idealistically organized the workers in your own father's factory in Brisk that produced uniforms for the czar. You were arrested, banished to Siberia and managed, with great travail, to escape to America where you felt you could freely continue to work for your Communist dream for humanity. I am American-born because in 1907 you arrived in New York. Had you not been sent to Siberia, there would have been no reason for you to leave Russia. You would have stayed to see Marx's world become a reality. And your children and grandchildren, had we been fortunate and saved from the Nazi and Communist purges, might well now be in Budapest preparing to emigrate to Israel, after a lifetime of disillusion and disappointment.

Grandpa, yours was a false god, but I could never convince you it was false. Now before our eyes we see how fragile your all-powerful, omniscient Communist god really was. The Union of Soviet Socialist Republics has split apart. The Iron Curtain is nothing more than a veil. And if you were leaving Russia in 1991, wouldn't you thank God that there was one place in the world, one land, which accepted you with no questions asked? Budapest is beautiful. One Jewish museum, which is still there, testifies to its rich Jewish past. I walked inside a synagogue built in the first half of the nineteenth century, which seats five thousand people, with acoustics so clear that the rabbi could be heard from one end to the other without a microphone. But the Nazis wiped out the vast majority of Jews, and the Communists wore down those few who survived. And now, with the fall of the old regime, Jews are emerging from the woodwork, awakening to their long-lost heritage. Believe it or not, ex-Communist Budapest is going through a Jewish reawakening, and streets that hadn't seen signs of a visible Jew in decades have become a way station for the Jews from Mother Russia on their way to Israel.

There are very few, if any, Jews left on Myrtle Avenue; the *shvitz* has long since ceased to exist; and there are no more meeting places where old and young Jews debate questions of

> ideology. But if we could meet again Grandpa, I'd want more than anything in the world for you to tell me if you still think "Rabbi" Marx was a greater teacher than Rabbi Moses. And I'd like you to know that, despite the vast difference in our lifestyles, much of what is me has come from you.
>
> Your loving grandson, Shlomo

* * *

Among the earliest memories I can recall – I don't think I was older than four or five – is a time when Grandpa came to our apartment with a gift for me, a finely crafted wooden stool that he had made with his own hands. I was truly thrilled – and that stool remains in our family to this day. He was obviously pleased at how delighted I was with his gift. He sat me down on the stool, and began what I remember to be my first adult conversation. In a very serious way he told me that we're Kohanim, priests, descendants of Aaron, Moses' elder brother, the first Kohen in history. He told me that we bless the congregation during the festival prayers, that we must teach everyone the message of peace, that we were Jewish royalty. And he showed me how to form the fingers of each hand into the letter *shin*, which is a prerequisite for the blessing. He seemed truly overjoyed when I arranged my fingers perfectly in the prescribed manner on my first try. But as I grew older, I was perplexed as to why this atheist grandfather, who didn't even attend synagogue on Yom Kippur, would find the *Kehuna* (priesthood) so important.

My answer came about five years later. He and I were riding on the train to his apartment on Kings Highway in Crown Heights, Brooklyn. There were two elderly Hasidic Jews sitting across from us in our train compartment, a rare occurrence in those years. Three "toughs" entered the compartment and started laughing, taunting and jostling the Hasidim. Grandpa Shmuel seemed to stop listening to whatever I was saying, staring intently at the other five members of our compartment. When the train came to its next stop, Grandpa (who was tall and strong as I remember him) suddenly lunged forward, grabbed the three toughs and literally threw them off the train.

He then returned to his seat next to me as if nothing unusual had occurred, and resumed our conversation. "But Grandpa, why did you protect those Hasidim?" I asked. "You aren't even religious." "Yes," he responded, "I'm even against religion. But they are part of our family. One Jew must always stick up for another Jew." No, Grandpa Shmuel was not religious. But he was a proud member of the Jewish family, who was deeply connected to every aspect of our ideological and cultural history. Would that many religionists today have his commitment to every Jew and his identity with our history – including the *Kehuna*.

Chapter Six

Being One of the Gang

I lived in Bedford-Stuyvesant. I knew there were street gangs, but somehow I was never in a fight in my life. I'll try to explain why.

There was a little library in Tompkins Park, on Tompkins Avenue. The librarian was a short, heavyset woman. She liked me a lot. Every Friday, after I finished any special errands for my grandmother, I would go to the library. I'd always pick out four books, the limit that one was allowed to take out. I'd bring them back the next week and take out four new books.

The authors were arranged from A to Z and my goal was to finish all the books in the library. Needless to say, I never did, but I read Darwin when I was quite young. I read all of Pearl Buck and found it fascinating. I found the whole world of books fascinating. No, I never got to Herman Wouk.

The neighborhood toughs saw me as kind of an anomaly, this little religious kid with four books; the books were probably higher than my nose when I used to come home with them on Friday. There were no ball courts in our neighborhood, but "the guys" played stickball in the gutter, and they always asked me to be there for the choosing of the sides. Everybody wanted me on his side, but I was never actually given a chance to play; I never got to bat. I was terrible at sports, rather uncoordinated physically. But they wanted me on their side because they saw me as a "good luck mascot."

I told myself that I was just as happy sitting on the side and reading, but like any other nine- or ten-year-old, I longed to be a really accepted member of the team! But, you see, not only did I never get into a fight; I was also completely protected. The African Americans were not only my friends; they were my godfathers! And because of that, I always felt safe.

On Shabbat morning I would always go to shul. When I was very young, the principal of the yeshiva I attended, a remarkably wise and warm educator named Rav Menaḥem Manus Mandel would walk several miles from his home in Williamsburg (a very religious Hasidic neighborhood), pick me up in front of my house, and together we would walk to pray at the yeshiva. He would then take me to his home, 83 Wilson Street, for lunch, until his very gracious and elegant wife tragically passed away. The walks with Rav Mandel, as well as the Shabbat lunches, were unforgettable. (He always remained my model for what a real "rebbe" must be.) When I grew older, I went to a neighborhood *shtiebl* to pray, and would make it a point to meet my grandmother walking home from a different shul and wish her a "*Gut Shabbos.*" One Shabbat morning, just as I left my house on the way to shul, two African American boys about my own age asked me if I wanted to go roller-skating with them in Tompkins Park. At first I refused, explaining that I didn't own roller-skates. They said they had skates to lend me. I'm sure that I already knew then that roller-skating on Shabbat was a forbidden activity, but I don't remember feeling terribly conflicted. I had compartmentalized my "religious" life at my grandmother's house and in the yeshiva, from my more "secular" life at home, and so I saw the roller-skating offer as a great opportunity to become "one of the guys." We went roller-skating together and I felt very good.

On the way home from Tompkins Park, roller-skates slung over our shoulders, I spied my grandmother returning with some elderly women friends from her shul (Rav Burak, Congregation Ohel Moshe Hevra Tehillim). As I said, I didn't feel conflicted. And I did want to wish my grandmother a "*Gut Shabbos.*"

So there I was, the "*yeshiva bochur*" grandson, accompanied by two Gentile friends, roller-skates over my shoulder, embracing my grandmother.

She kissed me and wished me a "*Gut Shabbos*." But for the first time, she looked at me with terrible disappointment. I'd never, ever seen her look at me like that. She had always looked at me before with enormous pride. Now I even saw tears welling up in her eyes. That look made me understand what I had done. And I think that was the last time I was ever knowingly *mechallel Shabbos*, the last time I ever knowingly desecrated the Sabbath.

I think about that often, because when I picture standing before God's heavenly throne, after a hundred and twenty years, it is not His punishment that I fear. After all, God is biblically described as, "Hashem, Hashem, *kel raḥum veḥanun*" – the God of love, who loves you both before and after you sin, the God of infinite patience and forgiveness. I think of God with too much love to ever be fearful of Him or of His punishments; that, too, is one of the legacies I got from my grandmother. But I am desperately afraid that maybe He will be disappointed in me. I would never want God, or my grandmother, to ever again look at me in disappointment with tears welling up in their eyes.

On my graduation day from the Yeshiva of Brooklyn, I learned a lesson that helped me immeasurably in my quest not to disappoint my Parent in Heaven. The lesson is the importance of time, and how we must plan every day and every hour of the precious time that God gives us. The guest speaker was Rav Alexander Linchner, founder of Boys Town, Jerusalem, son-in-law of Mr. Mendlowitz, the head of Yeshiva Torah Vodaas (Vodaath), and the inspiring teacher of Rav Mandel, who was so crucial to my early religious development. He looked at us, young and eager, and told us the following mesmerizing analogy from the Ḥafetz Ḥayyim.

Life is like a post card. You begin to write, and you leave a great deal of space between the letters, words and lines. After all, the post card is large and you don't have all that much to say. But then, as you come toward the end of the card, you realize that it was smaller than you thought, and that you had more to say than you thought. So you squeeze the words together, and you squash the lines in a mad, last-minute attempt to get everything in. Most of the time, you don't succeed. Often you leave out your most important thought. Tragically, you sometimes don't even have room to sign your name.

Chapter Seven

Shabbat with My Mom

After Rav Mandel's wife passed away, I would eat Shabbat lunch at home. My father would usually go to work on Saturday and would then go to the Turkish bath. My sisters were still quite young, and would generally eat before I got home from shul. It became private time between my mother and me.

My mother was a very special woman in her own right. During this period (the very early 1950s), our neighborhood was going from bad to worse and all of my friends, and my parents' friends, had moved out – to Flatbush, Queens, Long Island or New Jersey.

Every Sunday morning my mother would cut out the "House for Sale" advertisements, and our family would spend Sunday afternoon traveling by bus and train (usually two of each) to house-hunt. My mother always found something wrong with every potential home – the living room was too small, the windows could too easily be entered by thieves, and so on – so we returned to Bed-Stuy, only to make a similar trek the following Sunday.

Years later I understood that we could not possibly have afforded any house, anywhere, at that time. My mother just didn't want us to think that we were too poor to move; she didn't want us to feel deprived. She preferred to have us think that she was just too fussy, and that's why we continued to live where we were.

On Shabbat afternoons we would eat cold leftovers from the evening before. My mother smoked just three cigarettes a day, one after each meal. So after lunch she would smoke and we would sit and talk, and she would discuss everything, from family to politics. We really bonded during those lunches.

I was still in yeshiva elementary school, but by this time I had a Shabbat friend who was religious and who lived a few blocks away. His father was a rabbi in the area, presiding over a shul, most of whose congregants had moved away. His name is Sholem (Saul) Berman and he's now a leading rabbi, teacher and thinker, and we have remained good friends to this day. I would spend every Shabbat afternoon, after lunch, in his house.

And a fascinating household it was. His father, the rabbi, would be seated with his wife and children around a big table, with everyone doing his or her "thing": the rabbi would invariably be studying Talmud; his rebbetzin would read the Yiddish press, with its special supplements for Shabbat; the eldest son, Serayeh, was always studying something else, but something intriguing (I remember that during one period it was the *Guide for the Perplexed*, by Maimonides, in English); and the two sisters would read poetry and literature. Each would share anything that was thought to be of interest to the others, and everyone would stop what he or she was doing, to listen and comment. Sholem was then going to the prestigious Yeshiva Torah Vodaas while I was still in the Yeshiva of Brooklyn. Sometimes the two of us would review some *Ḥumash*, but usually we played Monopoly. Those afternoons were very special for me.

One particular Shabbat afternoon, when I was having an unusually lengthy conversation with my mother, Sholem came to call for me. I didn't think he even knew where I lived. I even remember exactly what I had eaten – cold lamb chops.

There was a knock on the door. My mother went to answer the door, and it was Sholem Berman. We were young kids, but he was already wearing a hat and a Shabbat overcoat. He was very "*Shabbesdik*," dressed especially for Shabbat.

Now my mother was very strong, firm and secure in what she

believed and in what she did not believe. She knew who she was and never made excuses for herself. Indeed, I had never before seen my mother nonplussed, or at a loss for words. But this time she was taken aback; she knew Sholem was a rabbi's son and she was embarrassed about the cigarette she was holding in her hand.

She held the cigarette behind her back, trying to hide it from view. I came to the door and I realized that both my mother and my friend were embarrassed. I told Sholem that I was finishing up lunch with my mother and that I would come by his house in about half an hour.

When my friend left, my mother looked at me and said wistfully, "You know, I think maybe God made a mistake putting us together. You should have had a rabbi and a rebbetzin for parents, or at least you should have been born in my house, to my parents. I'm not a traditionalist, so we just don't fit together."

Then my mother turned around, and corrected herself in her usual self-assured manner. "No," she said, "God didn't make a mistake. He knew exactly what He was doing. We do fit together. God put us together on purpose so that you would learn to also love people who aren't religious." I think my mother was right, and it was a message I've tried never to forget.

Chapter Eight

Harry's Place

My father, Harry Riskin, was my first, and in some respects my most important, teacher. We were so different that I only realized this fundamental truth in recent years. He was raised in the home of my paternal grandparents. My grandfather, Shmuel, the intellectual Communist, believed that religion was the opiate of the masses. My grandmother, Lena, a strikingly beautiful devotee of the Yiddish theater, knew Shakespeare in Yiddish virtually by heart. My father's home was Yiddish without being Jewish. He never even celebrated a bar mitzva.

Unlike his parents, my father was American, with interests more athletic than intellectual. He played semi-professional baseball (I believe for the Brooklyn Orioles), was an excellent tap and ballroom dancer, and loved a good card game. In spite of my being his eldest child and only son, I was the antithesis. I could hardly throw a baseball. By the fortunate "accident" of living in a low-income neighborhood with an educationally inferior public school, I was sent to a yeshiva. Dancing and card-playing were beyond the purview of what became for me acceptable behavior, yet my father and I enjoyed an uncommonly close relationship. From the time I was five years old, I spent Motza'ei Shabbat with my father (and grandfather for as long as he lived) at the Turkish bath, the *shvitz*.

And although I may have been the last to be chosen for a stickball team, I could take a lot of heat – an accomplishment that made my father proud.

The Turkish Bath – first on Myrtle Avenue in Brooklyn and later on Tenth Street and First Avenue in Manhattan – had a subculture all its own. Conversation ranged from the most profound philosophical and political debates to the banter of intimate male bonding. I never felt as protected as I did when receiving a rubdown from my father and grandfather – two tall bastions of strength who treated me with gentle sensitivity. Despite my young years, they made me feel that my ideas were significant. Even though I disagreed with them politically and theologically, they allowed me that right. My father and I continued our intimate conversations in the *shvitz* after I married, and even during my not infrequent trips to America after my *aliya* (in the Tenth Street and First Avenue baths in the Lower East Side). When my parents made *aliya*, my father and I would go regularly to the *shvitz* at the Ramada Continental Hotel in Tel Aviv, until a few months before his passing.

What was it that I learned from my father?

First and foremost, I learned to love people. My father initially trusted everyone unless they betrayed that trust, and he treated every human being with warmth and dignity, no matter one's background or station in life.

He was a people person par excellence, with a smile and a good word for everyone, old and young, his employers as well as those who swept floors.

He was the king of the *shvitz*.

He knew every waiter in his favorite restaurants by name.

He made pals whenever he stopped the car to ask directions even if he didn't get the directions he wanted. (My father had a pretty bad sense of direction and my mother often complained about his unnecessary "*farblundgeter*" miles.)

We were poor growing up. My mother said it was precisely because my father was so trusting and honest that he lacked the guile to outsmart others in business. He was the consummate good guy and probably a little bit of a *freier*. But I learned from him that it's better to allow others to take advantage of you than for you to take advantage of others.

It was also his gift of camaraderie and his guilelessness that made him such a successful salesman. When he began working for others – at Metalectrics, owned by the Rabinowitz family – his bosses loved and trusted him, and his customers loved and trusted him. As a teenager, I would accompany my father on his long selling trips. For me, it was a way to pass the time of summer vacation, and I saw how customers would invite him to enter their stock rooms and would order "blind" according to what he thought they needed.

It was my father's people skills that many years later gave me the confidence to urge my parents to make *aliya*. I knew that my mother would find her complete fulfillment surrounded by children and grandchildren, and that my father would make scores of new friends – Israelis as well as Americans.

And so it was. For so many of the Efrat children my father was "Poppi Harry." (He would always remark that the smartest and most beautiful children are to be found in Efrat.) He would "hold court" for many adults in front of Mordechai Goodman's pizzeria each afternoon.

Secondly, I learned from my father to love life, to savor all of the simple pleasures of this world.

When King Solomon said, "There is nothing better for the human being than to eat and drink and express the goodness of a life of labor…," he could have been speaking directly to my father, who certainly answered the Almighty in the affirmative when he was asked if he enjoyed God's world. He loved food, especially a good hot pastrami sandwich or a steaming bowl of kasha-noodle soup. He enjoyed the pleasantries of companionship, especially over a good card game. I once called him from one of my trips abroad, only to hear an unfamiliar voice answer the phone with "Harry's Place."

"I beg your pardon," I responded.

"Gin rummy, poker, refreshments and jokes – a harmless evening with the wild boys for whoever is interested," the mystery voice continued.

I asked in a rather upset tone of voice to speak to my father and heard the respondent say in a muffled voice: "Uh oh, Harry, it's your son, the rabbi. I'd better hang up so he'll think he got the wrong number."

A year and a half before his passing, my sister informed me in a panic that my father (who had severe cataracts, which his heart condition rendered inoperable, and that made it impossible for him to read or to distinguish images clearly) was taking driving lessons in order to apply for an Israeli license. I immediately went to his apartment, endeavoring to impress upon him that his eyesight would make driving hazardous not only to himself but to others as well.

"Do you think I'm stupid?" said my father in indignation. "I have no intention of actually driving! But the young woman who gives the lessons is a pleasure to be with…"

My father was truly "content with his portion." He assessed his situation not on the basis of what he lacked, but on the basis of what he had. From his perspective, he had the best: the best wife, the best children and grandchildren and great-grandchildren, the best city, the best mayor… My mother sometimes found it difficult to relate to my father's constant good cheer and optimistic outlook. "How can a person wake up smiling and go to sleep smiling?" she would ask, not without a little exasperation and perhaps envy. "It's because I'm married to you," my father would respond, only partially tongue-in-cheek. "I guess you have a point there," was my mother's response.

My father's optimism was the product of a natural, simple faith, an unshakable confidence in the future. Almost ten years before his death, my father had a serious lung-cancer operation. I flew to New York, and was allowed into the operating room shortly before he was to be anesthetized. "Why do you look sad?" demanded my father. "If God takes me now, I'll have no complaints. I was treated to a good life and have no right to ask for any more." And then he took my hand and said, "But, anyway, I'm sure I'll come out of this very well. We'll go to the *shvitz* together next month!" And we did.

A few years before he died, my father was rushed to the hospital on Rosh HaShana with a mild stroke. He could not speak and he could not swallow – the two activities he most enjoyed, the two oral expressions of communicating and eating that expressed significant aspects of his persona. I remember standing off to the side and praying to the Almighty. "Please God, heal him or take him, but don't leave him like this." (A prayer modeled after the commentary of the Ran in Tractate *Nedarim*.) And then, after a day of extreme discomfiture, my sister and

I watched a miracle unfold before our eyes as, in stages, our father "re-awakened," as it were, and regained his speech and swallowing reflex. When we were alone, I asked my father, "Weren't you terrified?" "No," he answered, "not at all. I knew I would come out of it."

Thirdly, my father taught me about commitment to family, especially to parents and children. Every Wednesday, starting from the week after his honeymoon, my father would return to his mother's house and clean the floors, literally getting on his hands and knees, because he knew how important cleanliness was to her. He visited his parents with the family. We trekked by foot and two buses every Sunday afternoon, and then again with my mother (until she balked as our nuclear family grew too demanding) every Thursday evening. When my paternal grandmother became mortally ill with cancer, my father was at her bedside every evening after work. When he came home, no matter how late at night it might have been, he would study from my *Reshit-Daat Hebrew Primer* to teach himself the language of the siddur in preparation for the inevitable. Although he had no religious training, after her death he never missed *Kaddish,* either during the first eleven months following her death or on the *yahrzeit.* It was that *Kaddish* year that brought my father into the synagogue, an activity that he truly enjoyed. In later years, when he lived in Efrat, he grew to love the synagogue even more, with his fondest "shul time" being the "Kiddush Club" as a *Haftara* substitute.

My father was a model husband who literally "loved his wife as himself and respected her beyond his own person." His pride in my mother's appearance, intelligence and house-management ability was total. He boasted that "the last decision I had to make was marrying your mother." (My mother would invariably respond with a laugh indicating that this wasn't exactly the case; had she waited for him to decide on marriage, such a wonderful family would never have come into existence... Apparently she had to force his hand, and they were both very happy that she did.) My father often quipped, "I always wanted my women weak and my coffee strong. God provided me with a strong woman who made me weak coffee, but He knew much better than I what I really needed."

It was not until my mother became ill with what was apparently Alzheimer's, however, that we began to view our father from a different perspective. He never lost patience with her, answering her same questions again and again and being there for her almost every hour of the day. My mother wouldn't allow him to leave her sight, and he almost always good-naturedly complied. Suddenly it became clear how emotionally dependent my mother was on my father, and that perhaps this had been a crucial aspect of their relationship all the years. My father's emotional strength had apparently been the source of my mother's ability to weather the various financial storms the family suffered over the years.

When my mother was comatose for months, my father would caress her and speak words of love to her as his body shook with sobs. And then, in the midst of my mother's illness, my father was felled by a stroke. Both parents were on the same floor of Shaarei Zedek Hospital, and, with grave concern, we saw that although our father's speech pattern and memory seemed to be returning, he never mentioned our mother or asked to enter her room. Could her illness have been so painful to him that he blocked it out of his mind completely? When we were able to take him home – he left the hospital in a wheelchair – he remarked as we passed our mother's room, "Tomorrow I'll see Mommy when I can stand on my own steam. If she would awaken from her coma and see me in a half-paralyzed state, she would never get over the shock." Indeed, we children began to understand that perhaps our father was the hidden bulwark of the family, after all.

Several years later, my father passed away on a Shabbat morning, surrounded by children and grandchildren. The night before, while I spoon-fed him some soup, together with his beloved granddaughter, Sara, he said that he had had enough, that he was ready to leave this world.

My maternal grandmother would always explain the Hebrew prayer, *Al tashlikhenu le'et zikna,* not as "Don't cast me into old age," but rather as "Don't *throw* me into old age; allow me to get used to it slowly, in stages and by degrees and then take me 'home.'" I am grateful that my father was like a ripened fruit, ready to be plucked from the tree of life in this world by the God in whom he trusted all his days. I am grateful for the person that my father enabled me to become, for the self-confidence one can only receive from a father who lets it be known that his son is the center of his universe. He may not have taught me how to learn a page of Gemara, but he did teach me lessons that are equally important: how to live, how to savor each moment of the joys of living, how to love, how to communicate with people, how to establish enduring commitments and relationships.

Chapter Nine

Tante Sadie

My grandmother had a younger sister, Sadie Goldberg. We called her Tante.

Tante Sadie Goldberg was a fascinating woman. She must have been a real beauty as a child and as a young woman, because even when I knew her in her seventies and eighties, people would still turn around in the street to look at her. She was also very bright and articulate.

She was actually the only family member of her older generation who spoke English, albeit with a Yiddish accent, hence she was the "American" and her advice was sought after by all her nieces and nephews, even grand-nieces and grand-nephews (Tante never had children of her own), for all matters pertaining to school or profession in the new world.

She lived in a fancy apartment building (with a doorman) in Washington Heights, at 20 Laurel Hill Terrace, overlooking the Harlem River. The younger families in her building also sought her counsel. I remember one case in which a young woman came to Tante in tears; she had three small children and was just told by her doctor that she was pregnant with a fourth. It was obviously an "unplanned" pregnancy. She begged Tante to direct her to a trustworthy gynecologist who would perform an abortion – but before her husband even found out that she was pregnant. She was then in her second month and Tante told her that indeed she knew exactly the right doctor, but "it wasn't yet time" to make an appointment with him. Each day the woman would ask if the proper time had arrived and Tante said, "Not yet."

When the woman entered her third month, Tante said that the right time had arrived. Now, however, the woman had changed her mind. As Tante had suspected, once this basically family-oriented mother felt the baby kicking, she couldn't possibly give up the potential life in her womb. "And," Tante wistfully told me, "I know what a precious gift from God a baby is." Tante eventually explained the reason for her delay to the woman, and she was the godmother (*kvaterin*) at the baby boy's circumcision.

My grandmother and Tante Sadie were the oldest and youngest daughters, respectively, that my great-grandfather Shlomo had with his first wife Mindel. The mother of these two sisters died when Grandma was eighteen and Tante was barely three. Grandma had just been married. Her marriage to Grandpa Ḥayyim took place in Lubien on a Friday afternoon, which was the custom at that time; after all, the economic condition of the Jews did not allow for lavish wedding meals in the middle of the week. This way the wedding meal was also the Friday night, Shabbat meal.

There was a river running through the little town of Lubien, and one of my grandmother's brothers, Yitzḥak, combined *mikveh* and a swim that Friday after the wedding ceremony. His mother gave him two *ḥallah bulkeleh* (small rolls) wrapped in a napkin to eat when he came out of the water. The *bulkeleh* were found at the river's edge, but his body never surfaced. Although my great-grandfather ruled that the wedding meal go on as scheduled, my great-grandmother's heart was broken and she died within a few months of this tragedy.

In time, my great-grandfather remarried and the second wife was a nightmare for the younger children, especially for Tante Sadie, or "Sorre" as she was called in Lubien. Hence, my newlywed grandparents basically adopted little Sorrele, and brought her up in their home.

Tante Sorre, who even then was sophisticated, wanted desperately to leave her wicked stepmother, Europe and old-worldism behind, so she married the first man who came along who was ready to take her to

America. This was Uncle Yiddl, and they were a classic mismatch. Uncle Yiddl was a sweet but retiring, simple kind of guy who never really made a living. The best he could manage was seasonal work as a "cutter by suits." Tante was a very strong, beautiful, passionate, impassioned woman.

Along the way she met a very wealthy businessman – Mr. C. He was a British gentleman who manufactured glassware. He had an unbeatable combination of a British accent and wealth, which gave him real "class" within our family, and Tante and "Uncle" C were almost inseparable. I remember once in my grandmother's house, my sister Judy asked, "How come everybody has one husband and Tante has two husbands?" and my mother slapped her. That was the only time my mother ever slapped any of us. My grandmother never tolerated any kind of gossip about Tante in her presence. She always said it's not what the gossip-mongers think; that they were just good friends, and I assume that was the case. But "Uncle" C went with Tante to the theater, to horse races and to the opera. Supposedly these were interests the two of them shared that their respective spouses did not find interesting. The two elderly couples shared a summer home in Long Beach where my parents, sisters and I spent two-week summer vacations for at least four summers. "Uncle" C was truly an intellectual. He read Shakespeare and Byron and would feed me with books when I was with them.

Tante and Uncle Yiddl were guests at my grandmother's home for every religious festival and sometimes the Cs also came. We, specifically my nuclear family, were invited for special occasions to Tante's house when she hosted "Uncle" C formally – especially Thanksgiving dinner. Tante wanted very much to be American and "Uncle" C gave substance to her desire. I always wondered why Grandma wasn't invited, but I now realize that Tante did not keep a kosher kitchen. At the time I was very young and naive and couldn't imagine Grandma's sister serving non-kosher food. Tante always served "leg of lamb"; an apparent specialty of hers that "Uncle" C loved. Tante certainly had a character that was molded by her religious upbringing in Lubien, despite her assimilation. Right before one of those Thanksgiving dinners was about to begin, there was a loud knock on the door. It was a poor "landsman" from Lubien, a Holocaust survivor, who came to America with Tante's address. Not only did she welcome him like a long-lost relative, but she sat him at the head of the table – where "Uncle" C usually sat – and served him the head of the fish (the perennial first course) and the choicest piece of meat. She explained to the disgruntled "uncle" that he always sat at the head everyplace he went and always received the best of portions; this landsman, a displaced person, had been bereft of real hospitality for many years…

Early into our marriage I suggested to Vicky that she order "leg of lamb" from Gruenspecht's, our Washington Heights butcher, and get the recipe from Tante. Vicky, who was similarly naive in this respect, called the butcher. I heard screaming from the other end: "Alfred, the Rebbetzin is asking for leg of lamb! Do you hear me? Help me, what should I tell the Rebbetzin?" So then, from the tone in the butcher's voice, I understood – thirteen years later. Embarrassed, I explained that I had a great aunt who had served that cut, and of course, the butcher explained that it could not be eaten because butchers in America were not skilled in removing the forbidden sinew from that part of the animal.

Tante Sadie lived in Manhattan, but she always traveled to Brooklyn before holidays to help my grandmother with her preparations. Grandma explained away much of Tante's "unorthodox" conduct as a natural by-product of her different childhood under the domination of "a wicked storybook stepmother." Even Great-Grandpa Shlomo felt guilty about her, blaming himself for not controlling his second wife in her behavior toward Sorre. Indeed, when my grandmother left Europe, and asked her father for a photograph of himself as a memento, he wouldn't have a photograph taken because he was a Gerer Hasid and considered a photograph to be a forbidden graven image. Instead, he gave her a *Shas* (complete set of the Talmud): "Since we learned Gemara together, you'll continue to study in America and that's how you'll remember me," he said. But when Tante Sorre left and she asked for a photograph, he did have his picture taken. Grandma realized that was not because he loved her sister more, but because he felt that Sorre had suffered a great deal as a child, and that the least he could do was to give her the remembrance that she asked for.

Grandma was also ready to forgive Tante almost anything because the latter had no children of her own; her life looked back on sorrow and had no real future to anticipate either. "I hope my children will treat her as if they were her children also," my Grandma would say. She would quote a proverb: "A person with many children often lives like a dog [because he must care for them and support them], but he dies like a prince, surrounded by his descendants. A person who is, God forbid, childless, may live like a prince, but will die like a dog – alone, unmourned and unloved."

Grandma was also sad that Tante had drifted so far from traditional Judaism. Therefore, she would conclude any discussion about Tante, "And you always have to treat people with love, because the only thing that will bring people back to God is love."

She would say this again and again and it was very important to her. This was truly her philosophy of Judaism, even beyond Tante. She always used to tell me the story of the Ba'al Shem Tov, the founder of Hasidism. A man once came to the Ba'al Shem Tov and said, "I have a son; he doesn't listen to me, he doesn't obey the commandments of God." The Ba'al Shem Tov said, "You have to love him." So the father says, "But it's worse than that. He's a *ben sorer umoreh,* a wicked and rebellious son, who desecrates the Sabbath and tramples upon everything that is sacred. I want him out of my house." "You're right," said the Ba'al Shem Tov, "I didn't understand. But God forbid that you banish him from your home; then he'll never come back. You must now love him all the more." And indeed it was easy to love Tante. As our American representative to the opera and the horse races, she added a tantalizing touch of culture and excitement to our lives.

Chapter Ten

Rav Menaḥem Manus Mandel: The Consummate Rebbe

The Bedford-Stuyvesant area of Brooklyn, New York, in which I grew up (1940–56) was a neighborhood in transition; the Jews were fast moving out as the African Americans and Puerto Ricans were moving in. The educational standards of the public schools were getting lower and lower as "gang wars" were developing in intensity, and as more and more students were coming to school with knives instead of school books. Rav Menaḥem Manus Mandel, an immaculately dressed, black-bearded young man ordained by the religiously right-wing Yeshiva Torah Vodaas, and a student-disciple of the Hasidic, outreach sage Shraga Feivel Mendlowitz, seized the opportunity to open a Jewish day school to attract the remaining Jewish families in the area. It was because of these conditions that my parents – who were then only minimally observant sent me to the Yeshiva of Brooklyn on Throop Avenue.

Largely because of my own bookish inclinations and my maternal grandmother's religious influence, I very much enjoyed, and excelled in, the study of Talmud, even from the tender age of eight. Early on I began spending Sunday afternoons with the eighth-grade Talmud teacher Rav Finkelstein (a Holocaust survivor whom I remember as a true Talmud scholar who could only speak Yiddish). Once, we lost track of the time and were locked into the school building; we both had to climb out of the window in order to get home in the evening.

Rav Mandel lived in a very Hasidic section of Williamsburg, about six kilometers from the school. He had started a Shabbat Morning Prayer service within the yeshiva building, primarily for the students and their parents. Knowing that my father would not take me, from the time I was ten years old he would pick me up in front of my building, bring me to shul and sit next to me during the prayers. I can still feel his caress as he would drape his prayer shawl over me during the *Kel Adon* song of praise to the Lord of the universe, and I still remember his whispered interpretations of the biblical readings between the *aliyot*. He would then take me to Williamsburg where we would stop in at a number of the Hasidic rabbis, at the later conclusion of their services, and end up at his home, 83 Wilson Street, for the second Shabbat meal. He taught me that a true educator sees his students as his children.

I recall his mesmerizing Friday morning *musar* (ethicism) sessions to the older students (seventh and eighth grades); lessons that I continue to find most valuable even to this very day. He would always begin with a provocative question, and surprise us with an unexpected answer – an answer that would totally reorient the way in which we looked at the world.

He once asked, for example, who is wealthier: the individual who has $100 or the individual who has $200? We all responded: the individual with $200. No, he said, the individual with $100. Why? It is the way of the world that for most people the material goods they have are never enough, and they wish to double whatever they own. At the same time, you can only truly assess what a person has by what he believes he is missing, because most individuals take for granted what they have and define their financial status by what they feel they lack. Therefore, since the person with $100 is lacking $100 (he wishes to double what he has), and the person with $200 is lacking $200, then the one with

$100 lacks less, and is thereby wealthier than the one with $200. And he would go on to prove to us how real wealth must be assessed in spiritual, rather than material terms.

One closing incident: I mentioned previously my childhood goal to read all the books in my local library. Early on in my mission (which, needless to say, I far from completed), I came to Darwin's Theory of Evolution and *The Origin of Species*. Perhaps I was eleven when I came upon this classic, and literally devoured his basic thesis over a weekend. I was fascinated by the ordered nature of the development of life, from the simple to the complex, which so closely paralleled the biblical account, which went from the earth, to the vegetative, to the animal, to the human. I was dazzled by my new-found understanding of biblical phrases like, "Let the earth bring forth grass" (Genesis 1:11), and "Let the waters swarm abundantly with swarming creatures" (Genesis 1:20). And since Darwin was a Gentile, I wasn't at all put off by his lack of faith in God; I had already decided for myself of course (in a more intensive and less elegant way than was stated by Henri Bergson), that the notion that the mind of an Einstein could "evolve" from an amoeba by accident, would tax the credibility of any rational individual. For me, the progression of each evolutional stage was necessary and even logical, but the fundamental evolutionary processes opened up many biblical passages; it beautifully explained, and even validated key expressions in my beloved biblical story of the creation of the world.

I couldn't wait to share my discovery with my rebbe, Rav Mandel, that Monday morning. I brought him the book, and showed him the relevant passages – totally ignorant of the "red flag" raised in religious circles by the mere mention of Darwin. Rav Mandel barely took the book in his hand; he slapped my face, and then kissed my forehead. "Your interpretations are magnificent, but it is forbidden to read such heretical literature," he said gently. I smarted at the slap, felt vindicated by the kiss, and continued to adore my rebbe even though I intuited then, and firmly believe now, that all of knowledge must be fearlessly explored, and that ultimately the truth of God and Torah will emerge supreme.

Chapter Eleven

The *Shtiebl* on Hart Street and a Lesson in Human Relationships

At the end of the block on which we lived, there was a small synagogue within a private house known as "Rav Gottesman's *shtiebl*." Rav Gottesman was a venerable sage, garbed in a shiny black kaftan on Shabbat and a pure white kaftan on the Holidays; his bearded, angelic face was graced with a fur-trimmed *shtreimel*. He seemed to have been transported into our changing neighborhood from another place and another time.

My first encounter with him was at the end of a day in early fall, at the conclusion of the High Holy Day season (so we were off from school); I must have been about nine or ten, and I was playing stick-ball with my friends in the street directly in front of the *shtiebl*, dodging the few cars and hitting the ball with great glee. The Rebbe walked into the very midst of our game, held up his hand to signal us to stop hitting the ball, and, in broken English, invited us all into the synagogue. "It is a Jewish holiday," he said, "the Holiday of our rejoicing over the Bible [Simḥat Torah]. We are dancing inside the synagogue, and everyone gets to eat apples [he pronounced it "eppels"] and drink beer." He then turned to the African Americans, who were laughing as he was speaking. He seemed to be oblivious to their derision, but embraced a few of them, saying, "It is your Bible, too, and you are welcome to dance with us and drink beer with us."

The magic word was "beer"; in our family, only my father got to drink beer with his dinner, and only on Sunday evenings (frankfurter night). I wasn't even allowed a sip from his glass. We all, including the African Americans, trooped into the synagogue (perhaps there were twenty regular attendees inside), joined the circle of dancers, hummed along to the melodies, waved the Israeli flags we were given to hold, ate "eppels," drank beer, and spent a most enjoyable half hour. I, the yeshiva student, found a neighborhood synagogue that I could easily get to by myself, and where I came to feel very much at home.

One of the Rebbe's sons-in-law would teach The Ethics of the Fathers (Mishna *Avot*) during the long summer Shabbat afternoons. Most of the regular congregants were Holocaust survivors who had only recently arrived in America and were just beginning to reconstruct their lives. The spoken language, as well as the language of the class, was Yiddish. Toward the end of the very first chapter of Ethics of the Fathers, Shammai teaches, "Accept every human being with good fellowship." One of the participants, a warm, smiley, good-natured father of twin girls (Mr. R), quietly added to the interpretation of the rabbi's son-in-law, "This teaching saved my life."

In measured and painful words he told the following story: "I was born in Poland, right near the German border. Every morning, when I would habitually go to synagogue, I would meet, almost face-to-face, a well-known and fairly well-to-do German citizen, who would always begin his day with a 'constitutional' walk, no matter what the weather. I would quietly greet him, '*A gut Morgen, Herr Guttmacher*'; he would give me a supercilious and sometimes even disgusted look, condescendingly muttering in semi-response, '*Jude*' [Jew]. His chin would nod slightly, and I was never quite sure if his one word was meant as a return greeting or an anti-Semitic reproach. Nevertheless, the dialogue between us continued every morning for at least two years; after all, I wanted to be true to Shammai's teaching.

"Then the Second World War broke out; our lives were shattered. I was taken to Auschwitz. Life became almost unbearable, but nevertheless, I desperately wanted to live; indeed, the only thing one lived for was to live another day. I became dreadfully ill with typhus, to such an extent that I couldn't even drag myself to the roll-call in the morning. And then there was another accursed 'selection,' when each inmate would march in front of a Nazi messenger of death; he would look each individual over for a few seconds, and then bellow either '*rechts*' (which meant continuation in the labor force) or '*links*' (which meant the gas chambers and certain death).

"I somehow managed to crawl to the selection line and unsteadily rise to my feet. I could feel the redness of my feverish face, and my bloodshot eyes almost made it impossible for me to see in front of me. As I came closer to my moment of truth, I wordlessly recited the *Shema*. And then, with double or triple vision, I looked up at my executioner, the Nazi face staring at me. With my last ounce of strength, I quietly said, '*A gut Morgen, Herr Guttmacher.*' His impassive face suddenly twitched; he looked at me hard. '*Jude,*' he muttered, and then, '*rechts.*'"

Chapter Twelve

My Bar Mitzva Suit and an Uneaten *Knish*

I have often down-played the notion of *yiḥus* (pedigree, ancestral lineage) as bestowing special privilege upon a proud and often arrogant descendant; if anything *yiḥus* could and should inspire noblesse oblige, empowering the descendant with the will and inspiration to follow in the footsteps of the respected forebear by dint of hard work and high ideals. Practically speaking, however, more important than who one's grandparents were, is who one's grandchildren will become!

I learned this lesson in an unlikely place when I was only twelve and my parents had just bought my first (bar mitzva) suit. But, you will ask, a bar mitzva boy is thirteen years old, not twelve? Yes, but Levy's Clothing Store, at 28 Elizabeth Street, Lower East Side, New York, was advertising a "once-in-a-lifetime" sale on suits, which my mother believed was too good an opportunity to miss. My parents hesitated a bit over whether "he would grow so much in the year as to make the bar mitzva suit unusable for its purpose," but they decided that the price made it worthwhile to take the chance.

That Sunday we set forth – on train and bus – for the Lower East

Side, and, two hours later, concluded a successful purchase. My father suggested we celebrate with a Yonah Schimmel's *knish* (Ashkenazi cousin to a Sepharadi *bureka*), an establishment widely known for its large assortment of tasty fillings for their well-baked *knish* dough: potato, kasha, blueberry, raspberry, cheese, etc. As we stepped up to the counter to give our order, I – the fearless and proud owner of a bar mitzva suit – asked if there was a *kashrut* certificate in the store; after all, I was the "yeshiva student" in the family. The salesperson looked rather surprised at the question, and directed us to management in the office next-door.

We opened the door of the office to find a large, oversized desk, behind which was seated a large, overweight man, wide of girth and bald of pate, whose head was uncovered and who seemed deeply occupied in consuming a corned-beef sandwich with mustard and pickles. "We were told to ask you about *kashrut* certification," I asked, in my most grownup voice.

"*Yungatsh*, young whippersnapper!" he said with annoyance. "You have a lot of *ḥutzpa* [arrogance], you know. Do you see that portrait right above me?" He pointed to a painting of a distinguished-looking gentleman, elegantly garbed in homburg hat and Prince Albert coat, his face framed in an obviously religious beard. "That was my father, Yonah Schimmel, bedecked in the Sabbath and festival garb he wore to the synagogue. He originated this establishment. And you dare to ask for a *kashrut* certificate?"

I was a bit full of myself, having just gotten my bar mitzva suit, so I was not at all put off by the boor in front of me. I rose to my full height, then well under five feet, and responded, looking directly into my antagonist's eyes:

"If you were hanging on the wall, and your father was seated in front of us, I wouldn't be concerned about the *kashrut* of the *knishes*. But since you're seated in front of me, and your father is unfortunately hanging on the wall – no, I cannot eat here unless there is a *kashrut* certificate!"

We closed the office door leaving a sputtering Mr. Schimmel, but I was disappointed in not being able to eat a *knish*. My father was proud as Punch, and that evening he sent a written description of our encounter to the editor of the *Jewish Digest*. The story was published, and the $10 we received in the mail became my first bar mitzva gift.

Chapter Thirteen

The Beth Moses Beit Midrash: My First Lesson in Zionism

It was the Shabbat of the weekly portion *Ki Tavo,* toward the end of the summer of 1952; I had known that the Rebbe of Sanz-Klausenburg had taken over the Beth Moses Hospital (the place where I was born), where he had built a very large *beit midrash-beit knesset* (study hall-synagogue), as well as a printing press to teach his disciples a trade, and I wanted to pray with the Hasidim that Shabbat morning. I also wanted to wear my new bar mitzva suit, which had very recently arrived from the tailor.

I had to conduct a long, hard negotiation with my mother, who was reluctant for me to take such a long walk alone in what was not a very wholesome neighborhood, and also adamantly opposed to my wearing the bar mitzva suit close to a year before my bar mitzva (which was scheduled for the following portion of *Emor*). At length my mother relented, but not until I promised not to get into any altercations with toughs who might start up, and not to partake of any *kiddush* if there was one.

When I arrived at the *beit midrash*, I was amazed by the sea of black and white, swaying figures that greeted my eyes, all newly immigrant Holocaust survivors. It was said about the Rebbe that, although his wife and thirteen children had been murdered, he had not sat *shiva* for any of them; he preached that those still alive must be saved with exit visas before one could be allowed the luxury of mourning for the dead. The Rebbe himself was among the last to leave Europe, insisting that the captain does not leave the sinking ship before its passengers. I took a seat directly behind the Rebbe, who stood at his lectern facing the eastern wall and the Holy Ark, with his back to the congregation. The prayer was the most intense I had ever experienced, with no talking whatsoever, and chance individuals even bursting out in tears during varying parts of the service, apparently in response to a sudden association with a painful memory.

Then the Torah reader began to chant the weekly portion. When he came to the passage known as "the Chastisement" (*Tokheḥa*: the curses that would befall the Israelites), which he began to read (in accordance with time-honored custom), in a whisper and very quickly, a sound suddenly came from the place of the Rebbe; he said only one word: *hecher*, louder.

The Torah reader immediately stopped reading, and seemed to hesitate for a few moments. I could almost hear him pondering. Did the Rebbe actually say "louder"? Would the Rebbe go against the custom of Israel, in all congregations, to chant the curses rapidly and in a barely audible voice? The reader apparently decided that he had been mistaken in what he thought the Rebbe had said, and continued reading in a whisper.

The Rebbe turned around to face the congregation, banged on the lectern, his eyes blazing: *"Ich hob gezogt hecher*, I said louder," he shouted out. "Let the Master of the Universe hear! We have nothing to be afraid of. We have already received all of the curses – and more. Let the Almighty hear, and let Him understand that the time has come to send the blessings!"

I was trembling, my body bathed in sweat. Many people around me were silently sobbing. The Rebbe turned back to his lectern, facing the wall. The Torah reader continued to chant the curses loudly, and distinctively and in a much slower cadence.

At the end of the additional prayers, after *Aleinu*, the Rebbe once again turned to this congregation, but this time with his eyes conveying deep love. "*Mein tayere shvestern un brider*, my beloved sisters and brothers, the blessings will come, but not from America. God has promised the blessings after the curses, but they will only come from the land of Israel. Let us pack our bags for the last time. Our community is setting out for Israel."

And, indeed, it wasn't very long after that Shabbat, that the Rebbe led his flock to settle in Netanya, where they founded Kiryat Sanz. The Rebbe established a large *beit midrash*, as well as the Laniado Hospital – and Netanya is still a major enclave for the Klausenburger Hasidim.

Part II

Yeshiva University College Years 1956–60

Chapter Fourteen

Harvard or YU?

I was graduating from high school and had received a full scholarship to Harvard. My parents were thrilled; they wanted me to be a lawyer, and so did I at the time. But I still felt conflicted. I very much loved learning Gemara and wasn't certain that I would retain my religious disciplines of learning and observance in a non-Torah environment. I often thought of a parallel situation when I had graduated from the Yeshiva of Brooklyn. I was accepted to Brooklyn Technical High School, a very prestigious institution, which offered free tuition for those who met their standards. Rav Mandel called me into his office. "There are two maps, Shloimele," he said, "one in this world and one in the other world, in God's world. In this world, New York is a great metropolis, as is London, as is Tokyo. But Mir is a small town, Slobodka even smaller and Telz doesn't even appear on some maps. In God's world it's the opposite. New York is miniscule and Tokyo hardly appears. But Mir is a large center and Telz is a major capital. It's the same with academic institutions," he lovingly concluded. And when the registrar of Brooklyn Talmudical Academy, Sam Levine, offered me a full scholarship, I gladly gave up Brooklyn Tech. But Harvard was different…

I spent Shavuot night at Yeshiva University (YU) a few weeks before my high school graduation and it was a delightful experience. We learned all night and just before dawn, Rav Dovid Lifshitz, a smiling, distinguished Rav with a black and white beard that looked like gently rippling waves, led us in a dance and song of praise to the God who sends us the morning star. The festival prayer was tuneful, heartfelt and filled with devotion. But for me, the climax came with *Birkat Kohanim*, the festival Priestly Blessing. The *mashgiaḥ ruḥani*, (spiritual advisor) of Yeshiva University at that time, was Rav Yitzḥak Lessin, a student of Slobodka, who spoke only Yiddish. He was tall, immaculately groomed in a black *kaputa*, graced by his forked white beard, and kindly facial features that exuded spirituality. I kept glancing up at him during that entire night of learning.

As it turned out, we were both Kohanim, and I found myself standing right next to him for *Birkat Kohanim* at the end of the repetition of the *Musaf Amida*. He had a beautifully sweet voice and enhanced the words of the blessing with a long wordless melody they used to sing at the Slobodka Yeshiva. I felt it must have originated from the Holy Temple itself. I was moved to tears thinking of Rav Mandel's maps, and of what my grandmother would want me to do. She had refrained from giving an opinion because she wanted to save me a tug-of-war between herself and my parents. Strangely enough, I also thought of my Communist grandfather, Grandpa Shmuel, and how he had taught me to separate my fingers into the letter *shin*, telling me, "Remember, we are Kohanim, and that's Jewish royalty. Always be a proud Jew." All these thoughts went through my mind as my soul soared to the sound of the melody. Before *Birkat Kohanim* concluded, I had taken an oath to go to Yeshiva University.

When I came home to my parents, I crashed down to earth. My mother was of course very upset because she wanted Harvard for me, but also, "because there's just no way you can go to Yeshiva. We can't afford the tuition. You have a full scholarship to Harvard." She even called Yeshiva University to ask about a scholarship, but they said it was too late to even apply.

That Sunday we happened to be visiting Tante, who lived just a few blocks from Yeshiva University. The issue of college came up, and to my parents' surprise and chagrin, Tante said to me, "Don't you want to go to Yeshiva University?" When I responded that I had indeed decided that that's where I wanted to study, and not at Harvard, Tante seemed genuinely happy. "Don't *vorry*," she said. "I'll get you in on scholarship. I'm on the *vall*." I was totally perplexed. Tante immediately arose, took me by the hand, signaled my parents to wait in the apartment, and led me to Dr. Belkin's office barely two blocks from where she lived. She was sure he would see us she explained, because her name was on a plaque on the donor wall for having contributed $100. I don't know where she got the money – maybe from Uncle C – but she had given $100 to Yeshiva University.

She walked directly into Dr. Belkin's office, imperiously saying to the secretary as she passed her by, "My name is Sadie Goldberg. I'm on the *vall* outside. This is my nephew, he's a genius. I have to see Dr. Belkin. I'm sure Dr. Belkin *vill* see me; I'm a contributor."

The secretary looked at her, and smilingly said, "Well, Mrs. Goldberg, the president is busy right now, but if you call for an appointment…" "*Vee* have no time for an appointment," Tante said, as she opened the door to Dr. Belkin's private office and walked right in. She literally dragged me in by the hand. You know, I wasn't a kid at this point; I was already sixteen years old, and I was mortified. "I'm Sadie Goldberg; I'm on the *vall* downstairs. This is my grand-nephew; he's a genius; he has a full scholarship to Harvard. I *vont* you to give him a full scholarship to Yeshiva University," she announced.

Dr. Belkin got up from his chair and smiled. He was a very warm person, and he patted my cheek, obviously understanding my discomfort. "Mrs. Goldberg, please wait outside for a few minutes, if you don't mind. I'll finish this meeting, and then I'll be glad to meet your grand-nephew." About twenty minutes later, Dr. Belkin's meeting ended, a person walked out of the office, and Tante walked in again and went through the same speech: "I'm Sadie Goldberg, I'm on the *vall* outside, this is my grand-nephew; he's a genius. I *vont* you to give him a full scholarship to Yeshiva University."

Dr. Belkin then said, "Thank you very much. You can wait outside or you can stay here. I want to test your grand-nephew." Tante sat there. He asked me which Talmudic tractate I was studying, spoke to me "in learning," and gave me a section of Gemara and the Tosafot commentary to read. He then came around the desk where I was sitting, kissed me on the forehead, and said to Tante, "You're right. He can have a full scholarship to Yeshiva University."

So I went to Yeshiva University and I never regretted the decision. My parents made their peace with it, my mother's only comment being that she hoped I would allow my own children the same freedom of choice that she allowed me. Dr. Belkin continued to "keep tabs" on me during my student years, especially when I became a Greek major. Greek was his field of scholarship and we enjoyed a warm and special relationship until he died.

I spent every Tuesday evening with Tante. Eventually Uncle C died, and Uncle Yiddl got very sick. Tante was constantly with him at the hospital; I visited every week, as did my mother. I'll never forget what Tante said to me: "When I'm sick, there'll be no one to visit me like I visit Uncle Yiddl. No one has to say thank you to a spouse who visits, or a child who visits. I know you'll visit me, and your mother will visit me, but I'll have to say, 'thank you.'"

In the beginning, especially after Uncle Yiddl died, I spent more and more time with Tante. At first it was just one burner on the stove that she reserved for me, but into my second or third year, she asked me to make her house completely kosher. By the time she died, she lived an entirely traditional Jewish life. Once again, Grandma was right.

Chapter Fifteen

Rav J.B. Soloveitchik

INTELLECTUAL INTEGRITY

Yeshiva University opened up a whole new world for me. I believe that I received there the kind of education I could not have gotten anywhere else – with Rav Soloveitchik for Talmud and Philosophy and Professor Louis Feldman for Greco-Roman civilization and the classical languages. Intellectually and spiritually I became exposed to true excellence, and I truly felt my mind and soul soaring.

But my entry into YU gave my parents one severe headache: they, especially my mother, were mortally afraid of my becoming a rabbi because I attended YU during an era in which Orthodoxy was in retreat and Orthodox rabbis barely made a living. They were generally dependent upon receiving payment for extra services rendered, like performing weddings and funerals, forcing them to rely upon the largesse of individual members of the congregation in a way that often became demeaning.

This was not my parents' dream for me. My mother, in particular, had seen me as the great white hope that would somehow lift the family out of the poverty of Bedford-Stuyvesant. She thought that I would make a very good lawyer. And I was, indeed, very much enamored of lawyers who courageously fought for civil rights and individual liberties. I was especially inspired by outstanding jurists like Clarence Darrow and William Jennings Bryan; I memorized the Cross of Gold speech, and saw myself speaking out in the courtroom on behalf of the disenfranchised and discriminated against.

At each juncture, when I went to Yeshiva University High School of Brooklyn, and then when I went to Yeshiva University, my mother would say, "We're letting you follow the course of your own mind, and that's fine. But remember, you promised you're not going to become a rabbi." I don't know if I actually promised that, but I certainly gave her to understand that I wouldn't become a rabbi, and I really didn't plan at that time to do so.

At YU, within the framework of the Secular Studies Department, I had to choose a language to study. I chose Latin because of the importance of Roman law as the foundation of the American judicial system – at least, so I thought. The professor of Latin and Intellectual History was Professor Louis Feldman, who at that time was a young faculty star who hailed from Trinity College as well as Harvard. He was the editor of the prestigious journal *Classical World* and was already a budding scholar in the world of classics. He also happened to be an Orthodox Jew, although he didn't wear it on his sleeve. I suspect that he was a *ba'al teshuva*, a penitent, having arrived at his Orthodoxy by choice.

So this classical scholar had come to YU and I was in his Latin class. I became taken with him as a teacher, as well as the whole intellectual pursuit in general, and the Greco-Roman civilization in particular. One could say that, in terms of my secular career, I fundamentally majored in Professor Louis Feldman.

From Latin, I progressed to Greek, which I especially loved. Early on, Louis Feldman had us reading Plato in the original, as well as Sophocles' Oedipus trilogy. I loved Greek philosophy – Plato and Aristotle, but mostly Plato. Professor Feldman was greatly admired albeit largely from a distance. His Greek course had three students, one of whom was my professor for English literature, Professor Fleisher. (I had two majors – English literature and classical literature, mostly Greek.) I had already given up on becoming a lawyer, and I even thought that perhaps I would become a professor of the classics.

And then, I entered Rav Soloveitchik's Talmud class.

Rav Soloveitchik, *z"l* (of blessed memory), was an extraordinary influence. He was a Jewish-Talmudical intellectual, way above anyone I had ever met. He brought Talmudic texts to life in a way that I never dreamed possible. When you sat in his class, not only Rava and Abaye, not only Ravina and Rav Ashi were arguing their cases before you, but also the Rambam would come in, and then the Ra'avad would ask a question of him, and the Rabbeinu Tam would have a whole other way of looking at the issue. And then the Rambam's view would be explicated so clearly that you realized nobody else had a leg to stand on.

The Brisker conceptual method of study, specifically through the lens of Rav Soloveitchik, was such that I began to see great philosophical constructs emanating from the pages of the Talmud, no less impressive and unifying than the Kantian or Hegelian philosophical constructs. Even more significantly for me, Rav Soloveitchik called himself a "halakhic existentialist" because he believed that halakha spoke to the most profound existential feelings of the human being.

Every year, on the occasion of the *yahrzeit* of his father, Rav Moshe, *z"l*, Rav Joseph Dov Soloveitchik would give a four-hour exposition; the first two hours were halakha, after which he would take the legal concepts that he had just interpreted in a novel and profound way, and he would go on to elucidate the philosophical, existential and humanistic ramifications of the Talmudic argument. For me, those four hours passed like just a few moments.

I began to realize that all I was looking for – the spiritual, the intellectual, the humanistic – could all be found within the pages of the Talmud.

I became a very devoted disciple of Rav Soloveitchik; my Yeshiva University experience was very much centered around the Rav, who became my religious and spiritual mentor.

Rav Soloveitchik's class was a difficult class. The film *Paper Chase*, which described the "agony and ecstasy" of a difficult law school class where students were sharply challenged and had to work hard to be up to snuff, was nothing compared to Rav Soloveitchik's *shiur* (Torah class). He lived in Boston and came into New York to teach at YU on Tuesdays, Wednesdays and Thursdays. During those first years, especially, I would wake up with an upset stomach on Tuesday morning, which wouldn't leave me until Thursday when he left. The pressure was very intense. We knew that he was greatness. We knew that it was a privilege to be in his presence. We would give anything for his praise, and we were in dread of his derision.

We strove to understand the Talmudic concept that he was explaining and he, especially in the early years (1957–9), would brook no foolishness. He wouldn't accept a foolish question, and could put down a less than perfect rendering of the Talmudic argument very strongly, and very bluntly. The classes were exciting and the material was intellectually invigorating. But there was a great deal of pressure. You didn't want to say the wrong thing. You didn't want to give a wrong answer. You didn't want to ask an unwise question.

I'll tell you at what point he completely captivated me, the incident that enabled me to understand the Rav's true attitude toward his students. There was one student I had taken under my wing. He didn't study in the Yeshiva section of Yeshiva University; he was, rather, in the less-intensive Teachers Institute Department. Since he was very bright, I tried hard to influence him to come over to the Yeshiva section, and he agreed. I also intervened when I thought he was ready to enter Rav Soloveitchik's class. There were about a hundred students in the class; many vied to get in, and it was a coup when my friend was accepted. I sat in the front seat, first row, and he sat in the last seat in the back row. But every week, I would encourage him to come up a row, until finally he was seated right behind me.

I remember exactly what we were studying when the incident occurred: *Massekhet Pesaḥim*, the topic of *tesha ḥanuyot*. It is a complex portion of the Talmud, and very difficult to understand exactly what the Gemara is trying to get at. It deals with the laws of presumption. Rav Soloveitchik had presented a whole construct as to how he thought the Gemara should be interpreted, and then he reversed himself completely and gave a wholly different understanding. I was very excited about the second way in which he was explaining the repartee within the Talmud and this new interpretation was truly novel and eye-opening.

Toward the end of the Rav's new explication, my protégé, we'll call him Cohen, now sitting right behind me, whispered a question in my ear. I thought it was an excellent question, even a devastating one to the Rav's construct. "Ask the Rav, ask the Rav," I whispered back, urging him on.

Now I want you to understand the atmosphere of the class. Rav Soloveitchik came in on Tuesdays. The class was supposed to start at 11:30 A.M., but you never really knew when it would start. In effect, whenever it started, it was 11:30. But from 10:00 Tuesday morning, nobody would so much as leave the study hall to go to the bathroom, nobody would eat anything, no one would ever leave the class in the middle. The classes could last anywhere from two to three hours, but no one would dare move from his seat. There was no emergency that could possibly take precedence over the Torah that Rav Soloveitchik was teaching. And it was rare that anyone would dare to ask a question in the middle of the Rav's exposition. Nevertheless, I thought this question was so good that it deserved to interrupt the Rav's development of the Talmudic debate.

So, I encouraged Cohen to ask his question out loud, and he did. Rav Soloveitchik exploded. "How could you ask such a foolish question? How could you ask me something like that? You shouldn't be here anyway. You're here because Riskin brought you in." And with that, he ended the class. I was devastated; Cohen was smashed to the ground.

During those years Rav Soloveitchik gave two classes back-to-back. One was in Talmud, for the younger students, and the other was in Codes (*Yoreh De'ah*) for the older students who were soon to receive their rabbinical degree. Although I still had a good deal of time for my rabbinical degree, I took both classes, as did a coterie of faithful students. So I stayed in the room after the Rav's explosion. We closed the tractate *Pesaḥim*, and we opened the *Yoreh De'ah*. Usually the Rav switched from topic to topic with barely an interruption, usually drinking a cup of soup in between. This time, Rav Soloveitchik sat at his desk with his head on his arm, the *Pesaḥim* still open before him, for at least twenty minutes. The class was long filled with the second group of students, anxiously expectant for the *shiur* to begin.

There was absolute silence. No one spoke. As long as the Rav remained silent, all of us continued to wait in silence. Then Rav Soloveitchik looked up at me and said, "Riskin, what's his name, the one who asked me the question?" I said, "Cohen, Rebbe." He said, "Yes, yes,

Cohen. Take me to him. Where is he now? Take me to him." I assumed that Cohen was eating. There was a restaurant right across the street that was called Tov Me'od, but we all called it the Greasy Spoon. So I said, "Rebbe, I think he's at the Greasy Spoon." "Take me to him!" he repeated.

Everybody was sitting in their seats as I followed Rav Soloveitchik out the door. The Rav had a rather distinctive walk. He walked very quickly and his hands swung on both sides. He rarely went into any of the restaurants; occasionally, he would eat in the Yeshiva cafeteria, but generally the Rebbetzin would prepare his food in their dormitory apartment.

When the Rav entered the Greasy Spoon, palpable shock waves went through the tables of diners. Out of the corner of my eye I saw Cohen, who was eating a scrambled egg and hash-brown potatoes with ketchup. I can see his plate in front of my eyes as I retell the story.

Everyone immediately jumped to attention at their places, including Cohen. He had just begun to recapture some color on his face, but at the unexpected sight of the Rav, his face turned a stark white. Rav Soloveitchik set his gaze on the hapless questioner: "Cohen, you're right and I was wrong. Your question was a very good question. It undermines my complete thesis. I have to give a whole different interpretation next week. Thank you, Cohen." And with that he walked back with me across the street and into the classroom. He was ready to open the *Yoreh De'ah*.

I understood at that point what intellectual honesty was all about. I also understood that Rav Soloveitchik was mindful of the fact that he was training future rabbis; future congregational leaders, future decisors of Jewish law. To his mind, a rabbinical student, no less than a medical student, couldn't afford to make a mistake. The *mesora*, the tradition that the Rav was giving over to our hands, must be treated with the same precision necessary in medicine. A mistake in a *mesora* was as dangerous as a medical mistake. And, after all, European Jewry was dead and Israel had not yet become a powerful and leading Jewish presence. The center of world Jewry had shifted to America, the preservation of our four-thousand-year-long tradition rested in our hands – and especially in his hands, our teacher.

The Rav believed in us; he believed in our mission, and he believed that it was his mission to properly train us. Teacher and disciple would only impart and receive our eternal tradition in the spirit of impeccable intellectual honesty and religious purity. That for me was a defining moment for someone who was beginning to view his mission as a teacher of Torah.

"IT IS TORAH AND I MUST LEARN IT"

My nighttime (or early morning) *ḥavruta* (study partner) was Shimon Eider, a very dedicated Talmud student who left Yeshiva University after the college years for the more religiously right-wing Lakewood Yeshiva at the time that I left for my year of study in Israel. He was a real *masmid* (diligent student), who barely attended his university classes, which he saw as an unwelcome intrusion upon his Torah study. I would meet him in the *beit midrash* at almost 11:30 most evenings – after I had done my secular preparations for the next day of classes – and we would learn together until 1:30 or 2:00 A.M. We were good for each other; he kept me glued to the seat, and I would usually second-guess what the Rav would concentrate on in the next day's classroom lecture.

The intense atmosphere of the class made every student reluctant to ask a question, especially when the Rav was first developing his thesis on how best to analyze the Talmudic passage under discussion. But Shimon Eider didn't understand the basic propositions upon which the Rav was developing his conceptual structure, and so he stood up and asked. The Rav looked up in astonishment, and then lambasted the questioner for his lack of proper preparation. Shimon stood his ground, quietly but firmly quoting what Maimonides rules that the student must say to an overbearing pedagogue: "It is Torah, and I must learn it; my mind is too small (to grasp what you are saying)." The Rav turned red, immediately spoke in a gentle tone, and asked my *ḥavruta* to please repeat his question. From then on, whenever Shimon Eider asked a question, the Rav patiently listened and responded.

THE RAV AND THE PRIME MINISTER: MEMORIES OF BRISK

Some years later, when I was teaching at Yeshiva University, I would generally request a meeting with the Rav on Thursday afternoons to ask my "questions of the week." He would usually give me from two minutes to an exceedingly rare, two hours, depending upon the pressures of his day. During one particular meeting, while the Rav was in the midst of showing me a passage from the *Guide for the Perplexed,* a telephone call came announcing that Menaḥem Begin, newly elected prime minister of Israel, would be arriving shortly. The prime minister of Israel is generally considered to be the prime minister of world Jewry, and this first traditional prime minister announced that during his first official visit to the United States, he wished an audience with the three religious Jewish leaders of the generation: the Lubavitcher Rebbe, Rav Moshe Feinstein and Rav Soloveitchik. Now that the revered head of state was about to enter the Rav's New York apartment, I knew that good manners dictated that I excuse myself; my curiosity, however, got the better of my gentility, and I opted to remain until I was specifically asked to leave.

When Menaḥem Begin walked through the door, the Rav quickly jumped up to meet him. As they embraced, the Rav seemed especially moved, with what appeared to me to be tears welling up in his eyes. These two Jewish world leaders, the foremost statesmen in the political arena and the foremost rabbi in the religio-philosophical realm, both shared a common "Brisker" (Brest-Litovsk, Lithuania) connection.

Rav Joseph Dov's illustrious grandfather, Rav Ḥayyim Soloveitchik (who pioneered a new conceptual methodology for the study of Talmud), was the rabbi of the main synagogue in Brisk and therefore of the entire city; indeed, he was known worldwide as the "Brisker Rav." Menaḥem Begin's father, Binyamin Begin – an avid Zionist, a devotee of the Revisionist Movement's founder, Ze'ev Jabotinsky, and in his own right a riveting orator – was the *gabbai* (lay leader) of that same synagogue in Brisk. And just to add some spices to the *cholent,* one of the three judges (*dayanim*) of that synagogue community was Rav Moshe Ḥazan, the father of Yaakov Ḥazan, founder and leader of Mapam and the initiator of the secular Shomer HaTza'ir kibbutzim in Israel – and the midwife who "birthed" all of the babies was the grandmother of Ariel Sharon. Menaḥem Begin had been born and raised in Brisk, and Rav J.B. Soloveitchik had spent significant Sabbaths there with his grandfather, including that of his bar mitzva.

After their initial embrace of greeting, both men stood looking at each other, respectfully, admiringly, nostalgically. The Rav seemed to burst out, "Mr. Prime Minister, you are so short, and your father was so tall." Menaḥem Begin responded, "*Kavod HaRav,* I will say two things. Firstly, you remember how my father looked when you were a small child, and all adults seem taller than they actually are, to children. But the real point is that my father was always a much taller and greater man than I."

And there they sat at the table and began to reminisce together, the one entering into the words of the other and finishing the other's thoughts and sentences. Clearly they felt transported to their childhood in Brisk, as their Yiddish words and gesticulations evoked that world. A world in which either the rabbi or the *gabbai* held the keys to the synagogue, and Binyamin Begin had gladly given up his keys to the illustrious Reb Ḥayyim when the latter accepted the rabbinical position. A place where a bar mitzva who was preparing to spend his biblical portion in Brisk, couldn't sleep a week beforehand because his revered grandfather insisted that every cantillation had to be exactly accurate or the entire verse would have to be repeated; an ideological climate in which Zionist leaders were either revered as forerunners of the Messiah, or reviled as rebels against God's rule over the cosmos.

And then they both recounted an incident together, the one dispute they remembered that had taken place between the *gabbai* and the rabbi, between Binyamin Begin and Rav Ḥayyim Soloveitchik. Theodore Herzl, the legendary father of modern Zionism, died, and Binyamin Begin planned to eulogize him in the main synagogue of Brisk. Reb Ḥayyim was an anti-Zionist who certainly did not believe it proper to eulogize a non-observant Jew who probably ate on Yom Kippur, in an Orthodox synagogue. Since it was the rabbi who had the keys, without any kind of discussion or debate, Reb Ḥayyim locked the synagogue door on the morning of the scheduled eulogy. Binyamin Begin, a powerful person in his own right, broke the lock, opened the synagogue doors wide, and gave his eulogy. He then purchased new keys and a lock, and left them on the doorstep of Reb Ḥayyim's home with a letter of apology and a promise that he would never do such a thing again.

Both men agreed to the facts of this. But the Rav added a fascinating postscript. He had heard of this incident from his father, Rav Moshe, who was a rabbi of a smaller town a considerable distance from Brisk. Rav Moshe asked his father, Reb Ḥayyim, how he had reacted to the *gabbai*'s defiance. Reb Ḥayyim, who was generally a lion in defense of what he considered proper Torah values, told his son that he decided not to react, that he inquired how many people had attended the eulogy, and found out that the shul was filled to the rafters with a large overflow outside, many more congregants than for *Ne'ila* on Yom Kippur. Reb Ḥayyim explained that "*a rav muz vissen ven tzu reden, un a rav muz vissen ven tzu shreigen,* a rabbi must know when to speak out, and a rabbi must know when to remain silent."

"Mr. Prime Minister, you apparently learned to be a principled Zionist from your father," said Rav Soloveitchik. "*Kevod HaRav,* you apparently learned to be a sage religious leader from your grandfather," said Menaḥem Begin.

At that point, the Rav suddenly took notice of my presence, made a very quick introduction, and gestured in a way that told me that my appointment had long since ended. I left the apartment happily, not at all guilty that I had overstayed my welcome. After all, this too was Torah, and I was glad that I had been in the right place to have learned it.

DON'T BE AN AGAINSTNIK

During my early years on the faculty of Yeshiva University, the Belfer Physics Center was being built on Amsterdam Avenue; a tall and imposing structure that seemed to dwarf in its shadow even the Portuguese, Moorish-styled *beit midrash* building barely two blocks away. A group of the younger Talmud instructors, myself included, took it upon ourselves to speak to the Rav of this "creeping" danger that threatened to usurp the paramount position of Torah study at YU; how could a heretical science building, whose classes would be co-educational, be constructed on a grander scale than the edifice that housed the central *beit midrash*? Wouldn't such a science center negatively impact upon the Torah mission of Yeshiva University?

The Rav, as well as the Rebbetzin Tonya, who was with him at the time of our meeting, patiently and politely heard us out, telling us he would take our arguments seriously and get back to us in due time. I was asked to be the spokesman for the group, and I attempted to convey our fears with all of the earnestness and intensity of a young, idealistic and fervent Torah teacher.

The next morning, when I arrived to teach my class, the Rav

asked to see me. "Riskin, I don't understand you. What are you afraid of and why are you an againstnik? Maimonides includes the study of science and philosophy (*ma'asei bereshit* and *ma'asei merkava*, the physics and metaphysics of Aristotle) under the rubric of Gemara, within the structure of our Oral Law. Ultimately, all of true science and wisdom can only deepen our understanding of the One Creator of the Universe and validate our sacred Torah. Never be afraid of knowledge and don't be against intellectual inquiry and discovery." I sheepishly left the presence of my rebbe, who had once again taught me an invaluable lesson.

WHAT WE GIVE TO ISRAEL

I was once in the Rav's apartment when a secular Israeli representative provocatively challenged him. "What do you religious Jews give Israel aside from money?" he asked. The Rav replied, "Recently I was at the airport at the same time El Al was flying off to Israel. There were two coffins, Orthodox Jews being transported for burial in Israel. And there were dozens of young high school graduates, setting out for a year's study in the Holy Land. What do we give you? We give you our dead and we give you our youth; we give you our past and we give you our future. What else can we give?"

Chapter Sixteen

My Greek Professor Helps Me Decide to Be a Rabbi

A few years after I entered Yeshiva University, we finally moved to a small apartment in Fresh Meadows, Queens. The new neighborhood was certainly better than Bedford-Stuyvesant, but there was no Orthodox synagogue within walking distance; the only synagogue in the area was Conservative, where men and women sat together. Since there were many children in the community, and the older congregants found their presence in the synagogue disturbing, I seized the opportunity to start a junior congregation. I got the permission of the rabbi (David W. Gordon) – because the rabbi was basically an Orthodox man in a Conservative synagogue, as was the case in many synagogues at that time – to have a *meḥitza*, a separation, between the young boys and the young girls in the junior congregation. So, although the main synagogue had mixed seating, the junior congregation that I led had separate seating, and it became very successful.

I also started giving a Gemara class for some of the older individuals in the community who liked to learn, and that class was also a success. I greatly enjoyed teaching Torah, and I began to realize that my true calling was to be a rabbi. But how could I ever break the news to my mother?

I called Professor Feldman because my professional quandary – and my perceived disloyalty to my mother – was making it difficult for me to concentrate on my studies. The Rav seemed too formidable for me to ask at that time, and I also felt that a secular professor's advice would have much more weight with my mother. I went through a number of agonizing days and nights, and although I really did not have to make the decision for a number of years – I was only a sophomore in college – I felt it was important for my peace of mind. The truth is that since Professor Feldman had such small classes, we felt a strong sense of camaraderie with him. His Intellectual History class was considered mammoth with about twenty students, but the Latin class was less than half of that, and the Greek class had only three of us.

Once, I was the only student who showed up for a class in Greek. I figured, if I am the only one, how can we have a class? I was speaking to Professor Feldman informally by his desk, but when the bell rang he looked at me and said, "Well, Riskin, I guess we'd better begin now." So I sat down. I wasn't sure what would happen. He looked around the class and he said, "Why don't you begin to read, Riskin." I remember that we were studying Plato's *Phaedo*. I began to read the Greek text from where the last class had ended. I went on for almost ten minutes, after which the professor signaled me to stop reading.

And then he looked around at the empty room and he said, "Are there any questions?" And then he looked around again at the empty room and he said, "Well, why don't you continue– you, Riskin." I continued, after which he again asked, "Any questions? Why don't you continue – you this time, Riskin." I was surprised to see that he wasn't smiling at all. It was hard for me to control my laughter. I wasn't quite sure what to do, so I left the room to go to the men's room. I came back five minutes later. Professor Feldman said, "Well, the class is almost over, but Riskin, in your absence we read the next two hundred and fifty lines. There will be a quiz next period." Then he looked up at me and said, "Remember, it doesn't matter how many people you're teaching. It only matters how well and how thoroughly you teach. Remember that every single human being is a world unto himself." That was also a very important lesson for me.

I knew I needed vocational advice. So one evening, when my problem felt especially acute, I called Professor Feldman from the dormitory pay-phone at almost 10:00 P.M. He lived at that time on Grand Concourse in the Bronx. I apologized for calling so late at night. I told him that I would very much like to arrange to meet with him the next day, that I had a pressing personal problem, and that it would be difficult for me to go to sleep unless I knew I had a meeting with him the next day. He waived aside my apologies, saying, "Why don't you come over right now?" I said, "But it's ten o'clock. By the time I take the train I won't get to you until close to eleven." "Whenever you come, you come. You will always be welcome," he cordially responded.

I got there around 11:00 P.M. His wife graciously served tea, coffee and cake, and he asked what the problem was. I blurted out the conflict that I had, how disappointed my mother would be and how passionate my feelings were becoming toward the rabbinate. He then gave me one of the wisest pieces of advice I have ever received, advice that I have repeated to my own students many times over the years.

He said to me, "If an individual is fortunate enough to have a vocation that is also his avocation, if he loves what he does and would do it even if he didn't get paid for it, he will live a very blessed life, and chances are he will do it well." He smilingly looked over at me, "If you're happy and successful, your mother will be happy too!"

That clinched my decision to become a rabbi.

The first person I told was my grandmother, and strengthened by her pride and tears of joy, I had the fortitude to break it to my parents. My mother was far more gracious than I thought she would be. She said she always thought that it would go that way. But she also said something that I never forgot. She said, "Remember, we as your parents, your father and I, always loved you and always respected you and always gave you the right to make your own decisions, even if we disagreed. You can repay us by doing the same for your children."

We do not own or control our children or our students. Our task is not to mold them into any predetermined shape. Our task has to be to try to make them as good as they can become, given their own predilection, and given their own inclinations. The most important thing one can give one's child or one's student is, I think, what my parents gave me, and that is to believe in yourself, and to know that you have the support of those who love you, even if you make the decisions that they would not necessarily want you to make, as long as those decisions will not do objective harm to you or to others.

Chapter Seventeen

A Mother's Gift

My grandmother passed away on the day of my senior dinner.

But this story is really about my mother.

Of course there was a graduation at Yeshiva University, but even more important than the graduation was the senior dinner. The graduation, the commencement exercises, were very formal; one graduated with the whole university, and there was no time or possibility for any kind of individual expression. But it was at the senior dinner that the valedictory address was given, and I was the valedictorian of my class. The various awards and prizes were also presented there; it was the more personalized element of the YU College graduation.

My grandmother was then at least ninety years old. She lived with my aunt, but she had her own efficiency room. At that time, she had become ill with cancer of the stomach, which was growing slowly and causing her to be in pain – although she tried not to show her discomfort.

I visited her every week, including just two days before the senior dinner. She had purchased a new *Shas* for me as a graduation gift, and she wanted me to come and take it. We both knew she would not be able to attend the senior dinner, although she did know that I was going to give the valedictory address, and she was very proud.

I remember that as I opened the door to her efficiency room, my grandmother looked up at me and said, "*Mein kind,* my child, that's what all of life is, an opening of the door and a closing of the door." She said, "I know in your mind you're a very young boy, really a young man, and I'm a very old woman. But my life passes before me in a flash, and from my perspective that's what life is, an opening of the door and a closing of the door. The important thing is to make certain that before the door does close, you let in enough good people and important ideas, and you go out in order to touch enough people significantly, to help them and to teach them." She saw that I looked upset because she had, in the last few days, become much more pale and frail. She said to me, "Don't worry. Don't be afraid for me. I'm not afraid. I'm going home." That was the Yiddish expression for death, *ich gay ahaim,* "I'm going home." "And God is doing me a great favor. He's weakening my body and making it much easier for me to accept the transition from this world to the next." Then she gave me the *Shas,* and I left.

Two days later was the evening of the senior dinner. I had not yet written the valedictory address. That morning at 6:00 A.M., the telephone rang. We had one telephone and it was in the living room, which also served as my bedroom. My mother ran from her bedroom to answer the call, realizing that I had also been awakened by the ringing. I heard my mother say, perfectly controlled, "Then I'll come, of course, and watch Mama today," and she put down the receiver. She told me that my aunt did not feel well. My aunt was Grandma's major caretaker since they lived in the same apartment, and my aunt did not have young children as my mother did.

My mother explained that she would be taking care of my grandmother that day. I asked if she thought she would be able to make the senior dinner, although I felt it was selfish to even ask the question; my mother naturally replied that it would depend on how my aunt would feel. She may have to stay late, so as not to leave my grandmother alone.

The day passed, and I wrote the valedictory address. My father and sisters attended the dinner, but my mother couldn't make it. At about 11:00 that night, my mother came home. She tiptoed in because she thought I was sleeping, went to her closet and took out non-leather slippers. I understood that my grandmother had died that day. Indeed the call that morning had relayed the sad news. But my mother understood that had I thought my beloved grandmother had died, I would never have been able to compose the speech, no less to give it. And she didn't want to take that milestone away from me. My mother was really one of the strongest women I have ever known.

So, that day became very bittersweet for me. But obviously, the legacy from my grandmother was what enabled me to become the valedictorian at Yeshiva University in the first place.

And so was the legacy from my mother.

Chapter Eighteen

Ordination – How to Learn and to Lead

For me, there were two very significant messages that I received from Rav Soloveitchik at the *Ḥag HaSemikha,* ordination ceremony, when I was ordained into the rabbinate. The first was the address that Rav Soloveitchik gave, a talk that I've carried with me all these years, and I've repeated often to my own students.

The Rav recounted a famous incident recorded in the Talmud (*Sanhedrin* 14a) about how, during the Hadrianic Persecutions following the abortive Bar Kokhba rebellion in the second century CE, the Romans were very anxious to find the Achilles heel of the Judeans, the best way to destroy the Jewish people. They quickly recognized that they would only succeed if they managed to neutralize Jewish religious leadership. Therefore, they forbade the granting of *semikha,* rabbinical ordination.

Rabbi Yehuda ben Bava decided to go into hiding in order to preserve the tradition. He found an obscure place between two cities, took five of his best disciples with him, and gave them rabbinic ordination while they were sequestered there.

In spite of his efforts, the Romans located them. They gave chase to the newly ordained rabbis and almost caught them, but the young men ran quickly. They tried to take their rebbe with them, but he felt he would slow them down and refused to go. The Romans captured him and mercilessly speared his body until he looked "like a sieve," but the tradition of rabbinical ordination continued. Obviously, as Rav Soloveitchik pointed out, this was an act of *Kiddush HaShem*, sanctification of God's name; although, as he also pointed out, it is difficult to understand because there are three sins for which a Jew is commanded to sacrifice his life rather than commit them: murder, adultery and idolatry. *Semikha* is not counted among those mitzvot for which one should die.

Furthermore, the Rav asked, what does the term *semikha* mean? It really means the "laying on of hands." This is, indeed, generally what happens. The rabbi places his hands on the head or the shoulders of his disciple and, in this way, confers upon his student the authority to give rabbinic direction and make *halakhic* decisions. What is the significance of this "laying on of the hands?"

The verb *lismokh* (from which *semikha* is derived) literally means to rely upon, to lean on. Now, one may ask, who leans on whom in the act of *semikha*? Many would say that the individual who receives the ordination leans on his teacher, on past generations, because his authority comes from the past traditions, from the generations of previous sages who have taught Torah. The young rabbi is a disciple, a link in that chain of tradition that harks back to Sinai, and he leans on those rabbis of the past whose tradition has been handed down to him.

However, Rav Soloveitchik said, "If you ever see an older man with his hands on a younger man, who is leaning on whom? Generally it's the older man leaning on the younger man!"

So Rav Soloveitchik looked at us during the ordination dinner and said to us, "You're not leaning on me; I am the one who is leaning on you. Whatever I've learned and expounded, whatever new approach, insight or interpretation I have formulated, will die with me unless it lives through you."

"Therefore," said Rav Soloveitchik, "Rabbi Yehuda ben Bava was not sacrificing his life by ordaining his students; he was rather giving himself eternal life. He understood very well that if the tradition had died, it would have been as if he had never lived."

It is this interpretation of this passage of the Talmud that I think of every year as I confer *semikha* upon my students.

* * *

The second intriguing message came during the dinner that followed the ceremony of the *Ḥag HaSemikha*. I was privileged to sit right next to Rav Soloveitchik with my family. Now, I had never seen anyone get involved in small talk with the Rav, his persona was the very antithesis of small talk.

So I used the opportunity of the dinner seating arrangement to ask him for advice. What counsel could the Rav give his student who is leaving the cocoon of the Yeshiva environment to take a pulpit in the much larger and more alien world roundabout (at that point, I did not know that I would be teaching at YU for another fourteen years and would have personal meetings with my rebbe almost every Thursday afternoon)?

The first, he said, was to go to *minyan* (a prayer quorum in synagogue) every morning. It sounded strange to me; of course I would go to *minyan*. I was responsible for waking up the other students to go to *minyan* every morning when I was a dorm-counselor at YU. But he said, "I know you'll plan to be at *minyan*. But you will be a busy rabbi, and you'll spend a lot time seeing people, and you'll work until very late at night, and you'll have to steal time until the wee hours to study – and your *minyan* attendance might suffer. But you have to understand that in every congregation there are people who keep the congregation alive, and those are the people who are in shul every morning, every afternoon and every evening. And they are the mainstay of the shul. It's critical that they see their rabbi in the shul every morning with them."

Secondly, he said, "Give *tzedaka* [charity]. Since a rabbi is responsible for the *ḥesed* [kindness] in the community, and as such, is in a position in which he asks a lot of people to give *tzedaka* to various causes, he can confuse his raising of money for *tzedaka* with his own giving. It's important that you give *tzedaka* personally."

His third point was, "Give a Gemara *shiur* to students every day, and not just to *ba'alei batim* [laymen]. The difference between a European rabbi and an American rabbi, when they each first receive *semikha*, is not at all great," he said. "No one is really a great *talmid ḥakham* [scholar] at age eighteen or age twenty. The difference, however, is that a European rabbi would take on a community, and would be expected to sit and learn for the next twenty years. His congregants would come to him with halakhic questions, and twice a year he would give a major sermon – on *Shabbat Shuva* [in between Rosh HaShana and Yom Kippur], and on *Shabbat HaGadol* [the Shabbat before Pesaḥ]. Other than that, he was immersed in Torah study. After twenty years in such a setting, the rabbi would emerge a respectable Talmudic scholar.

"But an American rabbi, even if he is very learned and bright when he receives *semikha*, becomes a busy community leader. The more successful he is, the busier he is. After twenty such years, he runs the risk of forgetting whatever he learned when he got *semikha* in the first place. Therefore," the Rav said, "make certain that you give a Gemara class every day to students, and that will always keep you fresh and in real, *emesdik* learning."

And finally, he said, "Get a PhD. I want you to know that I believe that no one's education is complete without a PhD."

I tried to the best of my ability to take his advice.

The first two instructions were almost natural, *de rigueur*. Attending *minyan* and giving *tzedaka* are expected of every Jew, and so I certainly expected it of myself.

Giving a Gemara *shiur* every day was not always easy, but I was a rebbe of a high school or a university class all the years that I lived in America, so I gave a *shiur* every day. And thank God I did, otherwise, having made the transition from America to Israel, I never would have been able to manage in Israel without having taught Talmud all those years.

As far as the PhD is concerned (from the School of Near Eastern Language and Literature, New York University), although I rarely use the title, my doctoral work dealt with "The Laws of Divorce in the Talmudic and Sharia Traditions." From that PhD dissertation came a life-long concern, almost obsession, with women's rights to divorce in halakha; it led to a book on the subject (a second edition went way beyond the dissertation in a halakhic discovery for a solution to a problem which still plagues our Jewish society); to the first school in history to train women advocates for the Rabbinical Law Courts (the Monica Dennis

Goldberg School for Women Advocates); to Yad L'Isha, a hot-line for women in distress and a legal-aid service to provide free counsel for women whose husbands refuse to give the *get* (Jewish bill of divorce); and a women's rights lobby organization that is working to continue the Talmudic efforts to enable women to be freed from recalcitrant husbands who take unfair advantage of their unilateral right to give a divorce.

Part III

Israeli Interlude 1960–61

Chapter Nineteen

Rav Kahaneman – Dreams of a Giant Builder of Torah

After graduating college in 1960, I wanted to study in Israel, so I saved up $200 for a one-way boat fare. Once again my parents were not happy, but again they respected the decision.

Yeshiva University had a division of the Religious Studies department that was known as the Teachers Institute (TI); it was considered to be less academically intense than RIETS (Rabbi Isaac Elhanan Theological Seminary, or simply The Yeshiva), but more Zionistic. This division encouraged its students to spend one year of study in Israel, at the Ḥayyim Greenberg Institute in Jerusalem (12 Reuven Street in Baka), where the classes were held in Hebrew. I was asked by the administration to accompany the students by boat, to see that they were well ensconced at Makhon Greenberg, as well as to accompany them on the touring that took place before the program began. In return, YU defrayed part of my expenses in getting to Israel, and left open the possibility that, were I to decide to live in Jerusalem for the year, I would remain as the counselor for the TI students during that period at the Greenberg Institute. In the meantime, I had planned to attend the Ponevezh Yeshiva in Benei Berak at least for the month of Elul and through the High Holy Days; I left an opening for myself at Makhon Greenberg in Jerusalem in case I would not be completely satisfied intellectually at Ponevezh.

My Elul, Rosh HaShana and Yom Kippur experience at Ponevezh was intriguing and meaningful. It was certainly a much more right-wing kind of environment than what I was used to religiously, but there was a spirited and intense learning in the *beit midrash,* and I reveled in the opportunity to devote the entire day to religious texts. I also enjoyed Rav Rozovsky's Talmud classes immensely. However, his approach was different from that of Rav Soloveitchik, and it was very difficult for me to get used to any other way of learning, or viewing, a Talmudic text.

When I first arrived, Rav Kahaneman, the rosh yeshiva (head educator, dean), was not there. When I did meet him, it was an unforgettable experience. He had been away on his frequent fundraising trips throughout the year (generally nine out of twelve months), but he would return habitually to the yeshiva for *Kol Nidrei* evening. He spoke to the entire yeshiva that night, and he had the uncanny ability, even when addressing hundreds of students, to make you think that he was speaking directly to you. He said that there were two crucial elements to Yom Kippur, our Day of Forgiveness. The first is the primacy of Torah, since the blessing of repentance, forerunner to forgiveness, begins, "Return us, our God, to Your Torah. Blessed be the Lord who desires repentance." The second is divine love. The Bible defines God, as it were, for Moses as "*Hashem, Hashem, kel raḥum veḥanun,*" a God of power, compassion and freely giving beneficence. The Hebrew for compassion, *raḥum,* comes from *raḥem,* which means womb. We all come from God's womb, and therefore we are all siblings, and have to love each other as siblings. And siblings don't throw stones.

He was referring to the ultra-Orthodox who would sometimes throw stones at cars on Shabbat. "Our way to reach the secular Jews is not by throwing stones," he said, "our way is through love. That's God's love, and that's the message of Yom Kippur." This made a very strong impression on me, especially within the context of that particular *ḥaredi* yeshiva.

I was privileged to have a number of conversations with Rav Kahaneman, immediately after Yom Kippur, because I had made a decision to leave the yeshiva, but I wanted to meet with him first. He asked me about Rav Soloveitchik, requested that I share with him some of the Rav's Talmudic interpretations, and asked why I was leaving Ponevezh. I explained that I had heard many great *shiurim* in Ponevezh, wherein a strong question was asked on the Rambam and a powerful answer was offered in response. I was left with a good question and a very good answer. In contrast, Rav Soloveitchik would ask what seemed like a devastating question on the Rambam; he would then return to the Talmudic source, offer a novel but logically brilliant interpretation of the Talmudic argument, after which it would become clear that since that was how the Rambam had interpreted the Talmud, there was no question whatsoever on how he had arrived at his halakhic decision…

I believe the most important outcome of my experience of being in Ponevezh was the fact that when Rav Kahaneman later came to America, when I was a rabbi at Lincoln Square Synagogue, I had the honor of spending time with him. For a number of years, he spent a Shabbat each year at my home and in my synagogue. From 1964–77, I had a full-time position at Yeshiva University, at the James Striar School (JSS), where I taught college students who had had no previous yeshiva or Torah training. It was a wonderful experience for me. The "Ponevezher Rov," Rav Kahaneman, met my students around the Shabbat table, and he would question them a great deal about their backgrounds and what had led them to Torah observance.

Then he became ill. He was admitted to Mount Sinai Hospital, and he asked to see me. He said he needed a blood transfusion, and asked if my students could donate blood for him. He said he would only take blood from *shomrei Shabbat*, Sabbath observers, but he would like Sabbath observers who are *ba'alei teshuva*, penitents, because the Talmud says that the place where the penitent stands, even the most righteous person cannot stand. So, of course I agreed to arrange that students from my classes in JSS would provide the blood for Rav Kahaneman's transfusions.

I spent several hours at his bedside. I knew what he had created. He had emerged from the jaws of the Holocaust and had succeeded in transplanting the European Talmudic Academy of Ponevezh to Benei Berak, Israel – and in a much bigger way than it had ever been in Europe. I also knew that he was just beginning to build a Torah complex in the then new city of Ashdod as well. I was truly in awe of this European Jew who raised money worldwide – from New York to Johannesburg – for the sake of Torah. He had even once told me, one Shabbat visit a few years earlier, that "he had sacrificed his own Torah on the altar of Torah." He had given up the possibility of writing Torah books, and teaching future Torah teachers intensively, in order to create the Torah Center of Ponevezh.

It seemed to me, whilst standing at his bedside, that he was depressed, and I said to him, "I hope the Rosh Yeshiva understands what a *zeḥut*, what a merit it is for me to have gotten to know the Rosh Yeshiva. After all, everyone dreams, but how many people are able to realize as many of their dreams as the Rosh Yeshiva was able to realize? What was accomplished at Ponevezh is a glory to behold. Most people are fortunate if they realize 10 percent. The Rosh Yeshiva must have realized 90 percent. The Rosh Yeshiva must have had great merit to have had such accomplishment."

He looked at me and he smiled. He then took my hand and said to me, "*Nein, nein,* Rav Riskin. True, for most people only 10 percent of their dreams are ever realized. No one dies unless 50 percent of his desires remain unrealized, is what our sages of the Talmud say. But in my case, it was also only 10 percent that was realized. I just had greater and loftier dreams."

More than anything else, I learned from Rav Kahaneman the importance of dreaming for Torah and the importance of trying to realize those dreams no matter what it takes. If you believe in a God who is invisible, you may well dream the incredible. And if you dream the incredible, with God's help you may achieve the impossible…, but make sure to set your sights high; at the end of the day, even the most privileged live to see only 10 percent of their dreams realized.

Chapter Twenty

Israel: Mirrors of Diversity

A YEMENITE FRIEND

When I first came to Israel by boat in 1960, I kissed the ground at Haifa. But I couldn't wait to come to the holy city of Jerusalem. I arrived by bus, and the first thing that greeted my eyes were *Fanny* posters. I was devastated. *Fanny* was an American musical comedy that had apparently come to the Jerusalem Theater – and the posters publicizing its arrival featured women dressed (or undressed) in colored bloomers, kicking up their feet in dance. This was my introduction to the holiest city in the world? I could not believe the desecration.

I slowly became adjusted to Jerusalem's reality: the European-like, old-world sanctity of Me'ah She'arim; the very special *Yakirei Yerushalayim*, veteran and venerable Jerusalemites; the soldiers with *kippot*; the screams of "Idiot!" which in reality was the hawking of the daily newspaper, *Yediot*; the intellectual excitement, as well as the heresies of the Hebrew University, at that time on the Givat Ram campus. I learned to love the very differences of the manifold smells and sounds, tones and textures of a polyglot of Jews of different racial colors, different dress and different cultural orientations.

I befriended a Yemenite boy my own age, who also lived in the Baka neighborhood where I was staying, and he invited me to his *sukka* on the first evening of Sukkot. I was shocked when his cute and wizened sixty-plus-year-old grandfather introduced me to a woman next to him with the words "Please come to know my wife" ("*na, takir et ishti*"), and then to the woman next to her and the woman next to her and the woman next to her, each with the very same salutation. Apparently he had brought his four wives from Yemen to Jerusalem. I was tantalized by the sharp fragrance and pungent taste of *kubana* and *hilbe,* and I was mesmerized by all of the children, some of whom still slept in cartons in an apartment not much larger than the *sukka.*

But most amazing of all was what decorated the *sukka* walls; three large *Fanny* posters. My friend told me that they had fallen from the lampposts and so could be retrieved at no cost; it was his grandfather, a lover of bright colors, who noticed their potential to make the perfect wall hangings for the *sukka.* He had already been instructed to save them for next year... I never learned a better lesson about our ability to sanctify every part of life!

I learned many lessons that year about understanding different cultures, and the importance of never calling ethnic groups whom we do not understand "primitive." I volunteered to be a counselor at a local elementary school in Baka, which had received a large influx of new immigrant children from North Africa. I prayed with them each morning and served as a "big brother" to several of them after school.

To the chagrin of the entire faculty, as well as their classmates, these new immigrants had never heard of a toothbrush or toothpaste. Thinking myself to be clever and resourceful, I bought these basic instruments of hygiene for all of my charges, and we all brushed our teeth together, in school, before daily prayer. Before long, one of my students told me that his grandfather, a *ḥakham* from the old country, wanted to meet me. He said there was a problem regarding the "tooth-brushing."

I braced myself for the meeting the next afternoon. The young boy interpreted for an ancient, wrinkled man with smiling eyes and a venerable beard, but without a visible tooth in his mouth (I probably couldn't have understood him even if he were speaking Hebrew, and I wondered what he could possibly know about tooth-brushing!). "You know," he said, after thanking me for praying with his grandson and inquiring about my American background, "our mouths are holy, especially when we pray to God. The Torah teaches that God breathed into the human being the soul of life, and the *Targum* interprets that as referring to our gift of speech, our ability to communicate with our mouths. When we sleep at night, our bodies rest, but our souls go up to heaven to give an accounting of our days' activities before the Creator of the universe. When we wake up, our souls return to our mouths. In particular, the first words we pray must be spoken in purity. Why do you make the boys put some extra substance, some dirty paste, into their pure and holy mouths, which have just come down from God?" I mumbled an embarrassed apology. From then on, we brushed our teeth *after* morning prayers.

A LESSON FROM AGNON

One of the courses I took at the Ḥayyim Greenberg Institute was in Hebrew literature with Professor Tuchner, a literary critic who was generally credited with having discovered the genius of S.Y. Agnon. For the final exam, each of us had to write an interpretation of Agnon's masterpiece, "The Orchestra." Three of the papers were read at the graduation ceremonies at the end of the year, and the great master-author himself was in the audience. I was chosen to be one of the "readers" – my position being that the story expressed the conflict between religion and aesthetics, with religion eventually emerging supreme. Two other papers – one was by Neal Kozodoy, today an editor of *Commentary* magazine – were also read, each purporting to extract a very different message from the same story.

As the *pièce de résistance,* Professor Tuchner asked Agnon to explain which interpretation was correct. The master declined to do so, but he did agree to tell a story:

There was a very small town in Europe, he began, a *dorf* so primitive that no one who lived there had ever seen a mirror in their lives. One of the townspeople went to a fair once a year, and that particular year he came home with a mirror for his wife, although he didn't really know what it was. When he walked into the house and unwrapped his gift, his wife began to shout, "You monster, you came home from the fair with another woman?! How dare you! Get her out of my house." The husband, taken aback by his wife's charges, for the first time looked at the gift he had brought her. Now he began to scream, "I am not the culprit, you are! This is what I have to find when I return home after my journey – another man in my house!" Their noise aroused the townspeople, who summoned the rabbi to arbitrate between husband and wife. The rabbi heard the two sides, looked at the gift and cried out, "I don't understand the argument. There is no strange man or strange woman in this house. There is only an old man with a beard, a rabbi who has achieved wisdom as the gift of his years..."

And with that, Agnon sat down.

Chapter Twenty-One

A Nun, a Monk and a Jerusalem Professor

During the winter semester that year I studied at the Hebrew University, where I was exposed to a panoply of stars: Professors Gershon Scholem, Efraim Urbach, Shraga Abramson. But one of my most fascinating classes was with Professor David Flusser, who taught the Gospels in ancient Greek. There were four students in the class including me; the others were: an Egged bus driver (only in Israel at that time could one imagine a Jewish bus driver who was also a Greek scholar interested in the origins of Christianity), Brother Yohanan (a monk from the Terra Sancta church), and a nun from Bonn, Germany.

The three men sat in front of Professor Flusser, while the nun sat by herself at the back and extreme end of the classroom; she took copious notes, but never spoke. I became quite friendly with Brother Yohanan. He was roughly my age, and we took hikes and went to the movies together.

Remember, this was before the Six Day War, and the Mandelbaum Gate was the closest we could get to the Western Wall. I would often confide to my Christian friend how anxious I was to pray at the Wall, to kiss its stones, to recite the priestly blessing in the protection of its shade. One day after class, he asked me to meet him the next day, with my passport, in front of the Terra Sancta church. He had some papers for me to fill out and, once the bureaucracy had been taken care of, he could arrange for me to visit the Wall along with the Easter pilgrims from the church.

My heart was thumping. I barely slept that night. I arrived even before the appointed time, almost afraid to anticipate the impending fulfillment of the dream that had given me no rest since I had come to Israel: to actually pray at the Western Wall of the Holy Temple. Brother Yohanan quickly perused my passport to ascertain that nowhere did it state that I was a Jew. He gave me a form to fill out with my birth details, American address, and my parents' names. I then came to the final line: "I hereby declare that I am a believing Christian," above room for my signature. My heart fell. "This I cannot fill out," I heartbrokenly told him. "And why not?" he asked. "It's not like you have to become baptized. Just sign it."

With tears in my eyes, I blurted out the whole history of Christian anti-Semitism in Europe, the autos-da-fé, the Crusades and their destruction of entire Jewish communities; the fact that we are forbidden from learning Torah on Christmas Eve, lest we congregate in a synagogue or study hall, and serve as easy targets for Christian pogroms against "Christ-killers." "But you're studying the Gospels with me," he charged. "Because I found out that Jesus was really a devout Jew," I responded. He returned my passport and I tore up the entry form. From then on we saw each other regularly in class, but he never spoke a personal word to me again.

At the end of the semester, the nun from Bonn hesitatingly approached me, speaking to me for the first time. "I'm interested in converting to Judaism," she said. She explained that she had been brought up to believe that, although the Jews were the first people elected by God, they forfeited their place and were doomed to wander the world, stateless and homeless, because they had rejected the messiahship and divinity of Jesus. But now she saw that we have returned to our land, and we are even flourishing. She therefore concluded that God's initial covenant remains in force, and she wished to become Jewish. I directed her to one of my teachers in Israel, Rav Zev Gotthold, who was then officially in charge of conversions in Israel.

I subsequently met her, several years later, already a converted Jewess in Me'ah She'arim, married to a "Reb Arele" Hasid and mother of three small children. Although she must have undergone an internal transformation, her external appearance, her garb, her "habit," seemed to be exactly as it had been when we studied together, including her covered hair…

Chapter Twenty-Two

A Dilemma: One or Two Days Yom Tov?

At the end of my year in Israel, I did not want to leave; I wanted very much to stay and make *aliya*. Obviously there was very strong pressure from my parents for me not to do that, as well as from a young woman in New York whom I had been taking out fairly regularly before I left. Truth to tell, however, the most powerful reason for my return to America was my plan to enter rabbinical school at Yeshiva University and continue my studies with Rav Soloveitchik.

One of the issues in the mix that was intensified by my indecision, and brought on by the upcoming festival of Shavuot, was the whole question of whether or not I should keep the second day of Yom Tov – the second festival day. According to Jewish law, only those residing in the Diaspora keep two days. Since I was now living in Israel, could I be considered a fully-fledged Israeli and keep only one day, or should I take into account my pull toward America and keep two days?

At the end of the year, during the post Pesah summer *zeman* (study session, semester), I was studying at Yeshivat Kerem B'Yavneh, the only high-level yeshiva in Israel that then combined Talmud study with army service. After a most successful and intellectually invigorating winter semester at the Hebrew University, I wanted to "taste" this first Israeli *Yeshivat Hesder* as well. The rosh yeshiva of Kerem B'Yavneh was Rav Goldvicht, but the *posek*, the halakhic decisor, was Rav Elimelech Bar Shaul, the chief rabbi of Reḥovot at the time. I had heard that he had been a *ḥavruta* of HaRav Avraham Yitzḥak HaKohen Kook, the first chief rabbi of Israel, *z"l*, as well.

Rav Bar Shaul would come to the yeshiva every Thursday evening, give a *shiur* and then invite us to place our questions in a large, square, black yarmulke. He would then pick out each question and answer it publicly. Before I went to Israel, obviously Rav Soloveitchik had been the authority with whom I consulted, but he had said that for questions that pertain to Israel, "You should find a rav in Israel, and ask him those questions." For me, Rav Bar Shaul became that man.

So along came the question of observing a second day of Shavuot, and I asked Rav Bar Shaul. "One day," he answered. "You must only keep one day of the festival. You are now in Israel."

By this time, Yeshiva University had announced its plan to open its first *kollel* for rabbinical students the following year, 1961–2, which would feature a special *ḥavura* with Rav Soloveitchik. I received a telegram inviting my participation, and my intense desire to continue studying with Rav Soloveitchik came back full force. Intellectually, financially, professionally and parentally – all roads turned back to America for me, although emotionally my heart belonged to Israel.

So I pressed Rav Bar Shaul, "But Rebbe, my intention is to go back to America." He grabbed hold of my hand and he pressed it very warmly, looked into my eyes, and said, "Who says you have the right to intend to go back? I don't believe Jewish law takes into consideration an intention that is not valid according to Jewish law. And Jewish law, Torah law, demands that you live in Israel: 'And you shall inherit the land and dwell in it' [Numbers 53:33]. So even if you do go back, it will be a temporary stay. By now, you know that your real home is in Israel. Therefore one day is what you must keep."

That left a very strong mark in my soul and I became firmer in my thinking about eventually living in Israel. But did I have the right to go back to America, even temporarily?

Once again I turned to Rav Bar Shaul, who sent me to Ḥakham Ovadia Yosef – who had already developed a reputation as an outstanding halakhic authority. Ḥakham Ovadia asked me what I intended to become, what I planned on doing with my life. I said I wanted to be a rabbi.

He asked me from whom I thought I could learn best in order to become the best kind of rabbi possible, and I said, "I believe from Rav Soloveitchik."

He said, "You must live now wherever you feel you can learn the most Torah. And if you are teaching Torah full time, and you are accomplishing a great deal in teaching Torah in America, you can even stay in America to teach Torah. You will be considered an agent of all of us in Israel.

"It is critical to teach Torah to Jews wherever they are."

Of course I understood that the best of all worlds would be to teach Torah in Israel.

Chapter Twenty-Three

Finding My *Bashert*: Zion and a Synagogue Director Share in *Shadkhanut*

Something else happened that clinched my decision about returning to America.

Since I was loath to leave Israel, I tried to prolong my stay for as long as possible. Yeshiva University had organized a trip to Israel for the summer that was led by Victor Geller. I applied to see if I could be a counselor for his summer program. That would give me an opportunity to spend an extra six weeks in Israel (room and board included), and then to get a free ride back. Since I did not really have the funds to return to America, this was a truly wonderful opportunity for me.

Vic was leading both a high-school and a college group. I was hired to lead the high-school group, but I was also scheduled to spend three days at a special seminar teaching the college group intensively. Its home base was on the Bar Ilan campus.

I arrived early the first day of my three-day stint at Bar Ilan, planning to speak right after the morning service, on the subject of prayer. The young men and women in the group were still praying when I arrived at 7:45 A.M. I was supposed to begin at 8:00 A.M., but I didn't, because I noticed that there was still one young woman praying on her side of the *meḥitza*. She was praying with great intensity, and I could not begin until she finished her prayers.

I can honestly say that, at that moment, I truly fell in love with that woman and decided that this was the person I wanted to marry.

While I was waiting for her to conclude the *Amida*, I asked Victor Geller about her; he said she was the most special young woman he had ever met. She was just about to enter Barnard. Obviously I thought that she was at least eighteen years old at the time. I had just turned twenty-one.

I gave my lecture and she asked very searching questions. They didn't at all disappoint me. Because I was rather shy, and since I still had a relationship with a young woman in the United States, I didn't really pursue what I hoped would be this new relationship. But the three days that I taught her at Bar Ilan only intensified the feelings that I had. I felt spurred on to return to America sooner, end the other relationship, and immediately begin dating Vicky.

Victor Geller told me her story.

Vicky came from a very non-observant background. Her mother was a third-generation American. The rumor in the family was that her great-grandmother, born in Davenport, Iowa, fasted on Yom Kippur. That was about the only relationship to Judaism that there was. Vicky's maternal grandfather's second wife was a German, non-Jewish woman. Her parents were not anti-religious, just areligious. Her mother had never been in a shul in her life until that point. They had had no background and no real interest.

At that time, my father-in-law, may he rest in peace, was doing very well financially. He was in the building trade and Vicky was an only child. Her parents sent her to the prestigious United Nations school, which was very "broadening"; students there were from all sorts of backgrounds – Hindus, Buddhists, Muslims. When she was fourteen years old, a teacher at the school led a tour to Europe for the summer and Vicky went on the trip. They visited Germany and she became very interested in history, especially Holocaust history. When she got back from the trip at the end of that summer, she told her parents that she really wanted to go to Israel the following summer. Her parents were not upset at this. They figured that it would also be "broadening." As I said, they were not anti-Jewish at all. They figured she would learn the history of the Middle East, the archeology of the Bible, and that some exposure to Judaism and Islam would be culturally enriching.

So when Vicky expressed the desire to go to Israel, her mother entered a synagogue for the first time in her life. Since they lived in Queens, she went into the Forest Hills Jewish Center, a very well-known Conservative synagogue, and asked the executive director of the synagogue about trips to Israel. "For whom is the trip?" he asked, to which her mother replied, "For my daughter." "Is your daughter observant?" he asked, and my mother-in-law (not understanding that in the usual jargon of knowledgeable Jews, the word "observant" means "observant of Jewish law, practice, customs," i.e., "Orthodox"), took "observant" to mean perspicacious, an intelligent and discerning viewer of people and events. "My daughter," she said proudly, "is very observant."

So immediately the executive director called Victor Geller, who led the Yeshiva University tour for "observant" girls and boys, and put him in touch with my mother-in-law. Vicky went on the trip, had a wonderful, unforgettable summer, and by the end of it she had truly become observant! Victor Geller lived about a mile away from where Vicky and her parents lived, and thereafter she became his regular Shabbat guest, spending every Shabbat with his family, meeting the family for prayers at the Young Israel of Forest Hills and then joining them for Shabbat lunch.

The following summer, Vicky went on the Israel trip again. This time she was sixteen and about to enter Barnard. That was when we met. Since she was with the college group, I never thought she was younger than eighteen. When I returned to America, I ended the other relationship and asked Vicky out. I remember that for our first date we went to see *A Man for All Seasons*.

Our relationship developed very quickly. We wanted to get married immediately. When she announced our intentions to her parents, who until that point had been very gracious toward me, they had a veritable "fit." And this objection went beyond the fact that she was only sixteen years old! (Indeed, when my daughter Batya turned sixteen, I wrote my in-laws a letter of apology; I began to understand a little bit of what they had felt because I know how great my objection would have been, had she – at age sixteen – wanted to get married to her first boyfriend.) They had initially gone along with her new-found religiosity only because they viewed it as a passing phase. They didn't really take it seriously. And then suddenly, this aspiring Orthodox rabbi comes on to the scene with no real prospects of making a living; I was also the first person that she had ever gone out with seriously. They were fit to be tied, to the extent that her father wouldn't even come out to speak to me when I would come to the house. He had always acted as a most gracious gentleman, but now he made it a point not to see me.

We used to have very inexpensive kinds of dates because I didn't have much money. I was a *kollel* student, so we had to use our ingenuity. I remember once we bought pomegranates and counted the pomegranate seeds to see if there were 613 seeds, like it says in the Gemara.

Then one day, when Vicky came down to meet me (since, at a certain point, it became easier for me to wait outside), she was crying. She told me that her mother wanted her to go to a psychiatrist. And her concern for her daughter's mental health was not only due to our relationship. Vicky had begun tearing the toilet paper on Friday afternoon, and that was the straw that broke the camel's back. To someone who has no religious background whatsoever, the actions of an Orthodox Jew do seem rather odd, to say the least. And now that I was in the picture, it only exacerbated everything.

Anyway, I told her I would go together with her to see the psychiatrist. I remember him – Dr. Carey, a non-Jewish gentleman, who was soft-spoken and wise. A few weeks later we were popping popcorn – that was another one of our dates – and my mother-in-law announced, "Well, Dr. Carey said he never saw two such mature young people, so I guess if you want to become engaged, you can get engaged. Just wait until you're eighteen to get married." And so my in-laws have, indeed, been absolutely wonderful throughout our married life. I grew to love them like my own parents.

From the moment of their "acceptance of the inevitable," their fundamental graciousness came through. My mother-in-law had always pictured a kind of Sunday morning, breakfast wedding in a very fancy place in Central Park, with finger sandwiches and classical music. We were talking about something that was entirely different, an event very strange and new to her. The fact that there would be hundreds of guests and no social dancing seemed bizarre. Nevertheless, she acceded to our wishes, and planned everything with great aplomb and elegance because she's that kind of person. And my father-in-law returned to being the perfect gentleman and wedding host.

At the end of the wedding, which was really, for us, very meaningful and beautiful, Vic Geller walked over to my mother-in-law and congratulated her. I overheard my mother-in-law respond, "For them it's the beginning; for us it's the end." Coming home from the wedding I repeated her mother's words to Vicky, and we promised ourselves that it was not going to be the end; we would see to it that, for her parents, it was going to be the beginning as well.

My mother-in-law, at that point, felt that she could not become observant. We decided that we would not allow our Jewish observance to be a barrier in our relationship. We could always eat tuna fish, a tomato, a cucumber in their home, using paper plates and plastic utensils. Eventually they kept special pots, pans and dishes exclusively for us, and Vicky would do the cooking. And subsequently, when we moved to Israel, the children even went to be with their grandparents on several occasions. They very much respected our wishes, so *kashrut* and Shabbat were never an issue. Each respected the others' lifestyle. My father-in-law was a real equestrian and rode on horseback into his eighties. Our son, Hilly, spent a lot of time on the Appalachian Trail with them.

Vicky's parents were very active, proactive grandparents for all of our children. They were extremely helpful and very close to us. My father-in-law shared his building expertise, first as the professional real estate advisor to the YU rabbis that purchased Camp Morasha, then in the building stage of Lincoln Square Synagogue, and later with Efrat. My mother-in-law was always there to help with the children growing up.

For us, they have also served as very important models of the possibility of adaptation. They have been loving people who taught us how members of the same family can maintain their own lifestyles and still retain mutual respect and love. My mother-in-law was in her eighties and my father-in-law in his nineties when they came to live with us in Israel, and – although we never asked them to – they adopted our observant lifestyle. My mother-in-law became an active partner in Vicky's thrift shop (*Maḥsan,* literally, "storage room"), which became a "Maḥsan Boutique" under her tutelage, and tried never to miss reciting the Grace after Meals, albeit in English.

They both proved to all of us that a loving family can overcome all barriers to relationships, and that it is never too late to change and grow.

Part IV

Teaching Minds & Touching Souls: Yeshiva University 1963–77

Chapter Twenty-Four

Power Lunches with a Power Educator: Rav Moshe Besdin[1]

It was June 24, 1963, the day I was to take the last of my qualifying examinations for rabbinical ordination at RIETS. It was also one day after my wedding, and two days after I had been informed that the Talmud class I had been scheduled to teach in Yeshiva University High School of Manhattan had been canceled due to a lower-than-expected enrollment. To say that I was panicked out of my mind would be an understatement. Here I was with a new bride (an eighteen-year-old Religions major at Barnard), a three-year rental contract for an apartment at 100 Overlook Terrace, and no tangible means of support. The telephone rang: "This is Moshe Besdin speaking." (Could it be the Rav Moshe Besdin, Director of the James Striar School for young men without yeshiva background –

1. This chapter is based on an article originally written for the 75th anniversary of Yeshiva University.

many of whom I had taught at Yeshiva University seminars – who had a legendary reputation as a master educator, but whom I had never formally met?) "I would like to offer you a full-time position, teaching Freshman Bible and Sophomore Gemara. May I depend on you?"

I was flabbergasted, frightened and flattered all at the same time. I mumbled into the phone my appreciation of the offer, but that I had never taken a course in pedagogy and I was more than a bit daunted by the prospect of teaching students who would only be a few years my junior (I was then just twenty-three years old – and looked about sixteen). He waved away my protestations, telling me that he would observe my classroom manner and have a weekly lunch meeting with me, during which time I would receive on-the-job training. "I'm a *beit midrash* watcher," he concluded, "and I've had my eye on you for a long time. I'm sure you'll do fine."

So began an association that was one of the most significant relationships of my life. From September 1963 until June 1977 – for as long as I taught at JSS – I ate lunch with Rav Besdin, Monday through Thursday, 1:00–3:00 P.M., at the Tov Me'od restaurant (the aforementioned Greasy Spoon). Rav Besdin loved to monologue, and I became his most ardent listener. He was, for me, a rebbe, a mentor, a personal counselor and a second father. Every skill I acquired in education methodology, every new initiative I established in the formative years of my rabbinate, every attitude I developed in my approach to Judaism and life, were shaped and refined by this generous, genuine, wise, incisive and consummately normal *talmid ḥakham*, who was both modest and decisive, inspiring and down-to-earth, and completely devoid of any modicum of self-importance or hypocrisy.

The James Striar School that he created – he was not only its first director, but he was the individual who shaped its contours, determined its curriculum and had the most abiding influence on four decades of its students – was probably the very first yeshiva for *ba'alei teshuva* in Jewish history. The student body (two- to three-hundred strong) was comprised of graduates of secular high schools from all over America, and occasionally even from far-flung areas of the globe (I had a student from Barbados, West Indies), each of whom had been influenced by some religious inspiration: a Yeshiva University seminar, a synagogue rabbi, a youth group, a religious relative or friend. Because Rav Besdin believed that a school was formed in its admissions office, he himself interviewed every prospective student; he made sure the candidate was serious about his Judaism, willing to assume an observant lifestyle, and able to read, although not necessarily able to understand, a Hebrew text. Each interview lasted at least an hour; by the time it was over, he had weeded out anyone whose main interest was merely getting into a private college and he had established an inextricable bond with anyone he had decided to admit to the program.

The JSS curriculum consisted of the study of traditional Jewish texts: the Bible and its classical commentaries (Rav Besdin himself taught this class to every one of the incoming students), the Mishna and the Talmud. Rav Besdin would regale me with his philosophy of education during those unforgettable lunches. "Teach *it*, not about it," which meant that he was against a paperback, even Artscroll form of Torah-in-translation, or a Judaism-lite article about biblical or Talmudic thought. His "*it*-ological" theory of learning meant that a serious student would welcome the opportunity to take the necessary intellectual plunge and grapple with the text itself – learn to read *it*, translate *it*, understand *it* and internalize *it*, slowly but surely progressing from *Ḥumash* to Rashi, to Mishna, to Talmud. He actually called himself a "*ḥeder*-ologist," after the *ḥeder*, the Jewish school system in the European *shtetl* that successfully taught numerous generations of Jews how to properly learn and understand a classical Hebrew text based on the single educational principle that if you cannot properly read and translate the original verse of Talmudic passage, you will never truly understand it.

Rav Besdin also had traditional notions of classroom management. He walked the halls before class was due to begin, making certain that each rebbe was on time, and he demanded thorough preparation and lucid application from every member of the faculty. Because we were teaching not only divine texts but also supremely human subjects – flesh and blood students – we were paid for two extra periods a week, at which time we were expected to meet with our individual pupils for regular counseling sessions. In all of this he remained *primus inter pares*, the master teacher – thoroughly knowledgeable, in love with his subject matter and his students, always accessible, and totally committed.

Rav Besdin detested pretense and pretension. There was a tendency among freshmen *ba'alei teshuva* to attempt to skip steps in the educational process and in their religious progression, to try to appear to know and to be more than what they actually knew and were. If he saw a beginner student displaying *tzitzit* or wearing a black hat, he would take him aside and warmly chastise him: "Remember, it is proper and even laudatory to attend a formal dinner with a tuxedo and top-hat. But if one wears a tuxedo and top-hat along with torn pants, he becomes a clown!" He understood that climbing up too quickly can result in crashing down just as quickly; true education must be a gradational, step-by-step process.

Rav Besdin was an accomplished Torah scholar – he knew *Yoreh De'ah* virtually by heart, with all the comments of the *Pri Megadim* – but I believe that his real love was the Ramban's commentary on the Bible. He also had great respect for world literature (he especially enjoyed quoting long passages of Shakespeare), he played a mean game of tennis, he was immensely proud of his charming and beautiful wife (he deeply believed in romantic love), and he gloried in the various successes of each of his children. Above all else, however, he was the consummate teacher for whom teaching Torah was not only his profession, but was truly the existential definition of his very being. And the Torah that he taught was constantly interspersed with the wise reflections of a renaissance man whose faith was profound, without being fanatic, and who genuinely believed that every individual was granted the God-given right to choose his or her lifestyle and life commitments. He saw the task of a teacher as the attempt to lovingly expose and wisely guide, never to forcefully coerce or underhandedly manipulate.

Rav Besdin had a clearly formulated philosophy of Judaism that stressed the Maimonidean "Golden Mean" and included a commitment to "Torah with *derekh eretz*" (both in terms of respectful interpersonal relationships, as well as professional pursuits). The source of his theological outlook was our classical Jewish texts, especially the Bible and its commentaries of Rashi and Ramban. The divine covenant with Israel was, for him, the very basis of the uniqueness of our nation, and so Rav Besdin was fond of explaining (in his interpretation of a difficult passage of the Ramban), that whereas a contract depends on the fulfillment by both parties of its stipulations, our covenant has the divine guarantee that there will always be a nation Israel through which redemption will eventually come, no matter what. A contract can be revoked if one of the parties reneges; the covenant is eternal. He had great respect for our traditions, and the vital force of a Judaism that has been transmitted – parent to child, teacher to disciple – for the past four thousand years. Indeed, he believed that Isaac's test in the *Akeda* was greater than Abraham's; after all, Abraham heard the divine voice ask for the sacrifice of his son, whereas Isaac heard it only from his father. In this fashion, Isaac is the truest representative of the Jewish people, who have constantly been ready to lay down their lives for their faith – not because they heard the command directly from God, but because they heard it from their parents and teachers.

And, in addition to all of this, Rav Moshe Besdin had a twinkle in his eye, a warm sensitivity, and sense of humor in his heart. Which one of his many students would not yearn to be lovingly called by him once again a *trumbenik* (ne'er-do-well), or doesn't think of Laban as a "villain with style"? I remember that Rav Besdin once suggested that we cut out the *knish* (generally kasha) with which we concluded our daily sandwich-and-salad each day; after all, calories and cholesterol were beginning to make a difference on both of us. But then, toward the end of our two-hour session, he looked at me seriously. "Reb Shloime," he said, "I've been noticing the woman who makes the *knishes* in the back. Do you know that in all the time we've been sitting here, no one has ordered a *knish*? She has had nothing to do. If she's fired, it would be on our conscience. You wouldn't want that to happen." I dutifully got us two *knishes*, as an act of *mesirat nefesh* on behalf of the *knish*-cook, of course.

So indebted did I feel toward Rav Besdin that I asked him to be the *sandak* (godfather) for my first son's circumcision; of course he acquiesced to my request. During our lunch together when I asked him, however, he seemed quite agitated. His son-in-law, with a PhD in Jewish History, was having difficulty in finding a suitable teaching position. "Plumbers," he railed. "Jewish children have to study to be plumbers. It's easier for plumbers to make a living than it is for Jewish educators." He went on and on, quite disturbed by the situation.

The next morning, the morning of my son's circumcision, I called

Rav Besdin at 6:00 A.M. I apologized for the early telephone call, but I explained that I had not slept all night. "I'm concerned about your *kavana* (internal intention) when you will be *sandak*," I explained. "I don't want you to intend my son to be a plumber. A plumber is fine, but I would still want that my son be a Torah teacher." Rav Besdin laughed heartily, "You surely know I wasn't serious," he said. "There is no profession as exalted and as satisfying as being a teacher. Even our morning blessing refers to the Almighty God Himself as a *melamed*, a teacher. A good teacher can always look in the mirror at night and know that he or she spent the day in a significant way. An educator paves the way for the next generation of Torah, participates in eternity. I wouldn't trade my life with anyone in the world." Neither would I – thanks to the many life-lessons I was privileged to learn from the greatest teacher I have ever known, Rav Moshe Besdin.

Chapter Twenty-Five

"Thank God It's My Leg and Not My Hand"

One of the students at JSS was a young man from Mississippi, Leroy (or David) Schild, who was so anxious to learn Torah that he would get up at four o'clock in the morning, work in a butcher shop from 5:00–8:00 A.M. in order to support himself, and arrive punctually for class at 9:00 A.M. In his second year, he developed a pain in his left leg, which he thought came from a fall during a soccer game. The pain grew in intensity, and when I realized he did not have money or insurance for medical help, I sent him to my physician. He was diagnosed with cancer, and had an emergency exploratory operation the day before Purim.

Just as we had finished reading the *Megilla*, the physician called my home: the student had listed me as next of kin, his leg had to be amputated, and the doctor gently suggested that I would be the best one to inform him of what had happened.

I immediately set out for the hospital. He was a regular guest at our Shabbat table; I loved him like a son. When I told him, he looked up at me incredulously: "But I can feel my leg," he said. I explained that it was the nerves he was feeling, but that in order to save his life, his leg had to be removed. With tears in his eyes, he thanked me for giving up the Purim celebrations to be with him. And then he said, "Thank God it's my leg and not my hand; I'll still be able to put on *tefillin* every day." Unfortunately, although he did live to graduate college and get married, he died shortly after his wedding – to a marvelous woman who loved him deeply and was fully aware of his medical prognosis before the wedding. He continues to inspire me with his faithfulness to God and His commandments until his very last breath. He was a rare Jew who did not keep the commandments in order to go on living, but rather valued every moment of life because it enabled him to keep the commandments.

Chapter Twenty-Six

Rav Akiva Eiger Calls Out to His Progeny

Another one of my memorable students started Yeshiva University as a seminar participant. (During the late 1950s and '60s, YU would run seminars during Christmas week for youngsters in public high schools who were becoming interested in Judaism.) He was then in his senior year at a Quaker high school in Lebanon, Pennsylvania, a good student who knew that his mother was Jewish although not at all observant, and who had suddenly and inexplicably become interested in exploring everything he could find out about Judaism.

Part of his search led him to the week-long seminar experience, where he was placed with nine other young men in my bunk (this was the winter vacation preceding my June 23 wedding). He became something of a "groupie," attending all of my sessions and asking very searching questions until late into the night. He even questioned what it was that I mumbled before falling asleep, and when I explained to him the law of reciting the *Shema* and a blessing over sleep before actually closing one's eyes, he asked if he could sit next to my bed and recite the words of the prayers along with me. Fortunately he had a charming manner, a ready wit and an interest in athletics, so that his intensity never appeared obnoxious or weird; actually, he was one of the most popular of that year's crop of seminarians.

On the last evening, he gave me a book (*The Catcher in the Rye*) as a farewell gift, with a beautiful inscription thanking me for being his "catcher in the rye." He then asked the question that gave me the key to his personality and the metaphysical reason for his quest: "Did you ever hear of a rabbi named something like Kob Eager?" "Of course," I said. "You must mean Rav Akiva Eiger. He was one of the most profound Talmudic scholars and greatest rabbis of the last two hundred and fifty years." "Well, he was my direct great, great-grandfather on my mother's side," he said. Apparently, the sage's DNA was working overtime, inspiring the soul of his young descendant.

I met with my new-found disciple once a week when we studied the Bible in translation, read and studied the daily prayers, and I concluded our sessions with a review of one of the more relevant responsa of Rav Akiva Eiger. Needless to say, he entered the James Striar School the following year where he was in my Talmud class, continued to study at Yeshiva University until his ordination, and is now the principal and rosh yeshiva of a yeshiva high school in the United States.

Chapter Twenty-Seven

They Are All Isaacs

There was one slightly jarring dampener upon my delightful teaching years at JSS. One of the older faculty members of the YU Talmud Department, a European scholar who had spent time as the chief rabbi of Argentina, Rav Avigdor Cyperstein, would often greet me in the corridor between classes with a cynical smile and a friendly, but nevertheless hurtful, query: "*Nu, HaRav Riskin, vufihl neshamos hut ihr oisgekhopt heint*? So, Rabbi Riskin, how many souls have you grabbed onto today?" I would invariably respond with an embarrassed smile, mumbling that I try to do the best I can, and he would give me a friendly pat on the back. Nevertheless, I was more than slightly discomfited by the repartee.

And then I had a student with whom I became extremely close, from Peoria, Illinois. He once called me in the middle of the night to tell me that his mother was in the hospital after a failed suicide attempt, that he was about to take a plane to Peoria to be with her, but that he would very much want a rabbinical figure to counsel him. I understood that he was hinting for me to travel with him, and I did.

He and his mother spent the Pesah *seder* with us, I studied with him privately for an additional two hours each week to attempt to answer his many philosophical questions, and I arranged a summer counseling position for him at a Miami Beach hotel so that he could be together with me and my family during our six week summer vacation.

During the next fall semester, our relationship naturally lessened in intensity since he went on to another Talmud teacher, but we still continued our private learning sessions. He never returned after the winter break; he suddenly and inexplicably withdrew from Yeshiva University, apparently left both academia and religion, and answered neither my phone calls nor my letters. I went through a kind of "teacher-trauma," mourning over this student almost as one would mourn over a lost child, and questioning my outreach activities.

Precisely at this juncture, in the halls of Yeshiva University, I met he who had become my nemesis, Rav Cyperstein. "So, Rabbi Riskin, how many souls…"

I didn't allow him to finish his question. "I've been re-thinking my priorities recently, after having been bitterly disappointed by a student to whom I gave a great deal of time. After all, all of those 'souls' whom Abraham and Sarah 'made' in Haran came to naught, we never hear of them neither in the Bible nor in the Midrash; only Isaac continued in the path of Abraham. So I've decided to forget my outreach, and to do more in-reach within my own family, with my own children. You were right to be cynical about my activities."

Rav Cyperstein affectionately pinched my shoulder, and took my hand in his. "*Nein, HaRav Riskin, hut nit kein far-rubel.* No, Rav Riskin, don't be at all insulted by what I said in the past. I was only joking with you. You dare not give up what you are doing; after all, you are working with Isaac's seed, with Abraham's grandchildren. God gave you a precious gift that you must continue to utilize. And don't be taken aback by a disappointment; remember, and respect, the freedom of choice God gives to every individual. You dare not force your will upon others. But continue to teach, to expose, to engage. All of your charges are Isaac's seed…"

I learned a world from those words.

Part v

Lincoln Square Synagogue: The Birth of an Outreach Synagogue 1964–83

Chapter Twenty-Eight

Three Rebbes and a *Meḥitza*

The first part of my personal and professional life was very tied up with the Lincoln Square Synagogue. But the story of Lincoln Square goes far beyond whatever it meant to one individual, because the Lincoln Square story is a microcosm of the development of the Orthodox rabbinate in America.

I had never thought of becoming the rabbi of a synagogue for many reasons. First of all, when I grew up in America, most synagogues did not have a *meḥitza*, a divider between the men's and women's prayer sections, and most did not even nominally subscribe to Orthodox Jewish law. I was committed to halakhic Orthodox Judaism, and I didn't want to compromise on those issues. Secondly, I was a Kohen, from the priestly tribe, and a Kohen can't perform funerals, or officiate at the graveside, which is a big part of the American rabbinate.

I was also very interested in academia. Right after I got *semikha*, I began studying for my master's degree, and I expected to go on and eventually attain my doctorate. I was on the faculty of Yeshiva University, first as a lecturer and then as an associate professor. I was really interested in making my mark in the world of academia.

I was making $4,200 a year in the beginning as a lecturer in Jewish Studies and I loved the teaching. At twenty-three, I wasn't much older than my nineteen- or twenty-year-old students. Many of them had been exposed to Torah teachings through YUSCY (Yeshiva University Synagogue Conference Youth), an offshoot of Yeshiva University's Community Service Division, which directed high-school-age youth groups around the United States and sent rabbinical students to special Shabbatonim and week-long seminars. Virtually every weekend I was in a different community, and, as a result of this outreach activity, many graduates of secular high schools came to attend the James Striar School where I was privileged to teach. They may have been university students without background in Jewish studies, but they were extremely bright, and quickly made up for time lost. Teaching them was challenging, exciting and heartwarming. And because of the fresh manner in which they viewed the traditional Jewish texts and our traditional lifestyle, combined with the profundity of their questions, they taught me at least as much as I taught them.

All of this provided me with much professional gratification, but with very little money to provide beyond our most basic living needs. I had attended Yeshiva University on a scholarship from my freshman year in high school straight through to rabbinical school and I desperately wanted to pay the yeshiva back in some way for the wonderful education I had received there. I therefore agreed to give ten free lectures on behalf of YU to wherever they wanted to send me, as a gesture of my gratitude.

It turned out that "anywhere" wasn't just in the New York area. It was anywhere in the United States and beyond. I went to Vancouver, Los Angeles and Las Vegas on behalf of Yeshiva University. But my most important "assignment," at least in terms of my personal future, was on the West Side of Manhattan.

Before continuing with this story (which turned out to initially define my rabbinical career), I must provide a word of introduction.

At that time, the most dynamic and popular stream of Judaism was Conservative Judaism, whose leadership was largely modern orthodox in practice but whose laity had mostly abandoned strict Sabbath, family purity and kashrut observance while they nostalgically held onto a more traditional prayer format (including a sprinkling of English readings) with their synagogues being filled only on the High Holy Days. In those days, their major departure from traditional Judaism was the removal of the *meḥitza,* the separation barrier between the sexes that defined the synagogue as a house of prayer rather than a social center. Rav Soloveitchik believed that this divider was cardinal to orthodoxy. The clarion call of the Conservative Movement, on the other hand, was "the family that prays together stays together." Rav Soloveitchik, known to be most "modern" in his espousal of university study and Religious Zionism, saw a mixed-seated synagogue with family pews as a flagrant departure from the tradition built into the very architecture of a synagogue. The *meḥitza* had thus become the symbol for the "great divide" between orthodoxy and conservatism and, in the 1950s, with old synagogues taking out *meḥitzot* and new synagogues being built without them, it seemed as though Conservatism was winning.

To counter this trend, YU was involved in what they called *kibbush kehillot,* the "conquest of congregations." They were interested in placing their graduates as pulpit rabbis in congregations, even if they were mixed-seated. It was to be hoped that in this way, these synagogues could be reclaimed for Orthodoxy, and it was expected that, in time, the modern-orthodox rabbis would succeed in re-establishing the separation of the sexes. (It rarely happened, however.)

At that time Lincoln Center was a newly developing area of Manhattan; it was the upper part of what was known as Hell's Kitchen, the place where the musical *West Side Story* was set. It had been a horrific area, made famous by its Mafia-inspired gang wars, but now it was becoming "gentrified."

An imaginative builder named Harry Zeckendorf began the process, building the Lincoln Towers luxury apartments. He felt that families would be desirous of moving back to the city from the suburbs, especially after their children got married or left home, and it was important to establish an inner city of luxury housing for the real estate industry as well as for the future of New York. The mayor at that time cooperated tremendously, envisioning a cultural center of the arts as the magnet for the return to the city. The Lincoln Center Opera House and Theater for the Performing Arts were all part of this process of gentrification that began in the late 1950s, early '60s.

I began teaching in 1963. I was newly married, living in Washington Heights (convenient for a faculty member of Yeshiva University), when the YU Community Service Division asked me to meet with the board of a newly-formed High Holy Day congregation at Lincoln Square, the Lincoln Center Community. Apparently the neighborhood was not at all religious, but there were many Jews living there, including one very interesting man named Danny Mars (previously Margolis). He had been trying to escape his Jewish past, but one day – two years before I came on the scene – he looked at the calendar and saw that it was the second day of Rosh HaShana. He felt a sudden desire to go to shul.

There was a Reform Temple called Habonim in the area, but since Danny had no ticket, he was refused entry. At first he was furious with the entire Jewish establishment, but then he decided that he should start his own shul that following year, which would be more user-friendly to those wishing a Jewish holiday experience.

He began by placing ads seeking people who were interested in starting a Rosh HaShana-Yom Kippur synagogue. That was all they were really interested in. Nobody cared about anything beyond that, not even about *Shabbat Shuva*, the "Sabbath of Repentance" that falls between Rosh HaShana and Yom Kippur. A number of people responded and met to discuss the nature of this "High Holy Day synagogue." After an argument as to whether it should be Reform or Conservative, they finally decided it should be Liberal Conservative.

They rented the Esplanade Hotel on West End Avenue and 74th Street and hired Rabbi N to conduct the services of the newly-formed High Holy Day Lincoln Square Conservative Synagogue. Rabbi N was an articulate rabbi in his forties who held a significant administrative position at the Rabbinical School of the Jewish Theological Seminary for Conservative Judaism, located on Broadway and 122nd Street.

Although the congregants were fairly satisfied with the arrangement, they thought it curious that their rabbi did not even try to introduce a *Shabbat Shuva* service. When they spoke to him the following year about continuing, he asked for a $500 raise. At this point, a board-member named Sidney Trompeter, who had been one of the founding organizers along with Danny Mars, said, "Listen, I bet we can get someone even cheaper, certainly cheaper than $1500, and maybe even cheaper than $1,000, if we are willing to accept a rabbi from Yeshiva University." And he added his belief that "Yeshiva University would be very accommodating and certainly wouldn't insist on a *meḥitza*."

They approached YU's Community Service Division, whereupon it was explained in no uncertain terms that whichever rabbi they chose, he would not broach the sensitive subject of the *meḥitza* until he believed the synagogue membership was ready for it. This was one of the ten speaking engagements YU asked me to take on.

There I was, twenty-three years old, attending a board meeting at the home of Sydney Trompeter. Danny Mars boycotted that meeting because he was against an Orthodox rabbi under any circumstances. From my perspective, I was adamant that it be made clear to them from the beginning by Yeshiva University that I was not interested in being their rabbi; I was only interested in talking to them about what Yeshiva University stood for, and what kind of rabbi could possibly be appointed to their synagogue. I was also prepared to answer their questions about Orthodoxy in the contemporary world.

I stayed at the Trompeter home talking with close to two dozen synagogue leaders until past midnight. They asked all sorts of questions about Judaism and about religion. At the end of the four hours they said, "Fine, we would like to hire you." I said it was made very clear from the outset that I would not come, because although Yeshiva University would service them without a *meḥitza*, I, personally, would not.

The more I said no, the more they said yes, which is perhaps part of the dynamic between rabbi and congregant. Since I was feeling gentle pressure from the Community Service Division – the neighborhood clearly had great potential – I sought the advice of my rebbe. Rav Soloveitchik discouraged me. "Look, it's not for you. The chances that you'll [get them to] put in a *meḥitza* are very slim. In the meantime you'll sully your reputation. If you're interested in the practical rabbinate, I'll help get you any available Orthodox synagogue you want. But it won't be to your advantage to begin your career in a mixed-seated congregation."

When I again said no, the president of Yeshiva University, Dr. Belkin, summoned me to his office, asking my reason for refusal. I explained that I had asked my rosh yeshiva and he had been negative. Dr. Belkin looked pained and said to me, "But I'm your rosh yeshiva." I hadn't realized the hierarchy – that the president of Yeshiva University is also the rosh yeshiva. I was very naive, and although I had enormous gratitude and respect for Dr. Belkin, I explained that since I had never studied Torah under him, I had to accept the halakhic boundaries set by my rebbe, Rav Soloveitchik. Dr. Belkin seemed less than happy. "Tomorrow your rosh yeshiva will tell you to go," he said, not without a certain degree of irony, and gently accompanied me to the door.

The next day, sure enough, when I went to teach, there was a note in my box that Rav Soloveitchik wanted to see me. The Rav said, quite correctly, that he hadn't given me a halakhic ruling not to go. He just felt that it wouldn't be wise for me, for my future. However, he said, Dr. Belkin had spoken to him. Since Dr. Belkin lived in the neighborhood, he understood the potential much better than he, and Dr. Belkin felt that the synagogue was young enough, being in its incipient stage, to change. Rav Soloveitchik ended the meeting saying unequivocally, "I agree with Dr. Belkin that you, Rav Riskin, should take the job."

I got home and was in a terrible quandary. I was afraid that I had been caught in a political tug-of-war. I was very confused.

I had always had enormous respect for the Lubavitcher Rebbe as the "leader of the generation," in the sense that he took responsibility for Jews worldwide, wherever they may be. (I looked upon Rav Soloveitchik as the Talmudic scholar of the generation, *lamdan hador*; Rav Moshe Feinstein as the religio-legal decisor of the generation, *posek hador*; and the Lubavitcher Rebbe as leader of the generation, *manhig hador.*)

I had never met with the Rebbe before. I called the Lubavitch headquarters and was immediately given an appointment for 2:30 A.M. that night.

I went to 770 (Eastern Parkway, Lubavitch headquarters), waited for about forty-five minutes and was ushered into the Rebbe's office. He seemed to know everything about me. "You have a wonderful rebbe and you should always listen to everything he says," he began.

"But what I really want to tell you," said the Lubavitcher Rebbe, "is that in every battle there are certain individuals who have to dress up like the enemy and get into the enemy camp. And although they believe that they're infiltrating from the other side, their compatriots will often think that they've sold out, and that they've become traitors. But if not for those people who infiltrate, the battle can never be won." And then he added with a smile, "And you will win the war."

It was maybe a three-minute interview. It was clear to me what the Lubavitcher Rebbe had said and I felt energized, empowered, by his words. I then went back to Rav Soloveitchik and agreed to take the position. The Rav made three clear stipulations.

The first was that I not move to where the synagogue was, to Lincoln Center. He said that I should remain in Washington Heights and stay nearby in a hotel just for Rosh HaShana and Yom Kippur; then, if regular Shabbat *minyanim* could be arranged – because that was obviously to be my goal – just to be there for Shabbat. He said that I shouldn't live in the community as long as there was no *meḥitza* in the shul.

The second stipulation was that I not accept payment of any nature as long as there was no *meḥitza.*

Thirdly, I could not pray with them, although I should lead the prayers. "*Daven* first by yourself, early, and they must know that you're not *davening* with them," he said. "If they think that it's all right for the rabbi to *daven* in a mixed-seated congregation, then they will think that it can remain mixed-seated forever."

Then Dr. Belkin asked to see me again. After congratulating me on my decision, he told me that he'd done a little bit of research and he understood that in addition to the $4,200 that I was making from YU, I was also earning an extra $2,000 teaching at Yavne Hebrew High School in Patterson, New Jersey, on Sunday morning and Thursday evening. Dr. Belkin explained that YU would pay me the extra $2,000 for my agreement to take Lincoln Center, and I would no longer have to teach at the high school. He felt that were I to be successful on the High Holy Days, turning the Esplanade Hotel three-days-a-year prayer hall into a regular synagogue would be more than a full-time job. I was grateful for the Yeshiva stipend of $2,000; the leadership at Lincoln Center truly felt they had gotten a bargain, a rabbi at no cost. So everyone was happy.

Chapter Twenty-Nine

He's the Rabbi Because She's the Rebbetzin

The first Rosh HaShana was fascinating. We held services in the Esplanade. They sold tickets and there were well over two hundred people in attendance, but there were also extra seats; if anyone came at the last minute and didn't have a ticket, they would be welcome. This was Danny Mars' critical legacy.

There were many intriguing people there – actors, musicians and other professionals. I had *davened* early by myself and I explained the services in English as we went along. Probably the most surprising thing that happened was that at the end of the services, Bernard Skolnik, one of the ushers (who has since passed away, but his wife is now the secretary of the shul we began), came over to me, put his arm around my shoulders and said, "Rabbi, I think you forgot something." I got terribly nervous. What portion of the service had I left out? I had thought we covered everything, but after all, it was my first time conducting adult prayers and I feared that I might well have forgotten an important part of the services. I could feel my heart thumping until he explained, "You forgot the final benediction." Greatly relieved, I realized that in Conservative synagogues the rabbi usually makes a final blessing. So I got up and I said the priestly blessing in English: "May God bless you and keep you…" He, too, seemed relieved and quite satisfied with himself and with me. "Now," he said, "the only remaining thing for you and your wife to do, is to stand in a receiving line to wish everyone *a gut Yom Tov, a gut Yahr* – a good Holiday and a good year."

Vicky and I stood in the receiving line. Vicky was barely nineteen and I was barely twenty-four. The first one in the line to greet us was Danny Mars. He was very complimentary, gave me a warm hug, and – before I could say Jackie Robinson – he kissed my wife! You can well imagine my discomfiture; I was fresh out of a *kollel,* not at all into the American custom of kissing and embracing with a first hello, and of course Orthodox standards of conduct between the sexes outside of marriage are quite strict. The truth is I felt like punching him in the mouth. And then Vicky resolved the situation by saying to him very demurely: "Danny, my mother taught me a very long time ago never to touch anything that doesn't belong to me." He got the point, turned around to the assemblage and announced, "No kissing the Rebbetzin!" Thus, proper conduct between congregant, rebbetzin and rabbi was established for the future.

POST SCRIPT:

The fact is that my wife was wise beyond her years and of immeasurable help to me all along the way. We had a *Shabbat Shuva* service, and on that Saturday night, between Rosh HaShana and Yom Kippur, we had invited the board to come to our home in Washington Heights. What ensued helped to set the tone for my entire rabbinate in the United States. I called my father-in-law (my in-laws lived only about a mile away, at 200 Central Park South) right after Shabbat. I asked him for a "crash course in home-style bar tending" because the members of the board were coming and I didn't know the first thing about serving drinks or mixing cocktails.

Vicky immediately got into the conversation and said to me, "That's not what's happening in our home. If they want to go for cocktails or get drinks, they can go to a local bar, or to homes more adept than ours at serving drinks. If they're coming to us they're coming for what we can give them, that which they can't get anywhere else, and that's a *melaveh malka*[2] the way you do it for your own students." I realized that my wife was right on, and we organized a *melaveh malka* for board members and their spouses, most of whom were Hebrew illiterate and devoid of traditional Jewish background. I invited one of my students, John Hellman, who, although not a cantor, had a beautiful voice; he led in Hasidic melodies while I interposed inspiring Torah thoughts. (He became our regular Shabbat cantor as soon as we started Shabbat services, and he is now a practicing psychiatrist in Jerusalem.) I told them a story of Rav Shneur Zalman of Liadi, the founder of Chabad Hasidism. He would always have the third meal, the last of the Sabbath meals, just before sunset with his disciples. This particular Shabbat – an especially cold and snowy day – he asked his *gabbai* to bring in the young Lithuanian peasant standing outside the synagogue door. In answer to the questioning look in the *gabbai*'s eyes, the Rebbe said, "I feel his Jewish soul; he is one of us."

When the young peasant entered, the Rebbe seated him to his immediate right. "Tell us of your parentage," he said in Russian. The youth replied that he was a foundling, left at the doorstep of a kind Christian couple with no children. But he had always felt an affinity toward Jews and Judaism, and he had even learned the Hebrew letters. "You were left by your parents, escaping a pogrom and certain death. You are a Jew," said the Rebbe gently but firmly.

The Rebbe then gave a learned Torah discourse, turned to the youth and asked, "Do you understand?" "*Nyet*," he replied. Then the Rebbe gave a brilliant analogy, interweaving a moving story with mystical symbolism. Once again he asked his new adherent, "Do you understand?" to which he again answered, "*Nyet*." And then the Rebbe started a melody, a wordless *niggun*, filled with heartfelt yearning for the Messiah, suffused with love of Torah and desire to joyously hold on to the departing Shabbat. The disciples sang, and the Russian peasant sang. The disciples danced, and the Russian peasant danced. With

2. The *melaveh malka* (lit. "escorting the queen") is a light meal, interspersed with song and story, traditionally held on a Saturday evening to escort the "Sabbath Queen" as she leaves us at the conclusion of the Sabbath.

tears streaming down his cheeks, the youth turned to the Rebbe and cried out, "Now I understand."

The way to bring Jews back to their roots is not through drinks, or even intellectual discourse. It begins with heartfelt song and joyous dance that enters the heart and the soul; it must then continue with the study of Torah, which will penetrate the mind.

Chapter Thirty

Location, Location – and More on the *Meḥitza*

Rosh HaShana and Yom Kippur really went well at our fledgling shul. We made an appeal and collected the first $5,000 toward the acquisition of a synagogue building. We began to look for an apartment where we could start some kind of a "first stage" Shabbat shul.

The board seemed not at all disappointed when I said I wouldn't be accepting money from them or living in the Lincoln Center neighborhood as long as there was no *meḥitza*. I imagine they were glad of the lower expenses.

We quickly found an apartment to rent for the shul from Alcoa, the Aluminum Company of America, which had bought up much of the real estate in the area ever since Harry Zeckendorf, midway through the development of the high-rise, luxury apartment blocks he had pioneered in the inner city, had gone bankrupt. The vice president of Alcoa, Vaughn Chase, actually had an apartment in Lincoln Towers, where there were many apartments available for rent. So after Yom Kippur, we rented apartment 1D of 150 West End Avenue to be used as a shul. Shabbat Ḥanukka, 1964, was to be our opening service.

The shul began with mixed seating for men and women but I was hopeful that I would manage to persuade them to bring in a divider. In order to find out if there were any observant Jews in the area with whom I could begin to develop a truly Orthodox synagogue, I did research through the butcher. We had a butcher by the name of Gruenspecht from Washington Heights, who gave special discounts to the religious faculty of Yeshiva University. They were known for their high-quality kosher meat, so I would have imagined that observant Jews living in the Lincoln Center area might well get meat deliveries from them.

I inquired if they had any deliveries in mid-town. It turned out there were a number of elderly women who were their customers, and, of course, I met with them and the adult children with whom they lived about joining the shul. Moshe Ḥayyim Tiefenbrunn was one of their customers who actually lived in the very same building that housed the shul. He would walk to another synagogue, an Orthodox synagogue more than half a mile away, called the West Side Institutional. I met with him, explained that I didn't expect him to come Shabbat morning when there was mixed seating, but that I would appreciate his membership and partnership in making the synagogue conform to halakhic standards, as well as his participation in the Friday evening and Shabbat late-afternoon services when women were not habitually in attendance. He happily agreed, anxious for an Orthodox synagogue closer to his home and appreciative of the religious outreach I was trying to do.

It was Shabbat Ḥanukka, 1964, 4:30 P.M. We scraped together ten men, most of whom were neither observant nor knowledgeable. Moshe Ḥayyim was the exception, fully expert in synagogue custom; in this he was more knowledgeable than I. He was also a fine *ba'al tefilla* with true expertise in proper *nusaḥ* (the traditional liturgical melodies), and exceedingly generous. He saw that there was no cover for the *bima*'s *shulkhan*, the raised table from which the Torah is read, so he ran up to his apartment (4M), took the white tablecloth off his table, and brought it down to serve as our "*bima* cover"; indeed, it remained so for as long as we stayed in the apartment, for the next six years.

He was a beloved and strong ally and we became very close friends. As soon as we had a *meḥitza* installed at Lincoln Square, he became the *gabbai* (ritual administrator; an unpaid, respected, and arduous task). In the meantime, he was extremely supportive in every way.

We had also started a late Friday evening *Oneg Shabbat* (8:30 P.M.) that consisted mostly of the singing of *Lekha Dodi* and *Zemirot, Kiddush* and refreshments, as well as a public lecture by a "person-in-the-news." (Among our guests were Mayor Beame and Isaac Bashevis Singer.) At this "service" men and women could sit together without violating religious law since it was not a statutory service; it was a kind of extension of my own Shabbat table. I felt that if this mixed-seated synagogue experience would be successful, perhaps a *meḥitza* for regular services would become more palatable.

I was trying to set the stage for the change that I hoped would come…

Then, on January 27, my eldest daughter, Batya, was born.

We used to stay at the Westover Hotel for Shabbat. The rooms, however, were somewhat shabby and drafty, and once our daughter was born, Vicky felt much more comfortable staying at her parents' home at 200 Central Park South. It was a lovely apartment, with a large picture window overlooking Central Park, but it was on the twenty-ninth floor. I would walk up and down twenty-nine flights, six times every Shabbat – Friday evening after the regular service, late Friday evening twice – before and after the *Oneg Shabbat,* twice on Shabbat morning, and once more on Shabbat afternoon for *Minḥa* (afternoon service). The people of the shul realized that it was very difficult. Also, since my in-laws did not keep a kosher kitchen, we brought our Shabbat meals with us, for us and for them. It wasn't so easy to do that week after week, but we managed – and it gave my in-laws a real taste of Shabbat.

A delegation from the shul came to see me expressing their wish that my family and I move into the area permanently; indeed, they had already arranged for an apartment at 150 West End Avenue, just one floor above the synagogue apartment. I thanked them, but said, "No thanks." Until there was a Shabbat *meḥitza,* my family and I could not move into the neighborhood.

Meanwhile, the shul was progressing, with forty to fifty adults attending services each Shabbat morning, and sometimes as many as

120 for the Friday evening *Oneg Shabbat* (with the numbers depending on the speaker).

I knew that Alcoa also owned a beautiful, open piece of land adjacent to Lincoln Towers that they were selling for $250,000. It would be the perfect site for the shul, just at the entrance to the Lincoln Center, and only a stone's throw from the Lincoln Center Cultural Complex.

I arranged a meeting with the vice president of Alcoa, Mr. Vaughn Chase, a tall and distinguished-looking man with a ruddy complexion. I told him that we had $5,000 in the bank, which I would like to give as a down payment to secure the property. We would immediately begin raising funds for a synagogue building. When he gave me a look that seemed to say it was preposterous to expect to tie up a $250,000 property for a $5,000 down payment, I proceeded to outline how advantageous the deal was for Alcoa. After all, the return to the inner city, even to the cultural Lincoln Center, was a yet unproven concept. Zeckendorf, for instance, had gone bankrupt in the midst of his Lincoln Towers building project. A synagogue would certainly stabilize and solidify the area. We would become partners in developing an upper-middle-class neighborhood in what had previously been Hell's Kitchen, I argued. He smiled and actually accepted my terms. But he wanted us to at least pay interest charges on the land, to which I happily agreed.

However, I continued to explain that since the $5,000 for our down payment was all that we had raised in our High Holy Day appeal, and we would somehow have to pay interest charges above that, I could not possibly manage to raise additional rent for apartment 1D. He agreed that the synagogue could occupy the apartment rent-free for the first year. I then added, "I also want to start a Hebrew school, which is crucial if we hope to attract young families, so I would need an additional apartment across the hall from the synagogue as well." He agreed to give us that also *pro bono,* but then he quickly terminated the meeting, "...before you convince me to give you the entire apartment building for free!" The fact is that we never ended up paying for the land at all. When Alcoa sold their estate holdings in 1972, they forgave us our $245,000 debt for the land. We hadn't paid it, you see, because we logically argued that we could not raise money for a building and pay for the land at the same time. And by the late 1960s, Alcoa was very anxious to get us out of 150

West End Avenue. By that time, all of the Alcoa apartments were renting well, the first-floor synagogue was bursting at the seams with well over a hundred people regularly attending services, and our flourishing Hebrew school, as well as our Shabbat crowds, were spilling over into the lobby. All of Lincoln Towers seemed to be an entranceway for the Lincoln Square Synagogue.

At the same time, Vaughn Chase knew that we had really helped stabilize the area, thereby enhancing their investment. So he encouraged us to build, and used the sale of his holdings as a good opportunity to deed us the land virtually for free. At my father-in-law's suggestion, he even gave us the air-rights above the building, which the synagogue has now – more than four decades later – put to very good use! He was a most deserving guest of honor at our first Lincoln Square Synagogue dinner in June of 1965.

Meanwhile, the board members, chief among them Danny Mars, were still pressuring my family to move into the area on a permanent basis. They felt (correctly) that I would not be able to manage the twenty-nine-flight walk-ups much longer – and they were worried that, were I to leave, the synagogue would lose its attendance.

I said that we could hold the late Friday night programs without a *meḥitza,* because the nature of the service did not require it, and that the Esplanade Hotel High Holiday services could continue without a *meḥitza* at least for the next season. But all services in the apartment would have to be conducted with the sexes separated.

They said they would bring up the issue of the *meḥitza* at the next board meeting, and they hoped it would pass. I disagreed. "You can bring *me* up at the next board meeting, regarding renewing my contract for another year, or two years, or for however long you want to renew it, and the board has to understand that if you extend my contract, I'm going to put in a *meḥitza.* If you decide not to renew, that's fine. You don't owe me anything. We all knew up-front exactly what the ground rules were. But if I'm staying, then by Purim, there will be a *meḥitza.* Vote on me, but not on the halakhic issue of separation of the sexes during services."

We had this conversation at the beginning of February, and Purim was to be four weeks later. I told them I would begin with a minimal, planter divider of forty inches (Rav Soloveitchik's minimum height of ten hand-breadths).

The next Shabbat, we had a guest at Lincoln Square. I did not yet know how the vote would turn out. In fact, the crucial board meeting had been delayed a few weeks, until almost the night before Purim, because Danny Mars wanted to do some lobbying with the board and there were very strong anti-*meḥitza* feelings. The Conservative movement had as their major slogan: "The family that prays together stays together," and this catchphrase had conquered American synagogue life.

There was a very interesting woman who came to the service that Shabbat, after which she stayed to ask me extremely intelligent and searching questions. She was Trude Weiss Rosemarin, the editor of the *Jewish Spectator*, which was the most important Anglo-Jewish magazine at that time. She was very well read, very well respected and very anti-Orthodox. (She had had difficulty receiving a *get*, Jewish divorce, from her husband and as a result, she abhorred the Orthodox establishment.)

At that time I did not know much about her background. She asked if she could interview me for her magazine after Shabbat. I agreed and we spoke for two or three hours. I thought at the time that our discussion had gone very well, since she was disarmingly charming; apparently I was very naive about the dangers of publicity.

The following week the *Jewish Spectator* came out with a lead story, entitled "Orthodoxy a la Lincoln Square." The basic message of her article was: Look at the hypocrisy of Orthodoxy at Yeshiva University. They argue about the importance of a *meḥitza*, and that's their big issue against the Conservative movement, and yet they send one of their most promising graduates into a gentrifying "yuppie" area in which they conveniently overlook the issue of mixed-sex seating.

Of course, when she wrote the article, she knew nothing about my ongoing discussion with the board regarding the *meḥitza*, and I naturally had not shared it with her, since it was an unresolved issue. I was also savvy enough to understand that any pre-publicity about the upcoming board vote could strengthen the anti-*meḥitza* forces.

For me, the article was devastating. Even worse than that, less than two weeks later, the *Jewish Observer*, which was the much respected publication of the more right-wing and anti-YU organization, Agudat Yisrael, prominently reprinted the Trude Weiss Rosemarin article in the *Jewish Spectator*, but added the final murderous punch-line: "Orthodoxy a la Lincoln Square makes Trude Weiss Rosemarin laugh. It makes us weep."

Anyway, I arrived the next morning for my class at Yeshiva University, and found (as was to be expected) students who were painfully aware of both articles, and, as a result, had serious questions about my religious credentials. Nevertheless, I felt that I could not speak about what was going on with the board. I could only say that I hoped that there would be other developments fairly soon, and that every step I was taking was under the direction of my rebbe, Rav Soloveitchik. As a novitiate, I was still rather thin-skinned, and despite the joyous satisfaction of the many individuals being brought closer to traditional Judaism as a result of Lincoln Square, I began to have second thoughts about the wisdom of my having taken on such a congregation in the first place.

A few days passed and Dr. Belkin asked to meet with me. He handed me a thick file of papers that had "Lincoln Square" written on it, saying, "You know I read the *Jewish Spectator* and the *Jewish Observer*, and many of our supporters read them as well. Please, just look at the first letter. All the others are very similar." That first letter was apparently from one of the more generous supporters of Yeshiva University. It said, "'Orthodoxy a la Lincoln Square' has convinced me to stop supporting YU. I'm ashamed to be an alumnus. Please cancel the remainder of my pledge."

Dr. Belkin continued, "Rabbi Riskin, what do you expect me to do?" I had no choice but to answer, "I understand that whatever you have to do, you have to do, even if it means disassociating the yeshiva from the Lincoln Square Synagogue. Yeshiva University, I understand, is bigger than any individual synagogue. I certainly wouldn't want in any way to cause an embarrassment to Yeshiva University."

Dr. Belkin seemed serious, even grim. "I'll tell you what I'm going to do. I found out from your secretary that family membership in Lincoln Square is $100. I believe in you, and have confidence in what you will accomplish. I'm making out a personal check for membership in Lincoln Square Synagogue. If anyone dares criticize you about the synagogue, you just tell him that Dr. Belkin, the president of Yeshiva University, is a member of your synagogue." And until he died, Dr. Belkin continued to send in a personal check for membership every year. And as the membership fees grew, his check grew.

That obviously gave me a tremendous amount of courage to go on. And with God's help the vote passed, and the *meḥitza* came in.[3]

3. Only one family left the synagogue over the issue of the divider.

Chapter Thirty-One

There's One in Every Shul

During the turmoil over the *meḥitza* issue, a man moved into the neighborhood, Mr. K. He was a tough character, and before he came to us he had been the treasurer of a Conservative synagogue in Manhattan. He expected the Lincoln Square Synagogue to be Conservative; he was also – unlike the other board members – very experienced in synagogue politics.

First of all, he started a men's club. There was already a sisterhood, and so it seemed that a men's club was a good idea. But every time I asked about programming, he said, "Don't worry – we'll work out our own programming."

One evening I came into the apartment-synagogue and saw a card game going on. I asked, "What's this?" He said, "Well, this is the men's club." I took all the money that was on the table and I threw it in the wastebasket underneath. And I said, "This is a synagogue. It's not a gambling joint. And there won't be any gambling as long as I am the rabbi here."

He turned red. He walked out and said, "You've just lost your men's club." My response was, "So be it! Goodbye and good riddance."

And, to the best of my knowledge, there is no men's club at Lincoln Square Synagogue to this very day.

It was the end of the men's club, but that was not the end of Mr. K. He stayed anyway, not only as a member, but as an active member. He soon became the accountant, *pro bono,* of the shul.

Along came the holiday of Sukkot, in the autumn, and we put up a *sukka* on the land that we had tied up from Alcoa. The only two families who ate in the *sukka* were the cantor and his wife, and my wife and I. The Tiefenbrunns were away that first Sukkot, so there weren't any others who even knew what the festival of Sukkot was.

I decided, however, to use the opportunity to introduce the children in the community to the concept of *sukka,* and to make a pitch for a Hebrew school, which I was anxious to start, at the same time. We invited all the neighborhood children into the *sukka*. We served frankfurters and fries and we had a party with a magician.

In the end, eight of the ten children who had come to our *sukka* party signed up for the new school. (One of them, Renee Miller, who at the time was Renee Brief, lives in Jerusalem today. She was the first enrollee in the Hebrew school, and our families remain very close to this day.)

And then something happened a few months later; it seemed inconsequential at the time, but led to a major episode.

My wife had given birth that previous January. We were still spending Shabbat at the Westover Hotel. The doorbell rang right before Shabbat. We only rented one room – a combination bedroom, living room and kitchen – and Vicky was nursing the baby. I went to answer the door and saw Mr. K standing there with a gift for the baby. I thanked him, but explained that I couldn't invite him in because my wife was nursing in the only room we rented. He left in a huff. Mr. K had also donated prayer shawls to the shul. He thought they were *tallitot,* but in reality they were small, narrow scarf-like shawls. Many non-Orthodox synagogues gave out similar prayer shawls to their congregants, but I didn't consider them appropriate for prayer.

I did not want to use the *tallitot,* but we had nothing else to offer. Moshe Ḥayyim Tiefenbrunn came to the rescue. "No problem, Rabbi. I will order regular 'kosher' *taleysim* [*tallitot*], and I'll pay the bill." The only prayer shawls we displayed that next Shabbat were the kosher ones bought by Moshe Ḥayyim. I explained my position to Mr. K, showing him the drawer in which I placed his gift, with a sign indicating their availability for those who preferred not to wear the regular sized *tallitot*. Once again he looked at me in anger, turning red as a beet.

Then the shul had a board meeting, the last one before the meeting in which they were going to bring up the issue of the *meḥitza*. Mr. K said that he wanted to talk to the board without my being there. It turned out that he brought up a number of very strong charges against me.

He claimed I had been guilty of misappropriation of funds; since he was the accountant, his word on this score became very weighty indeed.

First of all, he said, I had bought a *sukka* that was a private *sukka* just for me, and had charged the shul. Secondly, he said that I had bought meat and charged my private meat bill to the shul. Thirdly, he said that he had donated prayer shawls that were perfectly acceptable in every other synagogue, and that I had gone ahead and ordered other larger, woolen prayer shawls without asking anyone, thus incurring an extra expense for the shul. Finally, he charged me with disrespect for my elders. He had come with a gift for my baby, despite our altercation over the men's club, and I had left him standing outside like a beggar. I accepted the gift, he said, but I didn't even invite him in.

Afterwards, a delegation came to my house and raised all these issues with me. I explained that every self-respecting shul must have a *sukka* for the festival of Sukkot, no matter how few avail themselves of the opportunity to use it. I said that this was only the beginning, and I was sure that eventually scores of congregants would be eating in our *sukka* on Sukkot. (Five years later, we did indeed accommodate more than four hundred people in our shul *sukka*.)

As for the meat bill, I explained that that it was for a party we held to encourage kids to sign up for the Hebrew school. "You can go ahead and check it," I told the board, "because I remember exactly what I ordered." Regarding the *tallitot*, I had them check the matter out with Moshe Ḥayyim (who was not yet on the board), and explained that he had donated them for valid religious reasons. I also told them that I had apologized when Mr. K came with a gift, but my wife had been nursing.

Obviously, the accusations were dropped.

About two weeks later Mr. K had a massive heart attack. He was in Roosevelt Hospital in intensive care and I ran to see him. When he opened up his eyes he looked at me and he said, "What are you doing here, Rabbi. We're enemies." I said to him, "Mr. K, you're the meanest person I ever met in my life. Nevertheless, I want you to live and with all my heart, I pray for you to be healthy."

After that he became one of my biggest supporters and he left a generous legacy for the synagogue in his will.

I tell this story every year to my graduating rabbinical students. As a rabbi, you cannot allow whatever personal issues there may be between you and a member of the congregation to interfere with the proper religious duties of caring for the sick, mourning for the dead and being helpful in every other way. No matter what differences of opinion you have ideologically, it is crucial that you never let it get personal. It takes two individuals to get into a fight – so a rabbi must never permit a fight to develop between himself and a congregant, whatever the issue, whatever the provocation.

Chapter Thirty-Two

Moshe Ḥayyim Tiefenbrunn: *Ne'ila* and Faith after the Holocaust

One of the wisest, most down-to-earth, kindest human beings I have had the privilege to know and to learn from was Moshe Ḥayyim Tiefenbrunn, the *gabbai* of Lincoln Square Synagogue in Manhattan, and the most revered elder of Efrat until his passing at age ninety-two on Purim, 2002.

We initially met on the very first Shabbat of my rabbinate, Shabbat Ḥanukka 1964, when I conducted the inaugural Friday evening service in a small apartment on the ground floor of 150 West End Avenue. He was the tenth man in our *minyan* and the aforementioned provider of the tablecloth for our bima.

He was then a holocaust survivor of fifty-five, with a second family consisting of a wife and two young sons, and I was a beginner rabbi of twenty-four, newly married with a pregnant wife. Eventually we moved into that same building (apartment 2D) – and virtually every Friday evening, the young Tiefenbrunn boys, Shimshon and Levi, would come to our home for dessert, and on Shabbat afternoon Deborah Tiefenbrunn would send down a *cholent* for our Shabbat lunch.

Moshe Ḥayyim was a *Shaḥarit, Minḥa* and *Ma'ariv* Jew – whose generosity and common sense made his voice one of the most respected in the congregation. After nineteen years, when I announced my intention to move to Efrat, Israel, Moshe Ḥayyim and Deborah declared: "Rabbi, we were with you on the West Side and we will be with you on the West Bank."

And so they were. They built a home on the same street as mine, with Moshe Ḥayyim continuing in Efrat his New York custom of praying at the early *minyan*, supplying the Gemara volumes for the *Daf Yomi* (daily page of Talmud) class he attended each day, but adding swimming "with the boys" to his routine." Since we prayed, studied and swam together (*Daf Yomi* followed by "dip *yomi*"), I had great opportunity to get to know him intimately, and benefit from his counsel. But the most important lesson he taught me at the very beginning of our relationship was the lesson of faith – not a simplistic, simple-minded faith but rather a profound, thought-out faith; the faith defined by a faithfulness to a tradition that has forged the very fiber of one's being, and faithfulness to a God, even if He is incomprehensibly silent.

I came to learn this lesson because of a semi-humorous incident, which was one of my first challenges in the world of the practical, pulpit rabbinate.

We had to plan for our first Rosh HaShana-Yom Kippur service in the apartment, but as a small fledgling congregation in a largely non-observant environment, we had no funds to pay for the necessary officiates: the cantors, Torah-reader and *shofar* blower.

The responsibility for this "Orthodox" service lay squarely on my shoulders alone, because the main and official High Holy Day service of the congregation was scheduled to take place at the Esplanade Hotel, and it was still to have mixed seating. I had agreed to this, since I assessed that the board would not yet be willing to give up the High Holy Day mixed-seated service, which provided the yearlong funds for running the entire synagogue operation. But I was anxious that there be a parallel Orthodox service in the apartment; how could I arrange for all the necessary officiates?

And then a minor miracle happened. A visitor for Shabbat came to our apartment-synagogue, a Mr. Y, who had a beautiful voice and seemed rather accomplished in all ritual areas. When, at the end of Shabbat, he offered to be of assistance in any way possible, I thought he might have been Elijah the Prophet. And indeed he agreed to lead whatever portion of the services I desired – as well as to read from the Torah scroll and blow the *shofar* – with the single stipulation that he also be given the honor of leading the moving *Ne'ila* prayer at the closing of Yom Kippur.

I was overjoyed. I quickly gathered the other knowledgeable would-be officiates within our congregation – Moshe Ḥayyim, Mr. B and Mr. H – telling them of our good fortune and asking which portion of the High Holy Day prayers they would be willing to lead. Moshe Ḥayyim immediately begged off, insisting that he never officiated on the High Holy Days. The other two were willing to act as *ḥazan* (cantor) for any other prayer I would suggest – but each insisted upon receiving the honor of leading the *Ne'ila* prayer. At first I thought they were only joking – doing some good-natured baiting to see whom I would choose for the special honor of *Ne'ila*. But as the High Holy Days neared, I realized that they were serious and we were deadlocked: Messrs. Y, B and H would each perform gratis, but only with the condition that they lead *Ne'ila* – and, after all, there was only one *Ne'ila* service to be led.

In desperation, on the Shabbat before Rosh HaShana, I gave a sermon that caused most of the congregation to scratch their heads in bewilderment – except for our three potential officiates. I recounted a Yom Kippur in Berditchev, when the renowned Rav Levi Yitzḥak rose to lead the *Ne'ila* prayer as he was accustomed to do each year. Inexplicably, he stood silent for a goodly amount of time – seemingly remonstrating with some invisible being standing at his side. Suddenly he shouted in Yiddish, "If that's the case, then lead the *Ne'ila* prayer yourself!" – and the great sage took his seat among the regular worshipers. A stunned congregation sent someone else to lead instead, but after the fast ended, requested an explanation from their beloved rebbe.

"The *yetzer hara* [evil instinct] suddenly appeared before me as I rose to begin *Ne'ila*," he explained. "And with a twinkle in his eyes, he began to castigate me: 'You are different from most Jews! Virtually everyone else runs after me three hundred and sixty-four days a year, but shuns me on Yom Kippur. You, on the other hand, are the exact opposite. No matter how hard I try, I cannot get near you every other day of the year. But on Yom Kippur – I am right alongside you while you *daven Ne'ila* before the congregation. You know how much pride you take in the sound of your voice and the perfection of your traditional melodies.' I stood flabbergasted, finally telling him, 'If that's the case, then you lead the *Ne'ila* prayer yourself,' and resumed my place amongst the congregation."

With that, I concluded my sermon and took my seat. At the end of services, the three "targets" of my words came up to me a bit sheepishly. They each agreed to officiate in whatever part of the service I would designate – no strings attached. The leader of the *Ne'ila* would be solely my choice.

With the taste of my first rabbinic victory still in my mouth, I went to see Moshe Ḥayyim Tiefenbrunn to ask him to lead the *Ne'ila* prayer; he was deeply pious, had a good voice, enjoyed a consummate command over the proper *nusaḥ* – and he was the only one not to have insisted on *Ne'ila*. "I hate to refuse you, Rabbi, and of course I am greatly honored, but I told you I cannot officiate on the High Holy Days. You see, I ate on Tisha B'Av [the fast day commemorating the destruction of both Holy Temples]." I thought perhaps he was ill, and that his doctor had prevented him from fasting – but he assured me that that was not the case. And then, in an almost staccato voice, he told me the following story – which is one of the most profound lessons in faith I have ever received.

Moshe Ḥayyim's parents were very wealthy, very pious and very philanthropic Jews who lived in a small town on the border between Poland and Germany. They also owned a dacha (summer vacation home) deep in the forests of Poland. When the Nazis began to invade, no one could imagine the horrible cruelties Jews were to suffer under the Holocaust. Their only point of reference was the First World War, when the women, children and elderly were irrelevant, but the young men were conscripted into the German army where Shabbat and *kashrut* could hardly be observed. Hence the Tiefenbrunn parents, daughters, daughters-in-law and children were deposited in the dacha – where it was presumed they would be safe – and the sons and sons-in-law fled as far as they could go.

Moshe Ḥayyim himself (after a fortuitous meeting with Zerah Warhaftig, the man who persuaded a Japanese diplomat to issue thousands of life-saving exit-visas for refugees), was persuaded to go as far as Shanghai where he barely had enough food to eat, but punctiliously upheld the laws of Shabbat and *kashrut*. It was only toward the end of the war that a shocked Jewish community in Shanghai heard of the horrors that befell their loved ones trapped behind in Germany and Poland. And then, at the end of 1944, Moshe Ḥayyim received a telegram from a cousin that the entire family in the dacha had been saved. It would be impossible to describe his feelings of relief and joy. He borrowed from whomever he could – and prepared a most generous *kiddush* of thanksgiving to God, for the Shanghai Jewish community that Shabbat.

A few minutes before candle lighting, Rav Ashkenazy – the spiritual leader of the Jews in Shanghai – summoned Moshe Ḥayyim to his home. As gently as possible, he informed him that he had received the official lists of those Jews who perished in the Holocaust; the only family member of Moshe Ḥayyim who had survived was the one who had sent the telegram – and he was being hospitalized in a sanitarium for the mentally ill.

Moshe Ḥayyim was coming to the end of his account; he was perspiring, and his eyes were clouded with tears. "I walked out of Rav Ashkenazy's house with bitter tears strangled in my throat, and angry frustration raging in my heart. '*Let din, velet dayan*, there is no Judge and no judgment,' I shouted to the silent winds. My first reaction was to cast away my yarmulke, to divest myself of all of the religious commandments…

"But then I took myself in hand. If I were to reject the traditions of my forebears, then the beloved family I lost in the Holocaust – those who died only because they were Jews – will have lived and died in vain. I dared not allow that to happen. I bear a sacred responsibility to provide them with continuity, to give their lives and deaths significance by preserving those values by which they lived and for which they died. I would not give a posthumous victory to Hitler; Israel must emerge victorious.

"And so I went home and made the blessings over the Shabbat candles. But I eat on Tisha B'Av. It is my private rebellion against God – who inexplicably remained silent in the face of the horrific destruction of the most pious of His children. It is because I express my rebellion by eating on Tisha B'Av that I can continue to do all the other *mitzvot*, but as long as I eat on Tisha B'Av, I'm not worthy to lead the services on the High Holy Days."

I took Reb Moshe Ḥayyim's hand in my own, whispered that perhaps he might consider leading *Ne'ila* this Yom Kippur, and fasting next Tisha B'Av. He refused *Ne'ila*, but he did lead *Shaḥarit* both mornings of Rosh HaShana – and he did so every Rosh HaShana until he came on *aliya*. He also resumed fasting on Tisha B'Av.

Apparently his rebellion had ended.

Chapter Thirty-Three

The Cry of the Torah Scroll

And then something happened that completed the evolution of Lincoln Square Synagogue. Three years later, the two days of Rosh HaShana were followed by Shabbat, and we still planned for Orthodox services in the apartment, as well as mixed-seated services in the Esplanade Hotel. With a heavy heart, I concluded the time was not yet ripe for me to insist on separate seating for the Esplanade.

I specifically met with the general manager of the hotel, and explained to him that since Rosh HaShana was immediately followed by Shabbat, we could not dismantle the shul or remove the *sifrei Torah* (Torah scrolls) on the evening concluding the second day of Rosh HaShana, as we usually did. Everything had to wait until Saturday night. I asked him to please leave everything intact for Shabbat, after which I myself would come with some helpers to transfer the two *sifrei Torah*, the *Aron Kodesh* (Holy Ark), and all our other sacred items back to Lincoln Towers. I explained that it was critical that no one touch these holy articles during Shabbat, in our absence.

That Shabbat was *Shabbat Shuva*, the Sabbath of Repentance before Yom Kippur, when it was traditional for the rabbi to give a lengthy discourse on some aspect of these Days of Awe. I have always – from the very beginning of my rabbinate – put a great deal of time and effort into the preparation of this *derasha* (sermon) as has been customary with rabbis for hundreds of years. In the early years of the shul, twenty or thirty people would attend. But as the synagogue developed, two hundred, and then five hundred people would come for a two-hour discourse on a legal and theological aspect of the Holiday.

I was in the middle of the sermon in the apartment-shul when a man whom I didn't know, ran in, obviously very upset. He said, "I'm sorry to disturb you, Rabbi, but the *sifrei Torah* are on the floor in the Esplanade." I dropped everything and I ran the seven or eight blocks to the hotel, my prayer shawl flying in the wind. A number of the congregants came with me, including Sydney Trompeter, who was by then the president of this fledgling synagogue.

When we arrived, we found the makeshift shul dismantled, and indeed, the *sifrei Torah* were on the floor.

I began to weep. I had never before seen *sifrei Torah* on the floor. I picked them up, reverently kissed them and gently placed them on a table. The sheepish hotel manager apologized profusely and promised that he himself would stand guard to make sure no one would touch the sacred scrolls until I arrived later that night.

We returned in silence, where my faithful audience was patiently waiting. Before resuming the *derasha,* I made an announcement: "I see this as a sign from heaven. There will no longer be a mixed-seated service under the auspices of Lincoln Square Synagogue."

The incident was upsetting for all of us, including Sidney Trompeter. He didn't argue with my position.

The battle for the *meḥitza* was over and it was won by God's hand!

Chapter Thirty-Four

A Tale of Two *Sandaks*

It was during the second year of the Lincoln Square Synagogue apartment on the first floor of 150 West End Avenue. I lived on the second floor, Moshe Ḥayyim Tiefenbrunn lived on the fourth floor, and there was also a Hebrew-speaking young couple who occasionally attended services, living on the tenth floor. The husband was from Israel and his wife was from Munich, Germany, where her father served as the head of the Jewish community.

The wife's father would come to visit a number of times a year; he had a tall, very stately appearance, always immaculately groomed with a Vandyke beard, a black suit and a distinctive homburg on his head. He would always come to see me to pay his respects to the rabbi. His speech (he spoke to me in fluent Hebrew) was punctuated by rolling *R*s. He would call me *"HaRrrav,"* in a very nice way, *"HaRrrav hatza'irrr"* – "the young rabbi."

He always brought me flowers for Shabbat, and he let me know that he brought in catered food to eat with his children. His children refused to eat with us – he said he needed private time with them – but I always invited them to come in for a little *mashke* (whiskey), tea and cake for dessert. At first, he would come by himself; then the young couple began coming as well.

A year passed, and his daughter gave birth to a baby boy. Early on in the week, my doorbell rang at 6:45 A.M., half an hour before services. It was the head of the Jewish community of Munich. I wished him *mazal tov*, congratulations. He seemed quite preoccupied, however, saying, *"Aval HaRrrav, yesh lanu ba'aya ḥamura* [We have a very difficult problem]." Since he was clearly upset, his *R*s rolled all the more. What was the difficult problem? He was agonizing over who would be the *sandak*, the godfather (the greatest honor of the circumcision, the one who holds the baby on his knees during the ritual act). So I explained to him the custom was that the mother usually decides on the baby's name, and the father decides on the *sandak*, often selecting the baby's paternal grandfather for the first grandson's circumcision.

"That's our custom in Germany as well. But *HaRrrav*, my *meḥutan* [in-law] cannot be the *sandak*. He lives in Israel, he is a respected general in the Israeli army, *aval hu okhel shefanim*, but he eats *rrrabbits Rrrabbi Rrriskin*," he said, emphasizing the animal by repeating its name in English. Now it is true the halakha does say that the *sandak* should be someone who fears Heaven, someone who is a religious individual. Actually the *sandak* is compared to the high priest, and the place of the circumcision to the altar of the Holy Temple.

"And what do you suggest," I asked him, "that you be the *sandak*?" "Oh no," he said, explaining how that would usher in a third world war. In his mind, there was only one way out of this difficulty: *"HaRrrav hatza'irrr, kevodo, tzarrrikh lihiot hasandak."* I would have to be the *sandak*.

I never especially enjoyed participating in the mitzva of circumcision. I know how important it is, but for me, it is a very difficult commandment. I'm a bit squeamish, and so, when I am asked to be *sandak*, I close my eyes rather tightly. And I certainly would never ask for the job! Nevertheless, I felt that if it would extricate everyone from a difficult situation, I would be glad to step up. And as he explained it, I was the rabbi and this was the first circumcision in the synagogue; it was very common in Europe that the rabbi serve as the *sandak* at a circumcision in his congregation.

And so we thought we had solved the issue. The head of the

Munich community was in the synagogue every morning, and every afternoon, and he would remind me always, "*Rrremember Rrrabbi,* you must be the *sandak.* It cannot be the *meḥutan.* My *meḥutan* eats *rrrabbits*!"

Early Friday morning I came out of the synagogue after services and noticed a fairly short person with a bald head sitting in the lobby. He stood up from the chair as I was pressing the elevator button to go up to my apartment. He asked in a very strong Israeli accent, "Can you please tell me how I can find the rabbi of the synagogue?" When I responded that I was the rabbi, he burst out laughing, and he started speaking in Hebrew: "*Ata? Chuchik kamokha, ata harav? Ata zeh shemekalkel li et hasimḥa sheli?* You? A young whippersnapper like you – you're the rabbi? You're the one who's spoiling my whole joy at the circumcision of my first grandson? I came all the way from Israel to be the *sandak.* They tell me that you insist on being the *sandak.* How can you do this to me?"

I wasn't quite sure how to respond. I asked him, "Do you really want to be the *sandak*?" He said, "Of course. This is a very meaningful time for me. I was in four wars in Israel. I'm a decorated army officer. To me, it's great to be alive, to have lived to see the birth of a grandson. I came here in order to be the *sandak* at my grandson's circumcision." I told him that I would have to think about it. I skipped breakfast, and began poring over the halakhic texts dealing with the laws and customs of circumcision

Half an hour later the doorbell rang. It was my friend, the head of the Munich community, with flowers in one hand and a box of chocolates in the other. "*Kevod HaRrrav, halt fest,* ["stand strong"]. My *meḥutan* has *arrrived* [as if I didn't know], *tizkor, hu okhel shefanim! Rrremember,* he eats *rrrabbits*!"

I spent a very difficult day and an even more difficult Friday night. I did not sleep a wink. I studied and re-studied all the classical texts on circumcision, and then almost before dawn, I started to read *Arpilei Tohar,* a philosophical treatise by Rav Avraham Yitzḥak HaKohen Kook. There is a magnificent paragraph in which he writes that the soul of a Jew who is completely dedicated to the land of Israel and the people of Israel, stands on a higher rung on the ladder leading to heaven than the soul of a Jew who may very well be completely observant, but who does not have that commitment and that dedication to the people of Israel and the land of Israel.

I thought to myself, this is the answer to my problem. Yes, a *sandak* must be a religious Jew, but how does one define religiosity? And if a grandfather had fought in four Israeli wars and was a decorated army officer who had put his life on the line for the land and the people of Israel, then who am I, living in America, to disqualify him from being *sandak*? In a very profound way, he may well be far more religious than I!

That Shabbat morning, I ruled that the army officer from Israel should be the *sandak*. I introduced it, explaining that the *sandak* must be a religious Jew, and that I had learned from Rav Kook that religiosity is to be defined in no small measure by commitment to the land of Israel and the people of Israel. Someone who had put his life on the line four times for his people and his homeland is not only a religious Jew, but is also a holy Jew. And I told the congregation how fortunate we were that just such an individual was serving as *sandak* for our very first synagogue circumcision.

The leader of the Munich Jewish community initially held his head in his hands during my introduction. After the circumcision, however, he warmly shook my hand. "I understand," he said. "I think you made the right decision." And he continued to bring me flowers for as long as his children lived in the neighborhood.

Chapter Thirty-Five

A Holocaust Survivor and His Two Mistresses

During the days when the synagogue was still in an apartment, there was a man who used to come to shul every Shabbat and even often during the week, but he traveled a lot. He was in his forties, and he was a survivor of the Holocaust.

Two women came to see me one day. I recognized one who came fairly regularly to shul, but I was not at all familiar with the second lady. Both of them were European and both were Holocaust survivors. They also had something else in common.

As they introduced themselves, it turned out that they were both this particular "gentleman's" mistresses; one being the *vochedike* (weekday) mistress and the other being the *Shabbosdike* (weekend) mistress. Neither had known of the existence of the other until, when he was on his most recent trip, both of them came at the same time to clean up the apartment. He, apparently, was leading a rather active and carefree life.

When they first encountered each other, they were each jealous of, and angry at, the other. They then recognized the absurdity of the situation, wanted to put a stop to the advantage their "gentleman" friend was taking of them both, and felt that I – an individual whom he seemed to respect – was the best one to confront him and force him to marry one of the two.

Now, I was still a fairly inexperienced rabbi, not yet freed of my yeshiva student mentality. I must admit to having been quite shocked at the situation, finding it impossible to reconcile two mistresses with regular synagogue attendance.

Nevertheless, I asked to see him and when he came into my office, I read him the riot act. "You have to decide. Both women are on strike. They're not going to see you or talk to you until you decide which one you're going to marry. You can remain friends with the other one because they've become friends, but no more than friendship, no hanky-panky."

At first he was stunned. Then he smiled, understood his game was up, and he answered almost immediately: "Okay, I've decided, I'll marry 'X.'" So we planned a wedding in the shul apartment a week from that Thursday afternoon, catered by Meal Mart.

The guests were invited for three o'clock in the afternoon, with the ceremony (*ḥuppa*) scheduled for four o'clock. I was pleased to see that the "other woman" came as well; she even greeted everyone like a bridesmaid. I began to fill out the marriage documents, first the New York State marriage license, and then the *ketuba,* the Aramaic alimony-insurance policy established by the sages of the Talmud some two thousand years ago. Of course I had already ascertained that neither of them had been married before, so you can imagine my shock to read in the New York marriage license that the bride had indeed been previously married. With a sense of righteous indignation, I charged her with being foolishly duplicitous! "Listen, you told me you were never married before, but here it says in black and white that you were; this New York document even gives the date of your marriage and the person to whom you were married. Without a *get* – a proper Jewish divorce – from your first husband, this second marriage cannot take place."

There must have been close to a hundred guests invited, most of whom had already arrived. The woman had tears in her eyes, responding, "I didn't mean to lie. I married someone whom I knew from Auschwitz, but after we came to America, he converted to Christianity. Once he converted to Christianity, I left him and we got a civil divorce. But I assumed that since he was now a Christian, my marriage to him didn't count in the eyes of God, and no *get* would be necessary."

I explained to her that such was not the case: "Your reasoning would be correct if he were a Christian from birth. But since he was a Jew who converted to Christianity, he has all the obligations of a Jew, and he has to give you a religious divorce. Otherwise, we can't have a wedding."

She started to cry. I asked if perhaps I could contact her former husband and see if he were willing to give her a *get*. When she told me that he was a fine person who worked as an interpreter for the United Nations, and since our synagogue was but a mile away from the UN building, I called him immediately and explained the situation. He responded most graciously: "I finish work at 5:00 P.M. I can be there at 5:30. I will gladly do whatever is necessary."

Then I called my rebbe, Rav Soloveitchik; usually there is a three-month waiting period between a divorce and a remarriage, but since they had been legally separated and living apart for at least fifteen years, Rav Soloveitchik permitted me to waive the three-month delay.

Then I called Rav Melech Schachter, who was in charge of divorces for the Rabbinical Council of America at that time, and he also said that he would be able to be there by 5:30 with his "team" of two witnesses and a scribe. We told everybody that there would be a two- to three-hour delay for the ceremony; Meal Mart Catering packed our synagogue with hors d'oeuvres. The UN interpreter came on time; the scribe and witnesses came on time, we effectuated the *get* by 6:45 P.M. By 7:00, bride and groom were under the *ḥuppa* and, to the best of my knowledge, not one of the guests left in the interim (everyone was intrigued by what was going on behind closed doors in my office).

The former husband was the real hero of the tale. He even remained for the ceremony. Afterwards, I walked him to the door. "You've been so gracious about this," I said to him, "that I have been very much impressed with you. But I must ask you a question – and you may tell me it's none of my business. You were in Auschwitz; you went through so much suffering for your Jewishness. How could you have converted to Christianity?"

His reply is still ringing in my ear. "I don't believe in Christianity, and neither do I believe in Judaism. After the Holocaust, I can no longer believe in God, but I don't want Jews to suffer anymore. I came to believe that the only way to prevent Jewish suffering is by putting an end to the Jewish people. I am a very logical and consistent person. The result of my logic was conversion to Christianity, and that's what I did."

He walked out the door and then he came back. "But I am agonized by one question: by converting, wasn't I granting Hitler a posthumous victory? Wasn't I doing just what the Nazis would have wanted me to do? And when I look around and I see the State of Israel, and when I see the renaissance that religious Judaism is enjoying – and your synagogue is an example of that – I think maybe that I gave up too much too soon..."

I have never forgotten his words; what he said first, and what he said last.

Chapter Thirty-Six

A Rabbi Is a Johnny Appleseed

Also in the second year of our synagogue, I read a lead story in the *New York Post* of a heretofore childless, Jewish woman living in Lincoln Towers who had given birth to quadruplet boys. Although neither the woman nor her husband was a member of the shul or, to the best of my recollection, had ever come to services, I decided to visit her in the hospital with a *mazal tov* wish. When I entered the room and identified myself, she politely but firmly let me know that, although she appreciated my good intentions, she had neither interest nor need to speak to rabbis. More than slightly taken aback, I lamely suggested that perhaps I could recommend a certified *mohel* for the circumcisions. She cut me off, telling me that she and her husband had decided against circumcising their sons.

Two days later, I read that one of the quadruplets had died. Notwithstanding my previous cool reception, I decided to visit the hospital and offer my condolences and any other service she might wish. This time, the young mother seemed better disposed, even relieved to see me, even though she had been silently weeping when I entered her room. "I didn't know how to reach you, Rabbi. What am I supposed to do now?" I explained that until the thirty-first day after birth there is no mourning for the baby, but that there ought to be a burial; I told her that we already had a *ḥevra kaddisha* (burial society) in the synagogue that would take care of everything. "What is the charge?" she asked. I explained that there was no charge, that taking care of the dead – who cannot take care of themselves – is the greatest mitzva that there is, and it is a mitzva for which no one accepts any payment. She gave me a grateful smile, and began to sob quietly. Before I closed her door behind me, I mentioned that Jewish custom dictates that such babies who die before they have had even a minimal chance at life – and who are immediately taken by God and bathed by His tears – are to be circumcised right before burial, and that this too would be taken care of. I took her silence to mean acquiescence, and arranged for a private burial.

A week later, I received a most gracious note from the young mother, informing me that she had left the hospital, thanking me for my concern and apologizing for her initial bad manners. Three weeks later, she and her husband formally became members of the synagogue – and since the pediatrician had told her that the triplets would be ready for circumcision, she asked that I please provide for a *mohel*.

Despite this pleasant turn-around of events, I would never have looked upon this family as a Lincoln Square Synagogue "success story." They did begin attending High Holy Day services, but when it came time for the boys to enter school – and I met with the parents one evening to try to persuade them to send the triplets to a Jewish day school – they were sent to a private and exclusive French-speaking school in the area. They were, however, given some Jewish training in our afternoon school and were "bar-mitzvahed" at Lincoln Square Synagogue.

Many years later, after I had made *aliya* and had been prominently featured in the news for having led a peaceful demonstration against the then prime minister, Rabin, and had even been imprisoned for a day, I received a request for an interview with the prestigious *Life-Style* magazine. When I laid my eyes upon the young interviewer – who met me in a Manhattan hotel during one of my frequent visits to the States – I immediately recognized him as one of the triplets! And, even more remarkably, he was wearing a *kippa* (skullcap). "Yes," he told me, “I am an observant Jew today. We grew up with the story of a kind rabbi who visited us in the hospital and provided us with our circumcisions; I was always moved by your seminars and very much enjoyed my Hebrew school experience in the synagogue. And later, in college, I became fully observant. In fact,” – and he took out a scrapbook with articles about me that spanned decades, in various newspapers – “I was always somewhat of a student from afar, even though we didn’t spend real quality time together…”

Chapter Thirty-Seven

A *Kohen Gadol* with an *Etzba Elokim*

The forgotten festival in the early Lincoln Square Synagogue was Sukkot, the Festival of Booths, when observant Jews throughout the world build and dwell in small huts for seven days, reminiscent of the desert booths in which the outcast Israelites experienced God's protection for forty years after they left Egyptian slavery, four thousand years ago. Since the West Side consists mainly of high-rise buildings, there was usually no space for a *sukka*; hence, even the slightly more traditional Jews let the makeshift-dwelling aspect of this holiday lapse into assimilated oblivion. As a rabbi who prided himself on revitalizing many Jewish traditions for many "born-again" Jews, with regard to Sukkot, I was truly at a loss for ideas. How could I encourage *sukka*-building and living where there was no place to put a *sukka*?

At this juncture I met Mr. Adolf Katz, who truly taught me that if indeed you will it, nothing is impossible. This story begins not on Sukkot, but actually on first day of Pesaḥ 1966. Shortly before the beginning of the Torah reading, there entered a very tall, middle-aged individual, flanked by his two even taller sons, neither of whom had ever worshiped with us before. I immediately greeted them, ascertained that their family name was Katz, and confirmed that they were Kohanim, of our priestly lineage stretching all the way back to Aaron, elder brother of Moses, High Priest of the Israelites. (Katz is usually the acronym for *Kohen Tzedek*, righteous priest.)

I was jubilant, because until that time I had been the only Kohen at weekday festival services. Of course, we called up Adolf Katz to recite the first blessings over the Torah reading, which he knew by heart.

I promptly invited him to *duchan* with me as well, to bless the congregation with the biblical priestly blessing. With what seemed to me a profound sadness, he told me he could not do that. He held out his hands showing that two of his fingers were missing as the result of a work accident soon after he had come to America from Transylvania as a youth. A rabbi had told him that he had become a "blemished" Kohen, and so had lost the privilege of blessing the congregation.

I explained that since we cover our fingers and faces with a prayer shawl – so that no blemish is evident to the congregants – it is perfectly permissible, and even mandatory, for him to join me in the priestly blessing.

Once again he demurred, this time with tears in his eyes. "You see, when I bid my father farewell before getting on the train on the way to America, his last words to me were a reminder that I was a Kohen, a member of Jewish aristocracy, and that it would be my privilege and duty to bless the congregation each festival. But he added that for me to be worthy to do so, I must always keep the Sabbath day holy, just as I had in my home town. When I first came to America I scrupulously observed the Sabbath – so that I would remain worthy of blessing the congregation. But when my accident occurred, and the rabbi told me I couldn't bless the congregation anyway, I became lax in my Sabbath observance. That's why you haven't seen me in the synagogue for the regular Sabbath services until now. So I'm afraid that I cannot join you." I lifted my arms very high and embraced Mr. Katz: "So you'll resume keeping Shabbat from now on – and you'll rise with me to bless the congregation." I could feel the tears coursing down his cheeks as he shook my hand in a pledge – and he was in his front seat in the synagogue every Shabbat until he died several decades later.

Mr. Katz, a seasoned businessman with a great deal of common sense, quickly became a confidant and mentor – as well as a generous supporter of all of our projects. When I told him of my frustration regarding Sukkot, he asked for a few weeks to solve the problem. And solve it he did. He rented a large parking lot for the ten days surrounding Sukkot, from an Italian restaurant very close to the shul, put up a magnificent *sukka* that seated over four hundred people and subsidized catered meals for the first and last days. The Festival of Sukkot returned to the West Side!

POST SCRIPT:

Adam Katz, son of Curtis Katz, and grandson of Adolf and Erna Katz, recently dedicated the dining room of our Neveh Shmuel High School in Efrat – a dining room that provides three meals a day for close to two thousand students, many of whom we subsidize because their parents cannot afford to pay the tuition fees.

Chapter Thirty-Eight

The Power of a *Mezuza*

In the early 1970s, a widow named Ruth Belsky called Lincoln Square Synagogue, requesting of the secretary that the rabbi put up the *mezuzot* in her new apartment in Lincoln Towers. I visited her with alacrity, and found an intelligent and committed woman with an active history in charitable organizations, whose parents had been responsible for the maintenance of the *mikveh* in East New York, but who was consumed by loneliness. She had moved many times since her husband's death. When I asked her why she thought this move would be a more permanent one, she told me that her kitchen window looked out onto a park. "I cannot bear to eat alone," she explained. "In this apartment, I can eat facing the window and make believe I'm talking to the people sitting in the park."

I put up the *mezuzot*, and invited her to join us for the next Friday evening meal. She became a most honored and lively addition to our family for most Shabbat and festival evenings. But as closely involved as she was becoming with the Lincoln Square Synagogue family in general, and with my family in particular, she seemed rather removed – even alienated – from her own blood family.

She had two sons: one an engineer who lived alone, and the other a very prominent and respected internist, Dr. Marvin Belsky, who lived in Manhattan with his wife, Miriam, and their two children. He leaned to the left on the political spectrum, and was anti-religious on the theological spectrum. Ruth Belsky once told me that it was Marvin who prevented his wife from having a kosher home. She did try to maintain a close relationship with her grandchildren, especially with Annie, her granddaughter, who seemed especially interested whenever she came to visit, but the religious divide between Ruth and her sons caused her a great deal of anguish.

When I announced, at a regular board meeting, that I was going on *aliya,* Ruth Belsky was the first to react. "You can't leave us, Rabbi. If you're not here, who will say *Kaddish* for me?" I promised her that if I were physically able, then when the time would come, I would faithfully say *Kaddish* for the year. She seemed relieved – and I kept my pledge.

A few years after Ruth's death, I received a notice that her granddaughter, Anne Belsky Moranis, Marvin and Miriam's daughter, had tragically passed away. Although my contact with Marvin had been minimal, I called from Israel to express my condolences. Marvin told me he was sitting *shiva* and asked about the existence of a soul, the dimension of life after death. I was deeply impressed with the sincerity and intensity of his questions. We spoke at great length on the phone, and when I suggested a meeting when I was next in New York, he gladly accepted.

Thus began an odyssey, which has resulted in Marvin and Miriam's home becoming kosher, and Marvin – in addition to putting on *tefillin* every day – having become a complete Shabbat observer. He and his wife are now committed Zionists, and as far as Israeli politics are concerned, he now leans even to the right of my own position.

I often think about the transformation that has taken place in Marvin, and imagine his mother Ruth and his daughter Annie, looking down and smiling lovingly from above.

Chapter Thirty-Nine

Zalman Bernstein: The Most Unforgettable Person I Ever Met

Lincoln Square Synagogue began to develop as a vibrant, Torah learning, outreach synagogue. Every Wednesday evening I gave a Bible class followed by a topical lecture, which began to attract hundreds of steady attendees. Many of them were singles in their twenties to forties, looking for learning and looking for love.

One particular Wednesday evening I had finished my lecture, and all of a sudden someone, whom I had not seen before, jumped up and screamed out, "Hey Rabbi, I like your style. I want to say *Kaddish*."

I explained that since everyone was leaving and the men and women were mixed, it was not the proper atmosphere for *Kaddish*. "We'll have evening prayers, *Ma'ariv*," I said, "upstairs in the study hall, and then it would be fine for you to recite *Kaddish*." I asked for whom he was mourning, and he said it was for his father, who had passed away six months before.

We went upstairs, where about sixty people were gathered for prayer – sixty out of the four- or five-hundred-strong crowd who had been there for the lecture. He really did not know how to pray the evening prayer, but he did know *Kaddish* very well. Apparently, he had some Jewish background.

After the prayers were ended, he said again, "Hey Rabbi, I like your style. Too bad I can't be a member of your synagogue."

When I asked him why not, after all, we were an outreach synagogue, he explained, "Not me, you wouldn't take me. I've been married to a Christian woman for thirty years." This was all a public conversation and he was speaking rather loudly.

I suggested we continue the discussion in my office, but he wouldn't hear of it.

"Tell me here and now, Rabbi, will you take me as a member?"

"But why would someone who's married to a Christian woman wish to become a member of an Orthodox synagogue?" I asked.

He opened up his shirt to show me that he was wearing *tzitzit*, the ritual fringes. He said, "My father wore these, and after he died, I started to wear his."

I realized that there was a strong force pulling him back to tradition, that this was an especially sensitive time in his life. I took a deep breath and said, "You can take out a single membership for the synagogue."

There were tears in his eyes. He took out a checkbook. "How much is it?"

I really hadn't the slightest idea as to the price of membership so I simply picked a number. "Seventy-five dollars, but you have to study Torah with me every week."

"When do we start?" he asked eagerly.

"Tomorrow?" I offered.

"Fine," he said, meet me at one o'clock for lunch." And he gave me his card, "Sanford Bernstein Investment Brokers," in the General Motors Building.

"To which office shall I come?" I asked.

"To *my* office – Sanford Bernstein. I'm the president and chief managing officer of the company. That's me," he said with a flourish.

The next day, I actually biked over to his office, and arrived about twenty minutes late. I went up to the twenty-second floor. Everything was green, from the elevator door to the desk, to the telephones.

When I stepped out of the elevator, the secretary looked up and said, "You're the rabbi? One moment please... Mr. Bernstein would like to speak to you on the telephone."

I figured: we have an appointment, why the telephone? But I picked up the phone.

"Hey Rabbi, time is money. You kept me waiting twenty minutes; I keep *you* waiting twenty minutes."

"Mr. Bernstein," I responded, "time is not *only* money. Time is life. And life is far more valuable than money. If you cannot see me now because you're doing something else, I'll wait for you, even five hours if necessary – but if you're just punishing me, I will have to leave immediately."

He opened up the door to an inner office, which was even greener than the outer office. "I told you I like your style. Come in, but never be late again."

Believe me, I was never late for him again.

I sat down, and saw that there was a big sign on the wall in green letters that said "No Smoking," but he himself was smoking the biggest and smelliest cigar I had ever seen, puffing smoke right in my face. I looked at him and pointed to the sign. He said to me, "Listen, Rabbi, in your synagogue you make the rules. In this office, I make the rules. 'No Smoking' to me means 'No Smoking Cigarettes.' Cigars are fine."

I was sitting opposite him. He began to eat a cheeseburger sandwich – and I had never been in such close proximity to a cheeseburger before. He had prepared for me a hamburger with a stamp on it that read, "Glatt Kosher." I'd brought two Bibles, one for him and one for me. I had a whole lesson worked out for beginners, which would give insight into the entire Jewish philosophy of life, from the early verses of Genesis.

He concentrated very deeply and asked extremely good questions. When I gave an answer he liked, he would jump up and begin cursing like a drunken sailor. Anyway, about twenty minutes into our study, he looked up at me with real concern. "Rabbi, you look greener than the walls. What's the matter?" I felt as if the green walls were converging and the room was spinning.

As everything began to get dim, I gave the only explanation I could: "I'll tell you the truth. The stench of your cigar and the cheeseburger, your vocabulary and the words of the Bible all coming together are just too much for me to handle." He immediately opened the windows, squashed the cigar, tossed the unused portion of the cheeseburger in the garbage, and offered to give $180 to the Hebrew University for every vulgar word he used. I was beginning to feel a bit stronger and I said, "Listen, that's not real *charity*." So he said, "Oh, you want me to give to your yeshiva?" "No," I replied, "give to Chabad." At the end of that session we sent to Rav J.J. Hecht of Chabad a check for $1,800; Rav Hecht asked that I study with this gentleman three times a day and then he would be able to retire.

That was my first encounter with Zalman Bernstein.

The relationship became very intense, built around learning. He came to my home for Shabbat meals, together with his wife, and he began to grow in Jewish observance. Soon he became a steady congregant who attended synagogue every Shabbat – and while he was saying *Kaddish* for his father, he attended three prayer services every day.

He was a man of strong passions and deep convictions. It was a pleasure talking to him. We didn't always agree; the tones sometimes reached very high decibels, but there was always a great deal of mutual respect. His language toned down, though never became totally sanitized. More importantly, he became a completely observant Jew, a committed and philanthropic Jewish leader, and a beloved and very close friend.

Chapter Forty

A Grave Business

As Zalman Bernstein was growing religiously, and was learning about the importance of the land of Israel, he once told me that he wanted to be buried in Israel. I told him that my family and I spend our summers in Israel, and I would gladly arrange a cemetery plot for him. He wanted to be buried on the Mount of Olives. I contacted a close friend of mine, whose father was a member of the *Ḥevra Kaddisha,* the burial society, and we arranged for a single grave for him.

Toward the end of the summer, Zalman called me, and said that he was in France and that he'd like to stop off in Israel to see his gravesite. All of us – Zalman, three members of the *Ḥevra Kaddisha* and I – met outside the Mount of Olives cemetery. As a Kohen, I could not go into the cemetery, so I brought along a book of Psalms, and stood a considerable distance from the graves. Zalman went with the *Ḥevra Kaddisha* to "check out" his gravesite.

From where I was standing, I could hear very loud shouting, and I realized that there was an altercation going on between Zalman and the *Ḥevra.* Then I saw Zalman running hither and thither and looking at this grave and that grave, and that grave and this grave. I must admit, I was very curious and more than a little concerned as to what was happening.

When they came back together, with angry faces, Zalman told me that the grave was absolutely unacceptable. From his proposed gravesite, he had no view of the Temple Mount, and so he refused to be buried there. "I found a plot that's empty and from it you can see the Temple Mount very clearly," he said. "That's the one I want. I want to be switched."

The members of the *Ḥevra Kaddisha,* who had understood his background and realized why he was taking only one plot, looked at me and said, "He picked the gravesite two graves away from Rav Avraham Yitzḥak HaKohen Kook. We can't give it to him." I was both exasperated and ashamed. I angrily and embarrassedly said to Bernstein, "Listen, Zalman" (by this time he had changed his name from Sanford to Zalman officially). "Rav Kook is one of the holiest people who ever lived in this world, the first chief rabbi of Israel. You're just not on a sufficient spiritual level to be worthy of being buried next to him. And besides, when your time will come to use the grave, you will either be able to see everything or you will see nothing; but whatever you'll see or won't see will have nothing to do with the view from the grave itself." He looked at me in annoyance and then in fury. "Cancel the plot," he said summarily and, without contacting me again, he left Israel.

A short while later I received a letter from him. He began with an apology, writing that he had begun to do some research on Rav Kook. And then he explained that he understood very well that when the time came, the view from his grave wouldn't matter much. "But," he continued, "I pretty much messed up in this world, especially vis-à-vis my children. And it's too late now because they're on their own. I have only one opportunity left. There's a good chance that they will come to visit my grave from time to time. And the Temple Mount is the holiest place in the world. I want them to be able to see it; maybe they'll become inspired. Maybe I'll be able to do for them after death what I didn't do for them in life."

I went to the *Ḥevra Kaddisha* with the letter and translated it for them into Hebrew. I said to them, "I've been a rabbi now for many years. I guarantee you that this individual will be a complete Shabbat-observant Jew in very short order. He already puts on *tefillin* every day. Given where he came from and the direction in which he's going, I honestly don't believe that Rav Kook would be embarrassed to have him as a neighbor." They read the letter and they were moved. They gave him the gravesite without charging extra, and that's where he's buried today.

To the best of my knowledge, he only visited the grave one more time before he died. He wanted to "test it out," to lie down in it to make sure it was big enough, that it would fit the contours of his body. He had a picture taken of himself lying down in the grave, and he proudly hung that picture on his study wall for all his visitors to see.

Zalman became a devotee of everything that Rav Kook wrote and stood for, even sponsoring a very successful colloquium in Jerusalem on Rav Kook's writings. I suggested that a good friend and respected colleague of mine, Benny Ish Shalom, direct the colloquium, which featured many scholarly papers presented before a very wide audience. The event produced not only a fine volume dedicated to the life and thought of Rav Kook, but also Beit Morasha, the Robert M. Beren College, an important Torah institution in Jerusalem that combines serious Torah study with advanced university degrees. Zalman was inspired to give Benny and me the seed money for a unique Torah academy enterprise that would express the universalism of Rav Kook's teachings.

One of the joys of the rabbinate was to have become friends with such an unforgettable person, a great character with great character.

POST SCRIPT:

A very well-known American Jewish philanthropist, who had barely been cognizant of his own Jewish identity and had never been helpful to the Jewish or humanitarian community until he reached age forty (despite his considerable wealth), suddenly became a major contributor, and even an initiator of a major and very expensive project to train Jewish leaders.

One Friday night when we were together, I asked what had made him suddenly switch life-directions. What had triggered his decision to get married, have children, and become so involved in Jewish future?

"I had only one passion in my life," he told me. "I enjoyed money, but not passionately. My one passion was skiing, my only one. And then, when I was on a ski lift in Aspen, a storm broke out. I was completely isolated and I thought I might die. I wasn't afraid; I can't explain why not. I didn't make a bargain with God because that, I felt, would be infantile. But I became consumed with one thought: If I die, who will mourn me?

And I came to the conclusion that the only one would mourn me is my mother. And she would have done so even if I had died at birth. So I might as well never have lived.

"I thought further, what would there be to write on my epitaph? What have I done except have a good time? And so, I came to the conclusion that if indeed I would live through this storm, I would try to direct my energies to some ideal that goes beyond instant pleasures. I would try to leave something of enduring value behind me. Then there would be those who would mourn my passing because I had meaningfully touched them while I was alive. Then there would be significant words to write on my gravestone because I shall have left something behind. In the final analysis, the only thing we truly own is what we give to the future."

Chapter Forty-One

Women, Torah Scrolls and Three Rabbinic Opinions

It was Shemini Atzeret, the solemn assembly of the eighth day of the Festival of Sukkot, 1972, during our evening festive meal, when eight serious women of varying ages – all of whom were *ba'alot teshuva* ("born-again," penitent Jews), all of whom were intense students of the Bible and Talmud – knocked on my door just as we were beginning the Grace after Meals. Of course, my wife warmly invited them to join us in tea, fruit and cake – but these women hadn't come either to eat or to socialize. "Rabbi, we've come with a serious question. Tomorrow evening ushers in Simḥat Torah, when every male – even a male child – gets called up to the Torah, and is offered the opportunity to dance with the Torah. Every male is filled with such joy of Torah, such love of Torah…, but only the males, not us, the females. Why can't we read from the Torah and dance with the Torah? We all know how to do so – even letter and cantillation perfect. Didn't God call out His Sinaitic Revelation both to the sons of Israel – the men – as well as the house of Jacob – the women? Why aren't we adult learned women as privileged as a male child?"

I listened intently, and promised to give a reasoned response the next day. I heard the angst, frustration and even tears in their voices, and I knew first-hand how sincerely these young women had immersed themselves in the world of the commandments and their study. I was only saddened that they had not come a day before, so that I could have called Rav Soloveitchik for a ruling.

I was up the whole night, poring over the Talmud, the Codes, and the Responsa pursuant to women carrying a Torah Scroll and reading from it, separate from the presence of men. Ultimately, I concluded that all Talmudic sages and decisors agree, that a Torah scroll cannot become ritually defiled, and that a woman – even while menstruating – may touch, kiss, dance with, and read from a Torah scroll. I therefore met with them the following evening and told them that on Simḥat Torah morning I would allow them to lock the *beit midrash* door and conduct *hakafot* (circuit dancing with the Torah scroll), as well as a Torah reading by women and for women alone. I forbade the blessings over the Torah scroll because these special blessings had been established by our sages for the males, who alone were obligated to hear the public Torah reading. However, I did rule that it would be permissible, and even salutary, to permit these religiously sincere and committed women to embrace and dance with the Torah to which they had become so personally committed, on the Day of Rejoicing of the Torah.

The core group of women who had broached the issue to me, excitedly knocked again at my apartment door as soon as Simḥat Torah had concluded. Their ecstatic sense of fulfillment – and the many stories they told of women from fifteen to seventy-five, who had unabashedly wept with joy and pride the first time they had been allowed such close proximity to the Torah – made me feel that nothing less than a historically significant, religious experience had occurred that day at Lincoln Square.

And then all hell broke loose…

The rabbi of the West Side's Young Israel congregation, a revered Talmudic scholar, publicly announced in his synagogue the following Shabbat that if Lincoln Square Synagogue had allowed women's *hakafot* and Torah reading, then Lincoln Square Synagogue could no longer be considered an Orthodox synagogue. Suddenly I heard a "great rushing sound" of critique – and I felt truly devastated.

I immediately went to my rebbe, Rav Soloveitchik, in order to test the soundness of my ruling. I specifically requested that Mordecai Feuerstein (today a respected rabbi in his own right in Livingston, New Jersey, and who then served as personal attendant as well as faithful student to the Rav), be present at the meeting in order to verify afterwards the exact words and nuances of the Rav's reply. I carefully explained the events leading up to my decision, the fact that I was unable to seek his counsel because the issue only came up on the first day of the festival for a religious activity that had to occur (if at all) on the following day. I emphasized that there would be no problem admitting my mistake while still retaining my rabbinical position, if it be his decision that I had ruled in error.

The Rav could not have been warmer or more supportive. "You are one hundred percent covered halakhically," he said. He explained my predicament to be a political one – in terms of what other Orthodox leaders would say who were not faced with the challenges of my particular congregation, and who were less willing to depart from heretofore accepted procedures. However, reiterated the Rav, the weight of recorded halakhic opinion was certainly on my side. And then Rav Soloveitchik volunteered to give a *shiur* at Lincoln Square Synagogue, declaring, "Now I dare anyone to say that you and your synagogue are not Orthodox!" And he did.

For my own satisfaction, I continued to ask the same question of two other great Torah giants whom I also looked up to as revered Torah teachers. Rav Moshe Feinstein (whom I went to see accompanied by a good friend, Rav Dov Lesser, *z"l*, a student of Lakewood Yeshiva and a leader in the Torah Umesorah organization) said that had I asked him beforehand, he would have told me not to allow it – because, although he felt that my ruling was halakhically correct and that I would be capable of limiting the feminist requests to halakhically permissible activities, others, who might adopt these practices in their synagogues, may not be able to control their scope. Nevertheless, he added that if, were I not to allow a similar expression the next Simḥat Torah, it would cause even one woman to leave Orthodoxy, I would be permitted to continue the religious activity for the women. And the Lubavitcher Rebbe – after a far-reaching interview that dealt with many aspects of women in halakha and lasted for close to two hours – said in conclusion, "Not only may you do it [next year], you *must* do it." (I subsequently received a letter from the Rebbe that made it clear to me that his support of my position was limited specifically to my situation at Lincoln Square).

As I review my rabbinical and educational career in America and Israel, women in halakha has been one of the most challenging and crucial issues I have had to face; indeed, the Lubavitcher Rebbe defined it for me as the most significant religious challenge of the twentieth century. As I have faced each aspect from women's *hakafot* to women religious court advocates (*to'anot*), to women suing for divorce – I have tried to do so with humane and halakhic integrity, two factors that must drown out the "great rushing sound" from whichever direction it may come!

Chapter Forty-Two

A Meeting with Rav Yaakov Kamenetzky: How to Take Criticism

During the 1960s and '70s, I never refused a request to visit various communities throughout the United States and Canada – as varied as Phoenix, Arizona; Kerem, California; Houston, Texas; Denver, Colorado; Vancouver, British Colombia – to encourage the building of Jewish day schools and high schools, believing profoundly that there could be no Jewish future without intensive Jewish education. I went under the auspices of Torah Umesorah, a major Jewish organization whose *raison d'etre* was – and still is – organizing yeshiva educational institutions throughout the English-speaking Diaspora.

And then, when (in 1975) I established my own yeshiva high school in Riverdale, New York – Ohr Torah, under the educational directorship of the unforgettable Pinky Bak, *z"l* – Torah Umesorah wished to honor me with an award for "Educational Creativity" at their annual dinner.

Torah Umesorah was always to the religious right of Yeshiva University. Its halakhic spiritual guide was Rav Yaakov Kamenetzky of Monsey, New York – a great Torah luminary who had been the rosh yeshiva of Torah Vodaas, a major Talmudical academy at the time, which was philosophically and theologically critical of Yeshiva University (and Rav Soloveitchik) for its positive acceptance of secular university studies and modern Zionism. In addition, I had two more strikes against me for permitting women to dance with Torah scrolls (behind the *meḥitza*) on Simḥat Torah, and for teaching Talmud to women in our Ohr Torah High School for Girls (led by Dr. Rivka Blau). Hence, when the news leaked of my impending award within these more ultra-Orthodox circles, there was some opposition to my receiving the honor.

Amidst my willingness to gladly forgo the honor, and the confusion of those who had suggested my name in the first place, Rav Yaakov Kamenetzky (whom I had never personally met, although I had heard him speak at several public occasions) insisted I be given the award. He elected to present the plaque to me himself, but stipulated that I meet him at his home in Monsey on the day following the dinner. Although he could not have been more gracious during the presentation, and though the dinner itself turned out to be a most respectable affair (Rav Yaakov's role as presenter of the award silenced any lingering opposition), I nevertheless felt great trepidation throughout my journey to Monsey; after all, I was probably in for a serious questioning by a great Torah personality, who certainly opposed many of my religious and halakhic positions.

Rav Kamenetzky was then close to his ninetieth year; he completely disarmed me with his warm smile, jocular eyes and spry manner as he invited me to drink tea and eat cake. He then asked me to describe the beginning of Lincoln Square Synagogue and the Ohr Torah schools, and to chronicle everything that could be thought of as being liberal or "un-Orthodox," explaining the reasons and halakhic basis for these novel practices. He seemed to listen to me intently and encouragingly; I especially emphasized the uniqueness of our *meḥitza*, the *hakafot* for women, and our insistence on Talmud study for our women as well as for men, in the synagogue adult-education classes and in our schools.

After I concluded a rather lengthy exposition, he invited me to eat and drink some more while he shared with me an interpretation on the biblical portion of the week (which happened to be *Vayḥi,* the last portion of the book of Genesis).

He asked why it was that – although Shimon and Levi had previously been shouted at by their father Jacob for having destroyed all of the inhabitants of Shekhem – they were now given choice blessings: Levi was to be the tribal father of Aaron the High Priest, the progenitor of all Kohanim (teachers in the Holy Temple); and Shimon (according to the Midrash), the tribal progenitor of all Torah educators. If their destruction of Shekhem was a heinous crime, why do they merit such "plum" blessings, the privilege of producing the Torah leadership of the Jewish people? And if indeed they deserved such blessings, why did Jacob shout at them: "You have caused me to be muddied, to stink amongst the inhabitants of the land." (Genesis 34:30)?

Rav Yaakov smiled as he answered his own question. It was true that Shimon and Levi had acted forcefully and without due process, but they truly felt that they had no recourse. After all, while Shekhem and his father Ḥamor came to discuss marriage to Dina with the family of Jacob, the raped Dina was still being held captive in the city of Shekhem and with the knowledge of all its inhabitants. Indeed, their response to their father's seeming displeasure (in the concluding words of the chapter, the Bible's final words on the incident) is "Can we allow our sister to be made into a harlot?" They did what they did for the future security and pride of Israel!

Their father Jacob understood all this, and that's why he blessed them with the priesthood and the keys to education. Religious and educational leadership must take responsibility – and even risks – for the security and pride of our nation.

At the same time, however, leaders who act without due process – even with the best of intentions and even in the most necessary of situations – must be shouted at, must be reprimanded. Otherwise less sincere individuals, or weaker individuals who may not be able to limit or contain such activities to the specific moment or situation of exigency, may learn from them, attempt to copy them, and wreak havoc rather than salvation. Therefore, Jacob had to shout at Shimon and Levi, lest the wrong people learn from them. But at the same time, he had to give them the choice blessings so that they would continue to battle for the pride and security of Israel. Jacob had to shout, and Shimon and Levi had to act.

"This is my message to you, my young friend," Rav Yaakov Kamenetzky concluded. "*Zei muzzen shrayen un ihr muzt tuhn.* They have to shout and you have to continue to do." I left the sage's home gratefully and humbly; somehow, I never minded the criticism so much after that meeting.

Along a similar vein, early on in my rabbinate – during the first or second year of Lincoln Square Synagogue – our very nice *gabbai,* Reb Shmuel Asher, came up to me after I had delivered a sermon he particularly appreciated. "Rebbe," he said, "I give you a blessing that you should have enemies [*sonim,* in Hebrew-Yiddish]."

"What kind of blessing is that, Reb Shmuel?" I said with a smile. "It sounds much more like a curse."

"Not at all," he replied. "If you accomplish little, everyone will praise you as a fine individual, an upstanding rabbi. But if you do important things, there will always be room for criticism, and there will always be no lack of jealous friends just waiting to pounce on you."

As I tell my rabbinical students, you must decide to which audience you are playing, the congregants or God. I strongly urge you to choose to play to God, for He has a much better and longer memory than the congregants have!

Chapter Forty-Three

Everybody Needs Shabbat

During my time at Lincoln Square Synagogue, well-known rabbis and *rashei yeshiva* would often spend a Shabbat with us and speak to our congregation. One of my favorite guests was Rav Yitzḥak Dovid Grossman, famed rabbi of Migdal HaEmek in Israel, who was well known for entering Israeli prisons and inspiring the convicts to return to God and to Torah. His long *pe'ot* (sidelocks), charismatic warmth and sweet voice captivated my family and congregants alike. During one of his early visits – probably in 1971 or '72 – he suggested, after Friday evening dinner at my home, that we go for a *shpatzir*, a leisurely walk, down Broadway.

I must explain that I tried never to walk on Broadway on Shabbat. West End Avenue was residential, and I would often meet Shabbat observers on that street. Broadway was far more business oriented – filled with shoppers, transients and vagabonds – and exuded an atmosphere that was the very antithesis of Shabbat. I would take any kind of circumvented route to avoid Broadway from sundown on Friday evening to the proverbial "three stars" on Saturday night.

This was especially true during the particular period of Rav Grossman's visit. A large disco-bar had opened on the corner of Broadway and 72nd Street, called Tel Aviv. It was open 365 nights a year, including during the sacred *Kol Nidrei* prayer on Yom Kippur eve. I had attempted to reach the Israeli owner of the disco scores of times. I wanted to register my displeasure, to urge him to close the disco at least for the night of Yom Kippur, and to try to convince him to change the name from Tel Aviv to Manhattan – but to no avail. I finally received a message that he "didn't talk to rabbis." In light of all this, I certainly had no desire to "take a *shpatzir*" on Friday evening along Broadway with Rav Grossman.

Nevertheless, he seemed to really want to go there, and he was my guest.

We soon came to the corner of 72nd Street and Broadway, and from the big front window of the disco-bar we could see scores of people dancing inside. Rav Grossman motioned toward the window. "We must go in and teach them about Shabbos," he said. I vigorously shook my head, "No!" After all, I thought, Rav Grossman, with his fur Shabbat *shtreimel* on his head, long beard and *pe'ot*, could hardly be suspected of entering a disco on Friday night for the sake of enjoying the disco, but I – clean-shaven and dressed in a regular suit – might give rise to another story. Rav Grossman asked me if I had ever seen a mosquito trapped in a jar. "The mosquito engages in all sorts of dance-like contortions, and seems to be joyously prancing about. But in reality, the mosquito is gasping for air, stretching in search of oxygen and life. So it is with the people inside," he said. "They are dying of asphyxiation, in desperate need of fresh, clean air, of Shabbat oxygen, of essential life."

Before I could object, he had entered the disco, and so did I, right behind him. What happened was comical at first, and then truly amazing. I immediately recognized, on the dance floor, a few of our regular Shabbat-morning, single male worshipers, who turned pale and white then crimson red when they saw us enter. One covered his face and ran out; another ranted, stuttered and tried too hard to convince me that his mother's doctor had medicines to give him and had left word to meet him at the disco…The live band was Israeli, and when they saw us enter, they immediately stopped playing. Apparently they felt that they could not play their instruments on Shabbat in front of two rabbis.

Rav Grossman, still speaking Yiddish, urged me to take advantage of the silence and tell them about Shabbat. I told them the midrash about how, when Adam was banished from the garden of Eden, he complained to God that his punishment was greater than he could bear. After all, how could he cope with the tragedies of loneliness, illness, alienation and death, which characterize the unredeemed world outside of Eden? God heard the justice of his words, and gave Adam and Eve two gifts: the tear and the Sabbath. When things get really tough, we can weep and feel relieved. And once a week we get a chance to return to Eden, via Shabbat.

I described a family Shabbat: the lighting of the candles, the singing of *Shalom Aleikhem* to the angels of peace and *Eshet Ḥayil* to the woman of the house (or alternatively the *Shekhina,* the feminine aspect of God); the blessing of the children (no matter how old they may be); the delectable food; the melodious *zemirot* (Shabbat songs sung by the whole family together); an "oasis in time" that gives a foretaste of the love and harmony of Paradise…

Then Rav Grossman began to sing a *niggun,* a Hasidic melody. The musicians joined him, clapping to his rhythm without their instruments. And *mirabile dictu,* the disco dancers made two circles, one for the young men and one for the young women, and they danced as if they too were *Hasidim,* singing the wordless *niggun,* clasping the hands of their same-sex friends, for close to half an hour.

At that point, Rav Grossman and I left.

I wish I could report that a miracle occurred, and that they all became Shabbat observers. But that is not what happened. A few minutes later we could hear the band playing again, and understood that the disco dancers danced to the same songs in the same manner as they had done before our surprise entrance.

But two things did happen. For the next two years, many singles joined Lincoln Square Synagogue; they said they had heard me at the Tel Aviv Disco and became interested in experiencing that gift of the Sabbath I had spoken about. And the day before the following Yom Kippur, the Tel Aviv Disco closed down, reason unknown.

I came away with a crucial lesson from that experience. I learned that we must reach out to everyone wherever he or she is at – and that everyone desperately needs the pure oxygen of Shabbat air.

Chapter Forty-Four

The Rabbi and the Butcher

There was a very well-known kosher butcher on the West Side who cut corners in how he *treibered* (removed the fatty veins and arteries of the meat), especially the tongues. I was in charge of the West Side Kashrut Board at the time. I told him his *treibering* was insufficiently executed with too many leniencies, but to no avail.

I felt I had no recourse but to send out a letter to the congregation announcing that the *kashrut* standards of this butcher were unacceptable to me, and that anyone who uses his meat would have to consider his or her home non-kosher.

The following day the butcher put out a letter defying my opinion, insisting that his meat was fine and having his letter counter-signed by another rabbi whom he declared his new *mashgiaḥ* (*kashrut* inspector). I went to Rav Soloveitchik, asking what he thought I should do.

The Rav confirmed my halakhic position, but roundly criticized the ineptness with which I had dealt with the issue. "A letter such as the one you wrote to the congregants loses its force once you send it out. What you ought to have done in such a case is show the letter to the butcher *before* sending it out as a means of getting him to change his method of *treibering*. Once you send it out you've already used up your strongest ammunition and the butcher no longer has anything to lose. The only recourse he has left is to fight you." The Rav also said that he was familiar with this particular butcher store, and that it was very popular. His meat was of the highest quality – and he even shipped meat out of New York to Connecticut and Boston. When a housewife must choose between what her rabbi says and what her family likes – especially if the butcher has found another certifying rabbi – the contest becomes a no-brainer, with the rabbi on the losing side. As if I wasn't devastated enough, the Rav concluded with the words of Reb Ḥayyim, his eminent grandfather: "Two individuals don't understand the extent of their respective strength. The Russian Cossack doesn't realize how strong he is, and the rabbi doesn't realize how weak he is."

When I left Rav Soloveitchik, I was totally dejected, believing I had just irretrievably lost my rabbinical authority! My clever wife gave me the solution. She agreed that the women *do* like this particular butcher, and most of them would continue to use him – all things being equal. She then pointed out that most of his Manhattan clientele didn't order meat on the phone; they wanted to see precisely what they were getting before they made their purchases. So if I could set up a small study-group in front of the butcher shop, no member of Lincoln Square Synagogue would walk past *me* into the store.

I discussed the matter with Rav Besdin, the director of the James Striar School of Yeshiva University, where I taught. He agreed to take my classes for the next two weeks. I took the best students in the class and "set up shop," studying with them every day in front of the store. The housewives did not walk past me into the butcher shop.

After the first week, the butcher came to me agreeing to make any changes I wished, in order to receive my *kashrut* certification.

Chapter Forty-Five

The New Shul *Meḥitza* – and a Rabbi Learns to Fundraise

On Purim of 1965 we put in the first *meḥitza* at Lincoln Square Synagogue. It was a string of planters, forty inches in height, which eventually developed into a fairly attractive, wooden divider forty-eight inches tall.

We immediately began to raise funds to erect a synagogue building on the corner of 69th Street and Amsterdam Avenue. By 1967 we had raised $250,000, but when the Six Day War broke out on June 5, we had an emergency synagogue meeting that night and sent those funds to the Israel Defense Forces (IDF).

We made up those funds, however, and for the High Holy Days of 1970, we were ready to enter our new building, with the biblical words etched on the entrance: "Return to Me for I have redeemed you."

A great deal of planning had gone into the sanctuary design. We wanted it to be clearly in accordance with Jewish tradition, with a center-stage *bima* (platform from which the cantor would lead the prayers and from where the Torah reader would read the biblical portion of the week), and a clear separation between the men and women so that the sexes would not mingle during prayer. The point of such a divider was to ensure that the social dimension of the service take a back seat to the religious dimension; at the same time, it was crucial for me, as well as for the congregation, that the women definitely not take a back seat; that they be able to see, hear, and feel themselves to be an integral part of the services.

Hence the *bima* was in the center, and six banks of seats rose up in elevated fashion from the *bima*, dividing the sanctuary into two equal halves, one for the women and one for the men. The *Aron Kodesh*, Holy Ark, around which the rabbi, cantor and president sat, was on the highest point of elevation opposite the *bima*.

The sexes were divided by a five-foot-high partition, but this was alongside both the men's and women's sections, and didn't interfere with anyone's line of vision. A railing of forty inches stood in front of the men and the women in the front row and ran around the complete circumference of the synagogue. Due to the careful planning, the sexes looked and felt equal before God; no one's ability to see and hear the proceedings was impaired, although a clear division was maintained. This type of divider was halakhically affirmed by Rav Soloveitchik, my teacher and mentor, and one of the great religious legal authorities of the generation.

We conducted services in the main sanctuary one Shabbat before our official gala opening, as a kind of trial run. Everything looked fine, except that, when I took my seat for the first time next to the Ark, directly in front of me were the three elevated banks of women's seats, and the only railing was in front of the very first row. One woman happened to be wearing a mini skirt…

That evening I met with the synagogue president. "There must be wooden railings in front," I remonstrated. The railings would not obstruct the women's line of vision; they could incorporate handy shelves for prayer books and bibles, and they would protect the women's legs and thighs from being totally exposed to view.

The president was sympathetic, but firm in his refusal. "Rabbi, you agreed to the architectural plans, you even had your rebbe, Rav Soloveitchik, sign off on them. Such extra, wooden railings would cost at least another $20,000, and we're already in debt for what we've built. It can't be done." All of my arguments that we had not adequately visualized the result from the plans on paper fell on deaf ears.

My wife saw how upset I was. The trial Shabbat morning was, for me, a nightmare. She told me she had a solution, but it was a very radical one. The following Friday afternoon, a few hours before the gala opening of the new synagogue building, we went to the sanctuary and placed cardboard railings, which she had prepared, before every one of the women's rows. For that most special Shabbat opening, which attracted guests from far and wide, everyone entered to a magnificent sanctuary – with cardboard railings. To add insult to injury, many women rested their jackets on these cardboards – which soon fell from the weight of the jackets. I would then gently request the women in that section to please move to another section with a railing. The result was bedlam. The president looked at me with burning anger. "I know that I cannot control financial expenditure," I said, "but I do determine halakhic policy. I rule that railings are necessary; if wooden railings are too expensive, we'll just have to continue to make do with cardboard."

Somehow the congregation raised the additional $20,000 and attractive wooden railings were up for the next Shabbat. I also began to understand that had I raised the funds in advance, the problem would have been solved in a much more elegant manner. I realized that if a rabbi wishes to bring new innovations to his synagogue or community – in terms of physical structures or educational programs – he must be ready to raise the requisite funding to turn his dreams into reality. Fundraising is part of the responsibility of an outreaching and innovative rabbinate; it also leads to close friendships and devoted partnerships with outstanding individuals.

Chapter Forty-Six

Jewish Genes

True, in Judaism the religion of the child follows the religion of the biological mother (Mishna, *Kiddushin* 3:12). But the father's seed certainly has some effect – especially since Rabbi Yehuda HaLevi, in his philosophic work, the *Kuzari*, speaks of a special and essential quality of Jewishness, *segula* (uniqueness) or *inyan Eloki* (Godly matter or substance), which is transmitted from generation to generation, a kind of metaphysical "Jewish gene." Moreover, many decisors rule that it is much easier to convert a child with a Jewish father (*zera Yisrael*).

Here is a story that taught me that the indelible Jewish strain can never be obliterated.

When I served as rabbi of Lincoln Square Synagogue, a young woman began attending services not only on Shabbat, but during weekday mornings as well. She prayed intensely, always came early and seemed truly devout. I invited her to my home for a Shabbat meal – and was surprised to discover that she was not Jewish, that her father was an archdeacon of the Episcopal Church in upstate New York, that she was majoring in art history in a prestigious university, and that she wanted to convert to Judaism.

She became our regular Shabbat guest, she took many classes at our Adult Education Institute, I continued to be amazed at her devotion to and knowledge of Judaism – but I was hesitant to convert her. After all, she would certainly want to marry a religious Jew – and it would be exceedingly difficult to find a young man (or a young man's parents) who would feel comfortable with an archdeacon for a *meḥutan*.

After more than a year of gently delaying her desire for conversion, she suddenly called me for an emergency meeting. Her cousin was taking a graduate course in anthropology with Alex Haley at Harvard, and, in the course of writing a paper on his familial "roots," he discovered that their common great-grandfather had been the *Rav Av Beit Din* (rabbi and chief judge) of the community in Danzig. He had had three sons: one succeeded him as religious leader, and the other two converted to Christianity for business reasons.

She was the granddaughter of a converted Jew! She told me that it did not matter to her if she were to remain single for the rest of her life. She only desired to re-establish her family line, and to join herself to her biologically Jewish roots. She had her conversion ceremony before the week ended.

Though she had reconciled herself to the possibility of never marrying, the story does not end there.

She went on a vacation trip to Europe. When in Venice, she entered a glass-blowing factory. She was fascinated by the artistry of the owner – a tall, well-built Italian with a booming voice, a hearty laugh and a flowing black beard. She felt immediately drawn to him and began to choose a figurine to purchase, when he told her that he had to close shop for about thirty minutes.

Since it was too early and too short a time for a siesta, she asked the reason for the closure. "I'm going to a Jewish old people's home for the afternoon prayers," he explained. And he continued to tell her fluttering heart that although he had been born a Catholic, and had even been married to a Catholic woman, his marriage had been annulled by the church and he had converted to Judaism when he discovered that his great-grandparents had been Jewish *Marranos* (crypto-Jews) during the Inquisition.

They were married six months later – and the archdeacon danced up a storm at the wedding celebration!

Chapter Forty-Seven

A Miracle in My Pocket? Not This Time...

I have always defined the Rabbinate as taking responsibility for a Jewish community that must include a synagogue for prayer, and institutions of Torah education for every age and every level of learning. To that end I assumed the deanship of the Manhattan Day School, Yeshivat Ohr Torah, which was within the Lincoln Square neighborhood (on 75th Street, below Riverside Drive and West End Avenue), and I established the Ohr Torah high schools for young men and women in Riverdale, New York. When I was considering a principal for the yeshiva high school, only one name came to mind – Pinky (Pinchas) Bak, a wise educator and a charismatic leader who had that most rare ability to instill the best possible values of spirituality and ethics without demanding uniformity of outlook and spirit. On the contrary, he encouraged individual expression and respect for differences. The school we created together literally took the yeshiva high school world by storm, creating a new standard in religious, secondary-school education.

But three years after we opened, on Purim night when the entire yeshiva was celebrating and rejoicing together, the great light was extinguished. Rav Pinky Bak, my closest friend and colleague, the first principal of the first Ohr Torah High School in Riverdale, suddenly and tragically died.

I went into a tailspin, became tormented by survivor's guilt, raised $250,000 for his young widow, Karen, who was left with five children and twins in her womb, and then had the most problematic period of fundraising I can remember. Jerome Stern, a dedicated friend and supporter, came to the rescue that first month with a loan. Many of our largest contributors felt that I should have kept Karen Bak on our payroll, but that I should not have given out a large lump sum at one time.

Just when I didn't know where the next month's salaries would come from, I received a visit from Rabbi E, a genius in Talmud and an expert in extracting government funds. He had heard of our financial difficulties, and suggested that we apply to the Lunch Program of the U.S. Government, which would generate the needed revenue to balance our budget. When I told him that we did not meet the criteria, that most of our students did not live in the dormitory and were not entitled to lunch, he explained how to fill out the forms so that we would get the money anyway. I controlled my anger, and suggested that if he did not leave my office immediately, I would throw him out.

The following evening there was an engagement party for one of Jerome Stern's children, Ronnie's engagement to Ralou. It was snowing lightly, and I opted to walk across Central Park to air out my mind and attempt to figure out a way to make that month's payroll.

There were many prominent guests in attendance, and Jerome introduced me to one in particular, Mr. G, a man of about my height and build, who was one of the main contributors – to the tune of many millions of dollars – to Boys Town, Jerusalem.

I gave a *devar Torah*, wished the families well, and began to walk back home. I really wasn't in the mood for partying, given our school's financial crisis.

The weather had turned quite brisk, the snow was falling more heavily, and I put my hands in my overcoat pockets. Lo and behold, I felt wads of cash. Sure enough, in each pocket I found thousands-of-dollars-worth of bills, held together by a silver money-clasp.

I began to dance in the middle of Central Park, crying out my thanksgiving to God. I thought I had been repaid from on high for having ejected Rabbi E from my office.

Then I landed back on earth with a thud; I realized it must be someone else's overcoat. I took off the overcoat and examined it more closely. Vicky puts name tags in all my outer garments. No, it was not mine!

I returned to the Stern household as quickly as I could, feeling the pockets of my mistakenly borrowed overcoat burning as from fire. Most of the guests had already left. But then I spied Mr. G, agitatedly running back and forth, as if looking for something.

"Don't worry, "I said. "I have your overcoat. I apparently took it by mistake." And with that I began removing the coat.

"How do you know it's mine?" he asked, clearly relieved.

"Believe me, I know. It certainly isn't mine…"

No, he did not give me a reward, not even a single hundred-dollar bill. I don't remember how I made payroll that month, but I made it. I guess it is important to know that miracles do not always happen…or maybe they do. After all, Ohr Torah high schools continued to survive.

Chapter Forty-Eight

A Rabbinical Lesson: How to Prevent Burnout

During the early years of our married life, my wife and I would take two- to three-day midweek vacations at the famed Grossingers Hotel. My parents, *z"l*, would move into our apartment to watch the children, and we would go ice skating and hiking "away from it all."

As we were leaving the hotel one Thursday afternoon in mid-winter, Grossingers' *kashrut* inspector, Rav Charles Chavell, was just arriving with his rebbetzin. He was a most respected rabbinical figure, the author of many important books, among them a scholarly edition and interpretation of the commentary of Ramban on the Torah, a *tour de force* work that answered all the questions of Rav Akiva Eiger on *Mo'ed*, responsa and more.

He greeted me warmly, and invited us to be his guests that Shabbat, in a private cabin that the hotel made available to him. After checking with my parents, who agreed to extend their grandchild-sitting, and after a quick call to the Lincoln Square president, I accepted the opportunity to spend quality time with such a well-known Torah scholar from whom I had much to learn.

During the course of an unforgettable Shabbat, I asked how he could be such a prolific Torah author and still tend to his duties as a synagogue rabbi. "I always had small synagogues," explained Rav Chavell, "Small in every way, both with respect to the quantity of the membership, as well as to their individual mind-set. After all, many of the daily synagogue issues deal with rather picayune matters. And after a board meeting with the trivial and often petty complaints of Mr. or Mrs. So-and-So, the only way to retain my broad horizons was by opening the Ramban or studying Rav Akiva Eiger. Suddenly I would find myself transported to a completely different universe of grand ideas and cosmic ideals.

"It is my intensive study of Torah giants that inspires me to reach for eternity and strive to touch infinity, even while it is necessary – and even significant – to deal with much lesser individuals day to day."

I've often thought of the truth of his words – and the Torah commentaries and religio-legal articles I write provide a much needed oasis from what has been an active and often hectic schedule of communal activity. "Had the Torah not been my delight, I would have perished in my affliction."

Part VI

Soviet Jewry 1962–75

Chapter Forty-Nine

The Miracle of the Soviet Jewry Movement

One of the great miracles of the twentieth century was the exodus of Soviet Jewry from behind the Iron Curtain; more than one million of them came to Israel. I was privileged to take part in the Soviet Jewry movement from its very beginnings in the early 1960s, and it was one of the defining experiences of my life.

There were at least three million Jews behind the Iron Curtain at that time, Jews whom Elie Weisel had called "The Jews of Silence" because their own ability to speak out was repressed by the Communist totalitarian Soviet government, and there was no voice of world Jewry speaking out on their behalf.

In the early sixties I had met a fascinating Englishman named Jacob Birnbaum, a Herzlian figure with fire in his eyes and passion in his heart. His grandfather was the very famous Nathan Birnbaum, a leading *ba'al teshuva* intellectual who coined the word "Zionism."

Jacob Birnbaum had just returned from a fact-finding mission to the Soviet Union, which he had undertaken in disguise. He was highly charged with the necessity of activist work on behalf of Soviet Jews.

He envisioned world-wide demonstrations that would force the Soviet regime to either let its Jews live as Jews where they were, or leave as Jews for Israel.

The religious establishment at that time was against activist tactics; they felt it best to work through quiet diplomacy. A number of important rabbinic figures, most notably Rav Pinḥas Teitz, were then visiting the Soviet Union regularly, and managing to bring in matzot for Pesaḥ, *shofarot* for Rosh HaShana, and basic prayer-books for the few remaining functioning synagogues. It was believed that any activist demonstrations would endanger what they were now succeeding in doing in conjunction with the Communist authorities.

But I felt we had to learn from the mistakes we had made at the time of the Holocaust and take the offensive with public demonstrations against Soviet anti-Semitism. I believed that Jacob was right.

I went to consult with my rebbe, Rav Soloveitchik, about the advisability of this activist approach on behalf of Soviet Jews, and the Rav responded in a way that has crucially affected my whole philosophy of halakha. "I don't understand why you are asking me," he said. "You have to ask a top Sovietologist." He impressed upon me that when one is dealing with issues that are not necessarily halakhic issues discussed by the rabbis in the Talmud and the *Rishonim*, but are issues that have to do with historical and sociological trends and ramifications, one must go to the experts in those fields. I met with Professor Goldhagen, a leading Sovietologist of the day who taught at Harvard University, and when I reported back on the result of my research, the Rav gave his blessing for activist demonstrations.

At that time there were no national organizations for Soviet Jewry. The Jewish Agency gave small allocations to regular organizations, like Hadassah, for some Soviet Jewry activities, but there was no organization solely dedicated to being the voice of the three million plus Jews behind the Iron Curtain. And since each of these organizations zealously protected the funds that they received for their small Soviet Jewry departments, the established secular organizations also stood up against us.

Lincoln Square Synagogue was in its infancy, but it nevertheless became an important base for the burgeoning Soviet Jewry movement. Frieda Bluestone, soon to become Jacob's dedicated wife, and a very intelligent and active woman in her own right, was a devoted student in all of my classes, as was Glenn Richter, a crucial sparkplug for the entire movement.

First we founded the Student Struggle for Soviet Jewry, of which I was chairman, and then we began the more adult Center for Russian Jewry, of which I was president. (Rav Avi Weiss succeeded me.) The leader – "prophet" – of the movement was, of course, Yaakov (Jacob) Birnbaum, his right hand was Glenn and, together, they deserve the lion's share of the credit for our subsequent victory. I must add that Rav Shlomo Carlebach provided the much needed musical expression for our rallies (*Od Avinu Ḥai, Kakhol VeLavan*, etc.), as he did for the newly burgeoning *ba'al teshuva* movement; indeed it is difficult to imagine these two major activities – even defining expressions of the Jewish youth of the 1960s and '70s – without Shlomo Carlebach's music, which gave our words and goals soulful expression.

In the beginning, we were seen as young, maverick upstarts working against the establishment. Our demonstrations in front of the United Nations and the Russian embassy were small initially, as few as fifteen or twenty people. (For the record, all of this happened *before* Rav Meir Kahane got actively involved. He certainly was a leading activist, but his demonstrations, unlike ours, generally ended in violence.) But eventually we pulled off a rally of a hundred thousand people, and we certainly did succeed in bringing the issue of Soviet Jewry to the forefront of American Jewish consciousness. Even more importantly, with God's help, we succeeded in piercing through the Iron Curtain and enabling one million Jews to emigrate to Israel, America, Germany and elsewhere. The process itself – activist demonstrations and visits behind the Iron Curtain to give moral support to the refuseniks and even help to relieve their suffering – defined Lincoln Square Synagogue's mission and gave social-concern direction to a burgeoning Modern Orthodoxy; our success made me truly believe that "if you will it, it is not a dream," and that "if one goes to purify, he is helped from above."

Chapter Fifty

The Moscow Rav Visits New York

In 1969 the Soviet Union was beginning to suffer from all of the demonstrations and newspaper reportage about Soviet anti-Semitism, which were slowly beginning to emerge. Indeed, one of the earliest signs of our success was when the USSR felt it necessary to dispatch Rav Yehuda Leib Levin, who was the chief rabbi of Moscow, with a new siddur (prayer book) called *Siddur HaShalom*, the Siddur of Peace, to prove that the Communist government was indeed publishing Hebrew books. He was on a good-will mission of sorts, and he was scheduled to deliver a big lecture on a Sunday in February at Hunter College auditorium. He arrived a week and a half before the lecture, stayed at the Essex House, which was fairly close to Lincoln Square Synagogue, and had a *minyan* in his hotel room every morning.

Many of us who were active in Soviet Jewry went to pray with him. I was introduced as the rabbi of the nearest Orthodox synagogue, so he looked at me and said, "*Az, ir zant Rav hashechuneh*. You're the rabbi of the neighborhood," a concept familiar to him from the European model at that time. He invited me to have breakfast with him that Friday morning.

We had heard from our underground contact involved in Soviet Jewry that Rav Levin had come with a *ḥazan* from Leningrad, and with a *gabbai* who was a KGB agent. The *ḥazan* and the *gabbai* were always with him. While I had breakfast with them, I began asking questions. "Are there synagogues in the Soviet Union?" It appeared as though Rav Levin looked to his friends before answering, and responded to each of my questions with a question, such as: "Are there synagogues in the United States?" I tried again: "Are there yeshivot in the Soviet Union?" He replied, "Are there yeshivot in the United States?"

I realized we weren't getting anywhere and that he felt he couldn't speak. I asked him where he went to yeshiva and he told me Slobodka. So I asked him about Slobodka. He had attended the famed yeshiva during the Golden Age of the European yeshivot in Lithuania, and I was very interested in hearing about their methodology of study, the precise curriculum, which tractates they concentrated on. As an educator I couldn't hear enough about the course of study in a classical Lithuanian yeshiva.

Then the *gabbai* got up and went to the washroom. Suddenly Rav Levin, who had seemed very tense during our whole conversation, relaxed for the first time. Apropos of nothing, he suggested, "Let's sing a Shabbos *zemira*." And he started to sing *Ka Ribon*. The *niggun* that he used was very well known, and so I easily harmonized with him. And then he came to the stanza that begins, "*Elaha di lei yekar urvuta* … The God who has the honor and the glory, redeem your sheep from the mouth of the lion, and take out your nation from the midst of the exile." To my shocked amazement, he rocked back and forth and repeated those lines again and again, like a broken record, with tears coursing down his cheeks.

I began to tremble. I now understood the whole story. Through his rendition of these lines he had answered all of my previous questions. And then suddenly the *gabbai* came out of the washroom and Rav Levin turned colors, crimson red, and then chalk white. The *gabbai* screamed, "Rav Levin, *siz nuch nit Shabbos*! It's not the Sabbath yet!" To which Rav Levin mumbled, "I only wanted to show the young rabbi what kind of *zemirot* we sang in Slobodka. He was asking me all about Slobodka." That was the end of the discussion.

But that's not the end of the story. That Sunday I went to Hunter College, to attend Rav Levin's lecture. He opened with general *divrei Torah* apropos of the weekly Torah portion – interpretations completely devoid of any political allusions. He then announced the newly published prayer book, *Siddur HaShalom*. He spoke not a word about the kind of Jewish life that there was – or was not – in the Soviet Union. He just concluded with one rather ambiguous line: "Everything the Jews need, we have in the Soviet Union. You see the Siddur. The only thing missing is a *Beis Yaakov*." And that was it. The lecture ended.

Beis Yaakov refers to Torah schools for young women, which were started by Sarah Schenirer in Krakow in the late nineteenth century. Did he mean to say then that all that was missing for Jews in the Soviet Union was a yeshiva high school for girls? People were rather confused as to whether the chief rabbi had been forced to be an apologist for the Communist government in order to continue the paltry Jewish life he was struggling to maintain, or whether everything was really not as bad as we had thought regarding the Jewish situation behind the Iron Curtain.

In the meantime, with the conclusion of Rav Levin's lecture, it seemed as if the sky had opened up. It was raining, teeming rain, with thunder and lightning as well. The *gabbai* and the *ḥazan* were both busy trying to get a cab. My cantor and beloved friend, Sherwood Goffin, had also been to the lecture and, suddenly, I saw Rav Levin standing next to me on the curb and Sherwood beginning to enter his car. I literally shoved the rabbi into the car – and there were the three of us alone in the car for the drive back to the Essex House. I couldn't control my next question. "Rav Levin, I understood from the way you sang *Ka Ribon* what the situation is. How come you didn't say anything?"

He looked at me incredulously. "You mean you didn't understand me? I'm sure you realized I was limited in what I could say; I bear responsibility for the three to four million Jews left in the Soviet Union. I said there was no *Beis Yaakov*; I was using a double entendre, a name with two significances. Yaakov is Israel, our glorious tradition. The house of our tradition is non-existent in Russia. That's what I was trying to convey. And even more to the point: *Beis Yaakov* is a yeshiva for women. If women don't learn Torah traditions, families don't learn Torah. If the Jewish home – the *beis* – doesn't exist, Judaism cannot survive."

Then I truly began to understand the desperateness of the situation of Soviet Jewry.

It was during that car ride that I decided to visit the Soviet Union as soon as possible.

Chapter Fifty-One

The Search for a *Shoḥet* and the Discovery of a *Melamed Dardeke*

Shortly after Rav Levin's visit, I received a call from the office of the Lubavitcher Rebbe: the Rebbe wished to see me.

Almost as if he had read my mind, the Rebbe asked if I would go to the Soviet Union to establish four underground yeshivot – in Moscow, in Leningrad, in Riga and in Vilna. Obviously he had a "handler" ready in waiting to give me the names of contact people in each place, and to explain what had to be done and how to do it. I agreed that I would try to the best of my ability to do whatever he would ask of me.

I almost felt as if I were in a James Bond movie with a Jewish twist, because the Rebbe pressed on a phone he removed from his desk drawer, and said to someone in Hebrew, "Riskin agreed to go." He then handed me the phone. I was speaking to Neḥemia Levanon, the man in charge of the Soviet desk for Israel's Foreign Office. Levanon asked me if, at the same time, I would open up underground *ulpanim*,

Hebrew language schools, in each of these four places. Of course I said that I would do my best.

My trip was planned for the beginning of Elul, in late summer. I went with two friends from Lincoln Square, Danny Greer, who is a lawyer, and Richard Joselit, a businessman. Our first stop was Moscow.

I went with all sorts of strange feelings. On the one hand, my activity on behalf of Soviet Jewry made me rather knowledgeable about the degree of repression I could expect to find. But at the same time, my paternal grandfather had been an active Communist for whom the Soviet Union had been a virtual fatherland, and his life's ideal.

I traveled to Russia via Vienna. Prior to my trip, I had spent that summer in Israel with my wife and children; since I had been informed that I should not go to Russia with "Israel" stamped in an American passport, it was suggested that I "lose" the passport in Vienna and get a new one reissued there. Vienna was also the place where I bought food, so one of my valises was filled with kosher food, wine, matzot, cans of tuna fish, salamis. I had spoken to Rav Soloveitchik and he had said the only things I could eat in Russia were the *smetana,* a kind of yogurt, and *chyorniy khleb,* which was black bread.

When we arrived in Moscow, they did not even check our baggage. I had brought many Hebrew books with me, to be used for the underground yeshivot and *ulpanim.* My "handler" had explained that it was a crime to own a Hebrew book in the Soviet Union, but I could always claim to the authorities – if I were questioned – that as a rabbi, I needed the Hebrew books to study on my journey. I also had ten pairs of *tefillin.* I could always say I needed different versions – Rashi, Rabbeinu Tam – as well as weekday *tefillin,* Shabbat *tefillin* and festival *tefillin;* the same went for *tallitot* – I made sure that they each had different colors for different occasions.

I also took a few other religious items with me. Before I left for Vienna and the Soviet Union, I spoke one Shabbat in Ramat Eshkol, Jerusalem, and I mentioned in passing where I was headed. Afterwards, a man came over to me with tears in his eyes. "You have to do me a favor," he pleaded. "My old father lives in Russia. He is a *shoḥet,* a ritual slaughterer, and he lives in a small town outside of Moscow. I want you to take him an *etrog* (citrus fruit used ritually on Sukkot) because they are very hard to come by in the cold Moscow climate. And my son just became a bar mitzva. I want you to take the bar mitzva *derasha* [speech] of my son. It would give my aged father much pleasure."

I said I would be glad to do it. I met him later to get the *etrog* and *derasha,* and of course asked for his father's name and address. He broke out in a sweat and said, "I can't tell you my father's name." "But how else will I find him?" He said, "Listen, you ask for the *shoḥet* of Khaslava, a town outside of Moscow. Ask another religious Jew in Moscow. Everyone there knows him. He'll be accompanied by a young boy. The young boy is my brother's son. My brother is a Communist and is not living a religious lifestyle; he wants to get ahead in the Soviet regime. When my father saw how brilliant this grandson was, he asked my brother if he could take the boy and raise him, very much like when our patriarch Jacob asked Joseph if he could have his Egyptian-born sons Menashe and Ephraim to raise.

"My father said that if his Communist son would agree to let him raise his grandson, my father would give this son his own portion in the world to come, that he would certainly be forgiven all of his transgressions. And my brother agreed.

"My father spread the rumor that the boy is asthmatic; he somehow got doctors' letters of confirmation. Because of the "asthma," the boy never went to gymnasium [school]. Instead, my father taught him at home. The boy is an *iluy,* a genius in Torah, and he always accompanies my father. You'll see an old man with a beard, with this young boy, about eighteen years old. When you go to the Moscow shul, just ask for the *shoḥet* from Khaslava. My father and my nephew will find you after that. And they will let you know if it's okay for them to take the *etrog* and the bar mitzva *derasha.*" I skeptically took the materials but I really never expected to find the nameless and address-less ritual slaughterer and his genius grandson.

At any rate, when I arrived in Moscow, all the authorities did was write down the number of suitcases that I had. They never even asked me to open them up or to list their contents. I began to think that all the stories about the Soviet Union were exaggerated.

On my first afternoon I went to the main Moscow shul on Arkhipova Street. It was time for *Minḥa.* There was barely a *minyan* of men in shul. Between *Minḥa* and *Ma'ariv* there was an old Jew who gave a class in the tractate *Sota*. Everybody looked like they were well over seventy, except me, and the *maggid shiur*, the teacher, directed the entire class to me. After *Ma'ariv* he walked over to me and he asked who I was and where I had studied. When I told him I had studied at Yeshiva University, he said, "Oh, Rav Soloveitchik was my student." I blurted out, "You were the *melamed dardeke*? You were Rav Soloveitchik's rebbe when he was a young boy?" He assented vigorously. "Then you taught him *Bava Metzia* and continued to teach him *Tanya*." He began to weep. "How do you know? He must have told you. You mean he speaks about me, he remembers me?!"

I will never forget how, at the end of each year of classes, Rav Soloveitchik would always say to us, "Well boys, what would you like to learn next year?" It became a kind of joke, because we would always tell him our suggestions, he would appear to acquiesce to the desire of the majority, but then the next year he would teach whichever tractate he was interested in teaching, without so much as referring to the tractate we had decided upon a few months before and had spent the entire summer studying. During one of these year-end, rebbe-student conversations, a more brazen student said, "But Rebbe, you always choose the *massekhet* anyway, so why not tell us now and we'll get a head-start over the summer." Rav Soloveitchik smilingly said, "All right, *Bava Metzia*." One of the students foolishly blurted out, "I learned that already." I cringed, certain that Rav Soloveitchik would get very upset. But no, he was in a good mood. He smiled and merely said, "I know you learned it already. You probably learned it when you were nine or ten years old in *yeshiva katana* [elementary school]. But I'm sure you understand that we won't learn it the same way. I guarantee it will be a different *Bava Metzia*."

And then, like he was remembering something from long ago, he said that when he was a very little boy his father started him off learning with a *melamed dardeke* (teacher of small children), a *Chabadnik*. Actually, he told us there had been a difference of opinion between his father and his mother. His mother felt that her husband, Rav Moshe Soloveitchik, should himself teach his son who, even at the age of six, was already demonstrating his brilliance. But Rav Moshe Soloveitchik felt that the young Yosef Dov should first receive a foundation from an experienced teacher, and after he began to gain some proficiency, then Rav Moshe would take over his education. And so it was.

One afternoon, when young Yosef Dov was no older than seven or eight, he came home with smack marks (apparently from his rebbe) on his cheek. When his father demanded an explanation, and when the hapless student repeated his unfortunate questions that caused the slaps, his father, Rav Moshe, admitted that his wife had been right in the first place. From then on, he himself taught his brilliant son. Rav Soloveitchik looked at us and smiled. "Apparently there were two of us who didn't really know *Bava Metzia*: the *melamed dardeke* and I. But my father agreed that the *melamed dardeke* should continue to teach me *Tanya*. I loved those classes with him and they left an indelible impression on my life-long interest in *Torat HaNistar*."[4]

When I told the *melamed dardeke* that Rav Soloveitchik spoke of him often, that he told us that he learned *Bava Metzia* and *Tanya* with him, and that the *Tanya* classes had sparked his interest in studying *Zohar* and in appreciating Chabad, the teacher began to weep. He wrote out a note for me to deliver to the Rav.

Upon my return home, I delivered the note to Rav Soloveitchik; as he read it, he too, wept. He told me that he could still picture those "magical" classes with his childhood teacher; he told me that there was no profession more exalted, more sacred, than that of *melamed*.

Before I left the *melamed dardeke* in the Moscow shul, I told him that I very much wanted to meet the *shoḥet* from Khaslava, that I had gifts for him from his son in Jerusalem. He seemed to know exactly to whom I was referring. Perhaps I would get to meet grandfather and grandson after all.

4. *Torat HaNistar*: the study of the *Zohar* and kabbalistic texts.

Chapter Fifty-Two

"I Am Searching for My Brothers"

When I got back to the hotel after having met the *melamed dardeke*, a young man walked over to me. He apparently recognized the significance of the *kippa* I was wearing, as he said in perfect English, "You're a religious Jew? I'm religious, too. And I'm celebrating my thirtieth birthday. Please come to my house for my birthday party." So, instead of going inside the hotel, I went with my new friend "Sacha" to his house. I suppose I should have been frightened, or at least wary and suspicious, but I felt none of these emotions. I was on an adventure, a mission, and I was certain that I had special divine protection through the Lubavitcher Rebbe. Besides, I was an American citizen with an American passport, so I assumed that even the Soviet Union would not start up with me.

There were about fifteen people at the party and I brought along my friends and companions, Danny and Richard. I met Sacha's mother, and was surprised to discover that she and Sacha's father came from Allerton Avenue in the Bronx. They were Communists, probably more sincere Communists than most Jews are Zionists, because they had made their "*aliya*" to the Soviet Union in 1940. They had this son, and a daughter. The father had since died.

As we were riding on a bus on the way to Sacha's house, I couldn't help asking how, with Communist parents, he had become interested in Judaism. He drew the following autobiographical sketch:

"I was never bar mitzva, and I had no Jewish training at all. I was never even inside a shul. My parents were dedicated Communists who believed that religion was the opiate of the masses. I was a very good student and I became a physicist. In the physics laboratory where I worked, they gave two hours a day for library work to those of us who were very promising. I went to the library every afternoon, but suddenly I began getting headaches. Apparently something was bothering me, but I couldn't put my finger on what it was. I certainly couldn't concentrate on physics.

"The *lingua franca* in my house was English. The library had certain books on display in English especially for tourists, and one of them was the Holy Bible.

"I began reading the Bible and I became fascinated by the stories; I would spend my two hours of library time reading the book of Genesis, intrigued. I came to the stories of Joseph – which especially fascinated me – and how, when Joseph, sent by his father to look after the welfare of his brothers, was wandering about in the fields unable to find his siblings. And then he was asked by an unknown personage, 'For whom are you searching?' To which he then responded, 'I am searching for my brothers.'" Sacha then looked at me intently. "All of a sudden I realized that I too was searching for my brothers, but they're not in this library, and they're not in my physics lab. And, as if being chased by some kind of inner power that I didn't quite understand, I ran out of the library and began running toward Arkhipova Street, where I knew I would find the main Moscow synagogue.

"And lo and behold, there was a long line in front of the synagogue. I went to the end of the line and asked the person in front of me the reason for the line. 'For matza,' he replied. And I asked, 'What's matza?' He said, 'Tonight is the first night of the Festival of Pesaḥ, and matza is our freedom bread.' I stood in line and received a piece of matza. I put it in my pocket, went home and ate dinner with my family. When I went to the bedroom that I shared with my sister, before I went to sleep, I ate the matza.

"I got up the next morning and went to the physics lab. Everything that had happened the previous afternoon and evening seemed like a surrealistic dream. The dream turned into a nightmare, however, when the foreman greeted me at the door of the lab and informed me that I was no longer employed. 'Fired? What happened?' I asked. 'There was a hidden camera at the synagogue,' he explained sharply. 'You were in line yesterday in front of the synagogue. You can't work here or anywhere else anymore.'" And from then on, in enforced retirement at age twenty-seven, I began to study and practice everything I could learn about my Jewish heritage."

As he was telling me the story, tears suddenly welled up in my eyes and I said to him, "You're not going to believe this. In the book of Deuteronomy, at the end of chapter four, Moses gives a kind of historiography of what's going to happen to the Jewish people, about how there will be destruction and the Jews will go into exile. And then Moses makes a promise. 'When it will be difficult for you, the words of the Torah will find you … and you will return to God … because God is a God of love and compassion … and He will never forget the covenant He has made with your fathers' [Deuteronomy 4:30–31]. Sacha, the Torah is speaking directly to you, after almost four thousand years. The stories of Joseph in the Torah found you, and restored you to your brothers …"

When we got to his apartment, where the birthday celebration was taking place, we sat around the table talking to his friends. They began to speak of the Leningrad Trials, an event that was unknown in the United States. We had brought along a tape recorder, and I conducted an interview in Yiddish, recording how there had been a group of refusenik Jews who wanted to go to Israel, but were denied exit visas. One of the group had claimed to be a pilot and told the others he would be able to "skyjack" a plane and get them to Israel. He turned out to be a KGB agent, so when they arrived at the appointed time in the middle of the night to fly to Israel, they were all arrested and imprisoned. The trials were taking place at that very time, and people in the West knew nothing about it.

We continued to hear how, in the wake of the Leningrad trials, there was a serious crackdown on everything Jewish. If the authorities found a Hebrew book in one's possession, they would throw that person into prison. My two friends and I drew lots to determine who would become responsible for the tape, and Richard Joselit was selected. We taped the recording of the interview to his chest. As a result, he no longer accompanied us on our visits, in order to minimize the possibility of the tape being intercepted. He was simply to remain in Russia as a regular tourist, enjoy the culture, and then return with us to America, hopefully with the tape intact.

Danny Greer, the lawyer, immediately told Sacha that as long as his parents had not publicly renounced their American citizenship, Sacha was an American, and we could get him to America by right as an American citizen. We asked Sacha to get us papers that would prove the American citizenship of his parents. I gave him our itinerary, which was scheduled to take us from Moscow to Leningrad, to Riga, to Vilna, and then back to Moscow again where we had a scheduled KLM flight back to New York. Sacha would have a few weeks to arrange things, and if he could meet us at the airport in Moscow on the day of our departure, with his birth certificate, we would be able to get him out of the USSR. From America he could easily get to Israel. With this plan in formation, we embraced our newfound friend and bid him farewell.

For me, the most amazing part of the event was discovering how the verse from the Bible, so perfectly described Sacha's odyssey back to Judaism.

As for the tape, we ultimately gave it to Senator Jackson, who was known as a true friend of the Jews, and that became the basis for the Jackson-Vanik amendment.[5]

5. The Jackson-Vanik Amendment of 1974, introduced by Senator Henry Jackson (D-WA) and Rep. Charles Vanik (D-OH), linked American trade agreements with the Soviet Union to Jewish emigration rights from the Soviet Union. Israeli Minister and former Prisoner of Zion Natan Sharansky called it, "The first nail in the coffin of the Soviet dictatorship" (*Middle East Quarterly*, November 24, 2004). As a personally sweet closure of a circle, it was Irving Stone, the renowned philanthropist from Cleveland, Ohio (whose generosity gave Ohr Torah Stone its last name), who convinced his friend Charles Vanik to co-sponsor the amendment that originated with our tape and which was so important for Soviet Jewry.

Chapter Fifty-Three

The Anger of a Moment, the Satisfaction of Eternity

Permit me to add a difficult, but ultimately heartwarming postscript to the story of Sacha.

Sacha worked for the Voice of Liberty radio station when he came to the United States. He was a national hero, and his victory was quite a shot in the arm for the entire Soviet Jewry movement. Initially he lived in the Lincoln Square community, at the home of Bess and Leon Bergman. Then he established an independent residence and I stopped hearing from him altogether. I called, but he uncharacteristically did not call me back.

And then one day Sacha asked to see me. He had met a Flemish translator at the United Nations; a woman of sterling character and rare intellect, a woman with whom he had fallen in love. She was not Jewish, she was not interested in converting and they were going to get married anyway. He handed me a wedding invitation.

I am ashamed to record my reaction: I slapped him across the face, then I started to cry, and he started to cry. I said to him, "I'm sorry I helped bring you out of Russia. Had you stayed in the Soviet Union, you would have married a Jewish woman and you would have had Jewish children. I don't ever want to see you again." I felt hurt and betrayed, perhaps unjustly. We cannot control those we help out, and we must help them unconditionally. Nevertheless, I was left with a bitter taste in my mouth.

Then I lost contact with him, and all this after we had had such an intense relationship. To give you an idea of how close we were, and of how our closeness was bound up in Jewish tradition, CBS television wanted to do a special on "Sacha's first Friday night in my home in America, his first Shabbat experience in the free world, to be televised before millions of viewers on Shabbat. American television wanted to emphasize the religious message of freedom expressed by Shabbat observance. Obviously I refused, but I did say that we could film a simulated Friday night that would take place and be screened on Thursday night – as long as the program makers indicated that we were so doing. And so it was. We sang *Shalom Aleikhem, Eshet Ḥayil*; we made *Kiddush* (without mentioning the sacred name of God). Vicky prepared gefilte fish, *kneidlach* and soup, *kugel* – all the Shabbat dishes – on Thursday night. I realized very clearly that you cannot really make Shabbat on Thursday, although from the many responses we received from Jews and Gentiles alike, it was clear that this was a sanctification of God's name. It also demonstrated the identification of Sacha with traditional Judaism. And then, for the chapter to end like this, with intermarriage … I was devastated.

A little over a year later, I received a letter from Rav Vogel, one of the main Chabad emissaries in London. He wrote of a very serious young Gentile woman, already married to a Jewish man named Sacha, who had been enthusiastically accepted for conversion and who strongly requests that I be one of the rabbi-judges at the conversion. I was excited by the letter – but remained cautious. Declining to come to London, I stipulated that she come to New York alone and live in my house for a month. If at the end of the month I felt that she was a sincere convert, then I would either travel to London, or we would arrange to have the conversion in New York.

She came to New York and lived with us for a month. I was most impressed by her sincerity and her Jewish knowledge. The conversion took place in New York, after which she returned to London.

Before every holiday, and with every addition to their family, I received warm *berakhot,* greetings from them, which filled me with much satisfaction and joy.

* * *

Some years later, shortly before I made *aliya,* there was a wedding at Lincoln Square Synagogue, between Tamar and Alec Gindis, an expatriate from the Soviet Union. Many former Russian Jews were at the wedding.

During the reception, a man walked over to me. He was wearing a black hat and a long black coat. Trailing behind him was his modestly dressed, bewigged wife, and a goodly number of young children. Everyone in the family was speaking Yiddish to each other. The father said to me in Yiddish, "I'm asking you to please bless my children. You saved my life." I looked at him again, and I said, "You're making a mistake; you're confusing me with someone else." He said, *Noch a mol zolt ir kuken*" ("Look at me again"). It was Sacha, together with his wife. They had become Vizhnitzer Hasidim and moved to Brooklyn.

Chapter Fifty-Four

The Faith of the Young, the Faith of the Old

The next day in Moscow, I went to shul again for afternoon and evening services, and for the Talmud class between the prayers. I met the same cast of characters as had been there the day before, with the addition of an elderly bearded gentleman and a young man accompanying him. Could they be the grandfather and grandson for whom I was searching? But they didn't even so much as smile or nod in my direction.

Even though it was the late summer–early autumn month of Elul, it was very cold in Moscow, with more than a hint of snow in the air. I walked back to my hotel briskly and saw – on the other side of the street – the old man and the young man walking parallel to me. I was becoming certain that they must be the *shoḥet* and his grandson. I understood that they were probably checking to see that we were not being followed. It apparently seemed safe to them because they soon crossed over and we began to talk.

I gave the old man the *etrog* and the bar mitzva *derasha* I had brought for him, and then I started speaking in the language of "Torah learning" to the young *iluy*. I was teaching *Massekhet Kiddushin* at the time and he told me he knew five tractates by heart, one of them being *Kiddushin*. I saw that he knew the entire tractate backwards and forwards, including the major early commentaries, and I was exceedingly impressed. He told me that he had four students, but that not one of them knew of the existence of any of the others – for everyone's protection. They would each come surreptitiously to his home, at a different time each day. In this way, even KGB torture tactics would not compromise any of the other students who were studying Torah.

I then had a *kashrut* discussion with him that took an unexpected turn.

After my first two days in Moscow, I realized that, with leaving early in the morning and not getting back to my hotel until late at night, I began to feel weak-in-the-knees by midday. I had food in the hotel room, but I wasn't going to carry it with me. One had to stand in long lines at Gumm, the department store, to get fruits or vegetables, and the wait hardly seemed worth the spoiled and spoiled-looking wares that were on sale. Besides, I could not afford the time. There were, however, ice cream (*marozhinoye*) trucks, selling their sweet snacks on the Moscow streets. I asked the young man if "*marozhinoye*" was kosher.

He looked at me and smiled, saying in Yiddish, "*Oib de Rav trinkt dah de milch, megt ihr essen dah de marozhinoye* – If you drink the milk here, you can eat the ice cream here." From then on I decided that if he was careful about not drinking anything but supervised milk products (*ḥalav yisrael*) – even in the difficult conditions of the Soviet Union – then I could be no less stringent in this temporary situation.

About five years later, I met a Soviet refusenik who said that he had been one of this young rebbe's four students. He told me that his rebbe, the *iluy*, had been taken away by the KGB in the middle of the night, never to be seen again. His grandfather, the *shoḥet*, died a few weeks after his grandson disappeared.

As I began to weep, the young Soviet refusenik put his hand on my shoulder. "I am now teaching the Talmud tractates he taught me, to other Russian Jews in Maḥanayim in Jerusalem. I like to think that through me, my rebbe also lives…"

Chapter Fifty-Five

Torah Overcomes in Leningrad – Despite Lenin's Best Efforts

Three significant events occurred in Leningrad.

First of all, the Lubavitcher Rebbe had given me the names of people to contact, including one individual who was responsible for all those who remained Shabbat observers in Leningrad. No Shabbat observers could keep a job in Communist Russia, so they and their families had to be otherwise supported. The Rebbe had also arranged for me to take a good deal of cash for Michael, the Chabad representative in Leningrad, which I hid in a false heel of my shoe.

I was to go to the *mikveh*, leave the shoes together with my clothes while I was immersing in the water, and somebody would then come and take the money for later distribution, which is exactly what happened. The *mikveh* was freezing cold; it made the *mikveh* of the Ari (*z"l*), Rabbi Isaac Luria in Safed feel like a hot Jacuzzi in comparison. Nevertheless, there were men who went to the *mikveh* every morning and there were women who went to the *mikveh* in the evening, despite the danger and despite the cold. For me it remains a fact too wondrous to explain: the two most irrational practices in Judaism, family purity through *mikveh*, and circumcision, were specifically the two commandments maintained during the worst times of persecution in the Soviet Union.

The second event involves the rabbi of the main shul in Leningrad, Rav Lubanov, a man in his eighties who had been previously imprisoned by the Soviet regime for many years. I was in Leningrad for my first Shabbat in the Soviet Union, and, of course, I went to pray in the main synagogue. It was a very large, stately edifice with very many seats but very few worshipers. I tried to make eye contact with the rabbi because on that Shabbat in Ramat Eshkol, when I had met the *shoḥet*'s son, I had also met Rav Lubanov's daughter who gave me pictures of her grandchildren to give to her father. I had walked to shul with the photographs in my shoe, and now wanted to give the old rabbi a picture of his *naches* and continuity.

I could see that he was avoiding my eyes. At the end of the service, he called me to sit next to him. It certainly looked as if we were alone in an empty and darkened sanctuary, but every few minutes there was someone who would peer at us through a window, evidently monitoring his every move.

After I answered his questions as to my background, I whispered, "I have pictures of your grandchildren." He responded, "Let's talk Torah." And then he sort of muttered under his breath, "Let your prayer shawl drop to the ground with the pictures in it."

He then continued in a louder voice: "The Gemara says in *Ta'anit* that if you're present when a Torah scroll is burned or otherwise destroyed, you have to rend your garment, and you must rend the garment twice – once for the parchment, and once for the letters.

"However," he said, "there's a Gemara in *Avoda Zara* that states when Rav Ḥananya ben Teradyon was torturously murdered by the Romans during the Hadrianic persecutions, they wrapped him in a Torah scroll and torched him and the Torah scroll together.

"His students asked him, 'Rebbe, what do you see?' to which he responded, 'The parchment is burning, but the letters are flying up in the air, heavenward.'

"The two Talmudic sources contradict each other. If indeed the letters last eternally and cannot be destroyed by fire, if indeed they soar upward to the heavens, why does the Gemara in *Ta'anit* say that you have to rend your garments for the letters as well as for the parchment? I believe the answer is that it depends on who is destroying the Torah. If the Gentiles are the ones destroying the Torah, they have no power over the letters, the letters last eternally, and we need not rend our garments over the letters forever."

Just at that moment the *gabbai,* apparently a KGB plant, peered through the window. The old rabbi pointed in his direction, as if he were greeting him, and continued: "But if we Jews ourselves are destroying the Torah, if we are collaborating with the enemy, then you have to tear *keriya,* to rend your garment, twice: once for the parchment and once for the letters."

With those words, I understood the most diabolical part of the Soviet secret police, the KGB: that they did not even allow the synagogue to be a safe place for Jews. They "employed," or more correctly, blackmailed some of the *gabbai'im* and *ḥazanim* to be their spies and collaborators!

With that the old rabbi bent down as if to pick up something that had fallen, retrieved the pictures from the folds of my *tallit,* returned the *tallit* to me, and we bid each other goodbye. His last words were a whisper, "Next year in Jerusalem."

I never saw him again.

The third thing that happened in Leningrad was that a man came up to me who had seen me in shul. He was carrying a case in one hand and used the other to grab my arm with intensity. "I have a tremendous favor to ask of you. You have to take my best friend, my best friend in the world. He is in this case. He is a Torah scroll. My father-in-law gave him to me; my father-in-law went through the Holocaust. He managed to miraculously rescue a *sefer Torah* from his hometown and guarded it throughout the Holocaust, sleeping with it, running with it. He survived and he always attributed his survival to his best friend, the Torah scroll. Before he died, only a few years ago, he bequeathed his best friend to me.

"I kept the *sefer Torah* in the house. I would wake up in the middle of the night just to kiss it. I believe it protected us, just like it protected my father-in-law. Now our persecution has become intensified. The Communists are barely allowing the synagogues to keep sacred Hebrew books! Now, if the KGB finds a Hebrew book in someone's house, they throw him in prison and they destroy the book. I'm afraid to keep my Torah scroll at home any more. If anything were to happen to it, I would be violating the sacred trust of my father-in-law.

"Please watch over my friend. Bring him to a safe place. He'll watch over you, too."

I had to think quickly. I remembered that when I landed at Moscow, the authorities at the airport had only taken a list of the number of packages that I came in with, which were four. They never checked the content of the packages. One of those was for food, and since I would finish the food by the end of my trip, I could always claim that I had brought the Torah scroll in with me from Vienna. How would they ever know that the Torah scroll was from Leningrad? So I agreed to take the Torah.

I'll never forget how he kissed the Torah, crying and calling it again and again, "*mein besta freint*" as he left it with me. I told him I would guard it with my life. And from then on, wherever I went, I took the *sefer Torah* with me, safely ensconced and hidden from view in its case; I never even left it alone in a hotel room. It became my best friend as well.

Chapter Fifty-Six

A Tale of a *Tallit*

I was in Russia for two Shabbatot, and I spent the second Shabbat in Riga. Just as in Leningrad, the synagogue was magnificently large, with a high, vaulted ceiling. There seemed to be enough seating for five hundred people, with only several scores of Jews, all past sixty-five years of age, in attendance. In Leningrad, there had been *gabbai'im* who noted the attendees; in Riga, there was a visible seeing-eye camera over the Holy Ark, which took a permanent picture of whoever was there.

Friday evening in Riga, I noticed that there was one man who seemed much younger than the others, maybe forty years old. When I left shul, he walked behind me back to the hotel; when he saw that we were not being followed, he began to walk next to me. His name was Velvel and he told me that what he would want more than anything else was "a *tallis*." He had an old *tallit* that he had received for his bar mitzva, but it was literally in tatters and he would love a new one.

There was a little courtyard garden in front of the hotel where I stayed in Riga. I asked him to wait there while I went to my room to bring down an extra *tallit*. Would he like *tefillin*, too? He said no; he had *tefillin* that were quite usable. So, I came down with a *tallit*. We sat for a while talking in the garden. He told me to keep the *tallit* on my lap, not to give it to him for a while. At length, when he thought it was safe, he asked me to drop the *tallit* to the floor. He then picked it up and took it with him.

The next morning, on Shabbat, when I left the hotel, I found myself surrounded by four goons. I imagine that the KGB had begun to suspect what I was doing. I started joking with them, but they were silent and stone-faced. When I walked into shul, they walked in with me. I decided to play a little game with them. (Obviously, I did not realize the danger. I felt as if I were in a spy movie, memorizing telephone numbers, making contacts, giving payoffs and dispensing Hebrew books. And I was certain that my American passport, in addition to the fact that I was on a mission from the Rebbe, would make me invincible.)

So, I went to the men's room and my fellow Siamese quintuplets went with me. I opened a cubicle, and they were about to follow me in. Thank God I didn't have to go to the bathroom anyway. So I went back to the sanctuary and they took the four seats directly behind where I was seated by the *gabbai'im*. I apologized to them that I had not brought prayer shawls for them; they remained completely and stonily blank-faced. (Apparently, the art of humor is not in the KGB training curriculum.)

Then, to my dismay, who walks into shul with a new and sparkling blue and white *tallit*, but Velvel. I was sure he wouldn't bring the new *tallit* that Shabbat because then it would be obvious that he got it from me. I had been seated toward the back and off to the side, with some thirty rows separating me from the approximately forty other Jews in attendance, who sat fairly close to each other. A handful of women were in the balcony. The four goons were my only prayer neighbors.

It came time for the Torah reading and the *gabbai* gave me the honor of opening the Holy Ark. The goons surrounded me like bodyguards – but none of the worshipers seemed surprised. There didn't seem to be an officiating rabbi. I was carrying the Torah, and the cantor was singing, and we were marching around this immense, cavernous synagogue that was three-quarters empty. The cantor reached high crescendos as if there were hundreds of people in the shul.

When our small procession came near Velvel, he lifted the ritual fringes of his new *tallit* up in the air, about to touch the Torah scroll with the fringes, after which he would kiss them as is customary. But as soon as the cantor saw Velvel, he suddenly stopped chanting. And then everybody stopped chanting. It was a moment like an eternity; one I will never forget. The Holy Ark was open; Velvel's fringes were suspended in mid-air, close to, but not yet touching, the Torah scroll. All of us seemed to be caught in a freeze-frame, frozen in place, surrounded by an eerie silence.

All eyes were on Velvel. For the first time I realized what *ayin hara*, the evil eye is. The *ḥazan* was looking at Velvel with menace, Velvel was holding his fringes aloft and returning a hostile look at the cantor; it was a battle of the eyes. Who was going to let his eyes drop first, Velvel or the cantor (who was obviously an agent of the KGB)? I was sure that everybody must have realized that Velvel had gotten the new *tallit* from me; he had arrived at shul with it brazenly, and the *ḥazan* was letting him know that he was in a lot of trouble.

There was high tension in the sanctuary, silent drama. Neither Velvel nor the *ḥazan* so much as blinked. Suddenly, while still looking directly at the *ḥazan*, Velvel screamed out in Yiddish, "*Ich hob nit kein moyreh*. I'm not afraid! You've already taken everything that you can take away from me! When I began to come to shul and I lost my job as a result, my wife left me and she took the children with her. I have no job; I have no family. The only thing I have is my Jewish tradition. The only thing I have is this *tallit*. *Ich hob nit kein moyreh*. I am not afraid."

The *ḥazan* lowered his eyes. He started once again to chant, and the congregants chanted with him. Slowly, even triumphantly, Velvel touched the Torah with the fringes and very deliberately kissed them. The Torah was placed on the reader's desk as if nothing had happened. Velvel had won this battle.

Chapter Fifty-Seven

A Vort about Vodka

That same morning in Riga, in the middle of the Torah reading, an older man with a young boy came into shul with jackets over their faces, apparently to prevent their identification by the camera atop the Holy Ark. Each of them received an *aliya,* were called to say a blessing on the Torah – one after the other, despite the custom not to call father and son (as I assumed they were) consequentially. There were some muffled *mazal tovs*. It was obviously the young boy's bar mitzva. After the second *aliya,* they both ran out of shul. Neither of them had *tallitot,* nor did the synagogue seem to have any extras in stock. Apparently the jackets, which had never left their faces, served a double purpose, Soviet style…

As I took the Torah from the *ḥazan* and gently returned it to the Ark, the *gabbai,* a short man with a white, wispy beard, came up next to me, ostensibly to adjust the Torah scroll. He whispered to me in Yiddish, "We're thirsty for Torah. We have a *kiddush* downstairs after the service. We want to hear your Torah. Come down after the *davening* – but without your friends."

I was a bit nervous, but altogether rather pleased at the invitation. As for my "friends" – I could hardly be responsible for the goons' behavior. However, at noon sharp, the *davening* ended and miraculously, the four goons disappeared. I truly thought it was a miracle, but upon further reflection, I realized they probably had a lunch break from 12:00 to 1:00 P.M.; perhaps their assignment with me ended with the ending of the services. Anyway, they left at noon, and I went downstairs for *kiddush*.

It was black as pitch, like the darkness of Egypt. I found my way to a room where there were fifteen people around the table, most of whom I recognized from the earlier service. Set out on the table were bottles that looked to me like they contained water, slices of honey cake, and a chair of honor for me. The *gabbai* repeated to me, "We're thirsty for Torah." He poured me a full glass of the clear liquid, which did not smell like water, and whispered in my ear that it was vodka.

It was the first time I made *Kiddush* on anything but wine, and the first time I ever tasted vodka. I made the blessing, I gave a *devar Torah*, they sang a *niggun*, they did a dance. They poured me another vodka, I gave another *devar Torah* – a *niggun*, a dance, and again, more vodka, yet another *devar Torah*, a *niggun* and a dance… nine times!

By the ninth time, two things had occurred. First of all, I did not have any more words of Torah in my repertoire to give. I had said whatever I had to say on that week's reading, *Parashat Ki Tetzeh*.

The second thing that happened was that, until that point, everything had felt like black Tisha B'Av, and all of a sudden it began to feel like pink Purim. I felt very light; I felt very good. And I turned to the individual who had been the *ba'al koreh*, the Torah reader – I believe his name was Reb Yisrael Friedman, a Chabadnik (he has since come to Israel and I have seen him at the Kotel [Western Wall] putting *tefillin* on people). I said to him, "Please – you give this *devar Torah*; I want to hear something that I can bring back with me."

His *devar Torah* changed my life.

He began with a verse from the Torah reading: "'Do not withhold the wages due to your hired hand… that day shall you give him his wages' [Deuteronomy 24:14, 15]. By the end of the day, you must give him his wages. But," he said, "there seems to be something wrong with that law. There's a Gemara in *Kiddushin* that records a tragic incident. Rav Elisha ben Avuya, a Talmudic sage, the rebbe of Rav Me'ir, became a heretic, joined the Roman Epicurean Sabbath desecrators and consumers of non-kosher food. How could such a thing have happened? The Gemara explains that Elisha ben Avuya saw two incidents that caused his heresy. Firstly he witnessed a personal tragedy: He saw a father ask his son to please climb a tree and bring him down a pigeon. The boy went up the tree, sent away the mother bird, took the pigeon – and in so doing was keeping two commandments that, in the Bible, are specifically rewarded with long life – whereupon the young boy fell from the tree and died before his father's eyes.

"Elisha ben Avuya called out, '*Let din velet dayan,* There is no Judge and there is no judgment,' and he became a heretic.

"He further witnessed a national tragedy. During the Hadrianic persecutions, the Romans imprisoned Ḥutzpit HaMeturgeman, who was a sage with a mellifluous, stentorian voice; his Torah lectures drew great crowds of appreciative listeners. The Romans cut out his tongue, tied it to the tail of a pig, and sent the pig dragging the tongue throughout the streets of Judea. 'How can a tongue that spewed forth diamonds, now lick the dust? There is no Judge and no judgment,' said Rav Elisha ben Avuya. And he became a heretic.

"Rav Yaakov, his grandson, in the next generation, said, 'Had my grandfather understood a basic foundation of Jewish theology, he would not have become a heretic; There is no reward for performing commandments – in this world.' The reward for the commandments is in the world to come. Long life means long eternal life, in the dimension of the world of souls, at the conclusion of one's life in this world.

"But," continued the *ba'al koreh,* "how can Rav Yaakov be correct? How can that be? How could God tell us that we must pay the day laborer at the end of the day, when He Himself doesn't pay us for the commandments as soon as we perform them? How can God make us wait for our reward until the end of our lives? '*HaShofet kol ha'aretz ya'aseh mishpat*?' Will not the Judge of the entire world, Himself do justice? How can God set more exacting standards for us than He sets for Himself? If He wants us to pay the day laborer immediately, He should give us our reward for commandments immediately as well!"

After everything I had witnessed and experienced in the Soviet Union, I could well understand the overwhelming question Reb Yisrael Friedman was asking. Look at the commitment being displayed by these Soviet Jews day in and day out. Where was their reward? Even this very *kiddush*, with vodka and words of Torah, was placing every participant in mortal danger. There may have been permission for post-retirement Jews to pray in the synagogue, but the *kiddush* was technically a criminal act. Any minute the door to the basement could open, KGB police could enter, and all *kiddush* participants could be imprisoned – or worse. That is why we were sitting in the dark, hoping to escape notice. Where was the reward for these Jews?

Then Reb Yisrael answered his own question. He said, "There's a Gemara in the seventh chapter of *Bava Metzia* that differentiates between a hired hand or day laborer, and a contractor. Yes, a day laborer has to be paid at the end of the day, but a contractor has to be paid only at the end of the project. We, vis-à-vis God, are not day laborers; we are contractors. We each have a unique function to perform, given the talents with which we are endowed and the time and place in which we live. Our function begins almost as soon as we are born, certainly as soon as we can make decisions, and ends only when we die. Only then can we know and can God judge if we were involved in the proper function for us, and if we discharged our unique responsibilities adequately. That is why there is no reward in this world." And he looked at everybody there and he said, "The most important thing one can do in this world is to discover his purpose; how each of us can best improve the world even a little bit, given our abilities, given the time in which we live, given the place wherein we function. And then we must discharge our divinely given responsibility with as much integrity, devotion and grace as we can possibly muster."

It was at that moment in Riga, after nine vodkas, that I resolved in my heart that if I am privileged to be living in the generation of our return to our national homeland, how could I not use my one chance at life to fulfill my purpose in Israel? I thought of how much these Soviet Jews are sacrificing to attempt to get to Israel, when all I have to do is get on a *plane*. It was this *devar Torah* that inspired me at that moment in Riga to take an oath to make *aliya*, and attempt to contribute to world Jewry as a rabbi living in the Jewish State of Israel. I also silently vowed that once I arrived in Israel as an *oleh* (immigrant), I would make *Kiddush* every Shabbat afternoon on vodka.

I floated back to the hotel, deeply moved and inspired by what I had heard. I have tried to recapture a little bit of that resolve every Shabbat, after shul, when I try to make *Kiddush* on vodka wherever in the world I may be.

Chapter Fifty-Eight

Circumcision, Riga Style

That Saturday night, about two o'clock in the morning, there was a banging on the door. At first I thought I was dreaming; I didn't sleep very well in the Soviet Union anyway. The banging continued, and when I fearfully opened the door, I saw the short, wispy-bearded *gabbai* together with another man in his forties. The *gabbai* explained in Yiddish that this man had a son about to become a bar mitzva, and a two week old baby, neither of whom had been circumcised. A Jewish doctor was ready to perform the circumcision, but he didn't know the blessings and he would want some rabbinical supervision to ensure a proper ritual act. There was a cemetery outside of Riga called Rombula, and they asked if I would be the religious authority for the circumcision at the cemetery at four o'clock in the morning. They felt that this location in the middle of the night would protect us from unfriendly eyes. A car was waiting downstairs. Would I please oversee the circumcision, and make the necessary blessings?

I am very queasy about circumcision in the best of times, but I felt I could not refuse. I told them I couldn't go into the cemetery itself because I was a Kohen, so the ritual would have to take place on the outskirts of the cemetery, which they accepted. We set out, and everybody was told to lie on the floor in the car on the way there. We got to the outskirts of the cemetery before dawn, before even the rising of the morning star. The only anesthesia that was administered to both pre–bar mitzva and baby was the ubiquitous vodka (I also requested a shot to calm my fragile nerves). I braced myself, said *Shema Yisrael,* and intoned the blessings with added devotion that everything should occur properly, both medically and ritually. The doctor was apparently very skilled, and God helped out too; both circumcisions took place quickly and efficiently, without a hitch – until the end, that is.

Very relieved but with shaking legs, I recited the last blessings, the first over the wine and then the blessing that gives the newly circumcised Jews their names. (We were rushed for time, dawn was about to break, and so I agreed to do the two circumcisions together.)

And just when I came to the prayer "*Keshem shenikhnas lebrit, ken yikanes leTorah, leḥuppa ulema'asim tovim* – Just as he entered into the covenant of Abraham, so shall he become a bar mitzva, get married, and live a life of Torah and good deeds," the father became very agitated and screamed out, "No, no!" There had been hushed silence, even muted blessings until that point, and suddenly the entire atmosphere was dangerously interrupted by the father's shouts. "No! *Nit 'keshem'!* I don't want it to be 'just like'! I don't know why I'm doing this. I'm not even an observant Jew. I only know that I want my children to be Jewish, and that without being circumcised, I feel that they won't really be Jewish in the full sense of the word. But I don't want them to be bar-mitzvahed and married '*just like this, keshem,*' hiding in a cemetery, afraid of the KGB. I want future occasions to be in Jerusalem, publicly, without fear and with great joy..."

It was the most inspiring circumcision I ever experienced – and, indeed, the circumcision of this man's grandson, the elder son's son, did take place with great joy in Israel and I was proud to attend.

Chapter Fifty-Nine

A Departing Message from Vilna

We got to Vilna amidst heavy rains and gusty winds. We went straight to the only remaining functioning shul, the shul of the Gra, the sainted Vilna Gaon, Rabbeinu Eliyahu. Immediately after the Afternoon Prayer, the *gabbai* approached me with a warm "*Shalom aleikhem,*" noted that I didn't say *Kaddish* and asked if perchance I would give a short *devar Torah* before *Ma'ariv,* the Evening Prayer. I agreed with alacrity, and as I rose to a lectern that had perhaps been used by the Gra himself, I asked for a Torah, Mishna or Talmud text. A dour individual sitting at the back of the synagogue shouted authoritatively, "we have no texts." When I began to quote the first Mishna in the Tractate *Berakhot* by heart, this same personage banged on the podium, announcing *Ma'ariv.* The *gabbai* meekly objected that the schedule called for *Ma'ariv* in ten minutes. Undaunted, the "gentleman" from the back stepped forward and immediately began the Evening Prayer. I sat down quietly.

Back at the hotel, in the middle of the night, when it was still raining non-stop, I heard a bang at the door. I was used to nocturnal visits by now, so I wasn't frightened. The elderly, stooped *gabbai* of the shul was standing there, carrying a Torah scroll wrapped in a lot of newspaper to protect it from the rain.

He told me that there used to be twenty-two *sifrei Torah* in that shul, the shul of the Vilna Gaon, but that one Ḥanukka morning they discovered that twenty Torah scrolls had been mysteriously removed from the Holy Ark. They had not had a rabbi in Vilna for quite some time, and now they had a problem as to the validity of the second Torah. There was no real margin in the *klaf*, in the parchment, and they did not know if such a Torah scroll was properly "kosher" for use.

In truth I wasn't too sure myself. I knew there was a difference of opinion amongst the decisors about this issue, known as *mukaf gevil*, but without classical texts at my disposal, I had no way of finding out the final decision in the *Shulḥan Arukh*. Nevertheless, I took a deep breath, made a silent prayer and said that it was kosher. (It turned out that when I checked upon my return to New York, God had helped me give the right decision.) The old man thanked me with tears in his eyes because there are times when the service requires two *sifrei Torah*, and although they could make do with one, to have to do so would only exacerbate a most depressing and discouraging situation.

As he was leaving my hotel room, he added, "Can you imagine the shul of the Vilna Gaon left with only two Torah scrolls? I have a tradition from my father who heard it from his father, a tradition that explains what happened to us. They used to call Vilna the '*Yerushalayim deLita*,' the 'Jerusalem of Lithuania.' The tradition has it that once they began calling Vilna the 'Jerusalem of Lithuania,' the decree came from on high that Vilna had to be destroyed. After all, there is only one Jerusalem – in the land of Israel. Young rabbi, if you are able – go to Israel. That is the only future of our people…"

And he walked into the rain with the Torah scroll.

Chapter Sixty

For the Sake of a Torah Scroll

Danny Greer and I got back to the Moscow airport where we were supposed to meet up with Richard Joselit (with the taped interview attached to his body), as well as with Sacha, with the papers certifying his American parentage and, therefore, his American citizenship. I saw Sacha out of the corner of my eye, and my heart felt like it stopped beating. His face was bloody. His glasses were broken. His jacket and shirt were torn. He had come with the papers, but he had been beaten up by the KGB on his way to meet us. The truth is, he should not have come to the airport. As he approached us it was clear that he – and very soon our whole group – was being surrounded by KGB agents (who were not very subtle in their manner or comportment). We had to think quickly. Greer, Joselit and I were together when Sacha approached us. The most vulnerable was Joselit, with the tape that would incriminate all of us for espionage, but especially those Soviet Jews in Sacha's home who had given the interview, revealed the information, and were without American citizenship to protect them.

I had an idea. I started to scream, "Don't touch this package!"

indicating the package with the Torah scroll. It was a Torah scroll; there was nothing contraband about it. I really didn't care if they checked it. My main objective was to deflect attention from Joselit with the tapes. So, as all of the KGB agents, as well as many other onlookers surrounded me, I kept on remonstrating, "No, no, no, you can't touch it. Only a Jew can touch this. This is a Jewish holy book." The KGB men tried to wrest the Torah scroll from me for inspection, shouting *"Biblos, Biblos,"* and I was forcibly pulling it away from them. The crowds were gathering around me and bedlam was reigning.

When I saw Greer and Joselit get on the KLM plane, I grudgingly let the Soviets take the Torah out of my hands. They delayed the plane for two hours, checking every inch of the parchment. Finally they said to me, "Okay, you can go on the plane. We have to send this Bible to the Hermitage to be checked again." Ringing in my ears were the words of the man who had entrusted it to me in Leningrad: "It's my best friend. It will be your best friend too." And I felt that by taking it, I had given him my word that I would protect it with my life.

I had no recourse. "Look, I can't leave this with you. Either you let me have it to take on the plane, or I can't get on the plane." They said, "Okay, then you'll stay. And you'll go to prison for espionage."

The plane left without me.

I have to admit that at that moment, for the first time, I was truly frightened. I had no Russian money and no food left. I kept screaming about my rights as an American citizen, demanding to at least call my wife. Amazingly, they immediately complied. I tried to speak calmly. Expecting that my call was being monitored, I said to Vicky something like, "Remember the Torah scroll I purchased in Vienna? They think it belongs in Russia, and so they're not letting me out with it." Vicky was surprisingly rather calm; she had been nervous about the recent spate of skyjackings that had taken place, so she was initially relieved that I was not on an airplane. I had full confidence that she would know who to contact to make sure that an innocent American citizen would not languish in a Soviet jail-cell.

Then they took me to prison. Uncomfortable is not the word; there was a body search and torturous questioning. They tried to get me to admit to being a spy. I kept screaming that I was an American citizen and demanded to see the American consul.

The next day they took me to the American consul. He was an Irish Catholic, and a very good Catholic at that. He put on the radio when he talked to me in his office, so I understood that even he believed that the consulate may have been "bugged."

By this time I had not eaten anything in almost a full twenty-four hours, with the exception of a few chocolate bars that my prison guard gave me. The consul asked me what I could eat, and I said that I could have fruit, vegetables, *smetana* and black bread. He stood in line with me for some half-rotten apples, got me a few *smetanas* and chocolate bars and told me that my imprisonment was fast becoming an international incident. The Soviets did not want any trouble, but they were obstinate in not letting me out with the "*Biblos*."

The consul really worked very hard to try to find a solution. At his suggestion, I was allowed me to sleep at the Consulate. After three or four days, he said, "Trust me. Leave the Torah with me. I'll send it to you by diplomatic pouch." I asked him if he had a copy of the Gospels. When he confirmed that he had, I asked him to swear on the Gospels that he would get the Torah to me. He did. On that basis I agreed to be on the next Aeroflot flight back to New York.

* * *

I got back. The new Lincoln Square Synagogue shul building had finally been completed. It was 1970 and it was the first Rosh HaShana in the new shul. Everybody was worried that I would not make it, but I got back in time, thank God. I was entering the High Holy Days, however, with a heavy heart. I felt responsible for the Soviet Jews I had left behind – and especially for Sacha, who had looked awful at the airport. After all, he had gotten in trouble with the KGB because of my suggestion about his American citizenship.

Then Vicky had a great idea. Barry Farber was a very well-known New York radio personality with a midnight-to-4:00 A.M. show every night, on which I had been a frequent guest. Barry had run for Congress against Bella Abzug, and in the heyday of their contest, I had invited them both to Lincoln Square to debate. When Bella Abzug couldn't show – for a very good and legitimate reason – I made the decision to host only Barry Farber, who spoke to a record crowd. He lost the election, but he won our district by a very large majority.

He called me up after the election and said to me, "Rabbi, I have the memory of an elephant and the gratitude of a '*shtetl yid*.' If you ever need a favor, call me. I appreciate very much what you did by allowing me to speak alone..."

That was a few months back, before I went to the Soviet Union. The night of my return, when I stayed up for hours telling all of my experiences to Vicky, my wife immediately sensed that Sacha was the perfect vehicle to get America fired up about the plight of Soviet Jews. Emphasize his American citizenship and his desire to come here, she advised. No American will feel sympathetic to a regime that does not allow an American citizen to come home. "And," Vicky added, "Barry Farber is the one who can do it for you. Call him up and test his memory and his gratitude." I did, and he was terrific. He used his very popular radio program to widely publicize the plight of Soviet Jews, with the case of Sacha as the focus for American identification.

And so I worked through the media, and Danny Greer, who had excellent political connections (he had been the New York Director of Ports and Terminals), got the American State Department to intercede with the Soviet Union government to free Sacha. Our rallies attracted more and more people. The American Jewish political establishment even agreed to finally work together with us, as well as to create a separate organization single-mindedly devoted to the plight of Soviet Jews.

Some of the mottos that we used to call out at these rallies were: "Let them live as Jews or let them leave as Jews – Let them live or let them leave," and "Two, four, six, eight: open up the Iron Gate." Americans could not really conceive that someone could be a prisoner in a country that he does not want to live in. Slowly but surely, the issue of Soviet Jewry in general, and Sacha in particular, drew international concern.

We finally got the call that Sacha was being released from the Soviet Union. The whole Lincoln Square Synagogue came out to the airport. There were thousands of people there to greet him, including Mayor Lindsay. Together with Sacha, we appeared on the Mayor Lindsay

TV show. His entry to America was on the front page of the *New York Times*, the *New York Post* and the *Daily News*. At first he lived in our Lincoln Square community, and he learned a lot about *Yiddishkeit*. We even arranged for his circumcision at Beth Moses hospital.

About three months later the *sefer Torah* came by diplomatic pouch, and again thousands of us went to the airport to pick it up and to deposit it at Lincoln Square Synagogue. The Lubavitcher Rebbe sent word that he would like to dance with it on Simḥat Torah, and of course we were most honored to honor his request.

The entire chapter of the Soviet Jewry movement was among the most exciting events in the last two thousand years of Jewish history; it probably ranks second only to the establishment of the State of Israel. One visionary leader named Yaakov Birnbaum, together with Glenn Richter and a handful of students, initially stood up to the mighty Iron Curtain and proved that the red wall was far from impregnable. It can justifiably be argued that the freedom of Soviet Jews was the beginning of the fall of the evil Communist empire. And it proved to me that, with God's help, there is no limit as to what a few individuals can accomplish. One must never remain silent in the face of injustice, no matter how impossible the odds for success may appear to be. Ultimately, to be alone with God is to be with a majority of One.

Part VII

Avinu SheBaShamayim: Airplane Stories

Chapter Sixty-One

The Pastor's Son

I was in Florida vacationing with my family, and was scheduled to speak at what was then called the Brandeis Institute in Simi Valley, California. I had actually been invited to dialog with Professor Mordechai Kaplan, the founder of Reconstructionist Judaism – a completely rationalistic philosophy of Judaism without a personal God, which stressed Judaism as an entire civilization rather than a mere religion. Our audience was to be a group of bright, largely uncommitted college students. I was very much looking forward to the intellectual excitement of the encounter, as well as the exposure to so many searching Jews.

I was supposed to leave Miami on a Thursday afternoon and then spend a long weekend in the Institute. Thursday morning at 6:00 A.M., the airline called me saying that my flight had been canceled and they suggested I take a Friday morning flight. I didn't want to travel so close to Shabbat, and inquired about the possibility of getting on another plane that Thursday. They said that if I could get to the airport within fifty-five minutes I could make a flight. I was rather discombobulated, but I did it.

I got onto the plane, found my seat, and then I saw my seatmate. He seemed to me to be about seven and a half feet tall, a veritable giant (maybe he was 6′2″ or 6′3″, but to me he looked enormous). Actually, since his "shirt" consisted of two strips of denim material displaying a mammoth tattoo across his chest; he looked like a walking tattoo atop very short jeans-shorts. As soon as he took his seat, he began reading a paperback novel, the cover of which displayed a woman clad, or rather unclad, in a way that caused me to turn my eyes in the opposite direction.

I thought to myself, what did I do to deserve this? I'm pretty friendly. I like to speak to my seatmates. What can I possibly have in common with this tattooed giant?

I was, at that time, writing a translation and commentary of the Jerusalem Talmud *Beitza* for a course in the Bernard Revel Graduate School of Yeshiva University. So I was busy with my literature – writing, and he was busy with his literature – reading, and there developed a kind of invisible *meḥitza* between us. I noted that the stewardess came over to him early on, giving him a special form to fill out because he'd been bumped from first class. I remember thinking, in a rather prejudiced way, what does this guy have to do with first class?

Then breakfast arrived. I was very upset because my kosher breakfast had been canceled along with my flight. I drank a few glasses of water and tried to feel optimistic about my enforced diet.

After a few hours, lunch was served. Suddenly my seatmate turned to me and said in rather imperious tones, "Hey bro, order a **** [expletive deleted] lunch."

I looked at him quizzically. What was it his business whether I ate or not? I said firmly, "I don't want lunch."

Again, almost shouting at me, he said, "You **** Orthodox Jew, order a **** lunch."

I thought to myself, there are stewards and stewardesses on this plane, my people won the Six Day War; I have nothing to be afraid of. "I don't want lunch," I said again.

"You fool!" he came back at me. "You haven't had anything at all this morning except a glass of water. Look at this **** lunch: a salad of vegetables and a hamburger. You order a **** lunch. I have a **** lunch. I give you my salad of tomatoes and cucumbers. You give me your hamburger. You'll eat and I'll eat."

Suddenly, I gained newfound respect for my clever seatmate. I ordered a "**** lunch." And then we began to talk. It turns out that he was the captain of the football team of a southern university. He was traveling on official school business, and therefore he was supposed to have been in first class, but the carrier had canceled its first-class seats on that flight.

More importantly, his father was the Chief Baptist Minister of the entire southern region of the United States. This pastor's son was very well versed in the Bible. He knew exactly what I could eat and what I couldn't eat as a *kashrut*-observant Jew. But after giving me this background, he added quietly and sadly, "I haven't spoken to my father in ten years. He never spoke to us, his family; he only preached at us. He had time for the congregation and the whole world, but he never had time for us."

I was then a young rabbi with a young family. I tried to explain to him the tensions and the difficulties of balancing career and family. You're reading a story to your daughter and the telephone rings. A congregant has been rushed to the emergency room at the hospital. You know this congregant is alone in the world; her children live far away from where she lives. You stop reading the story and set out for the hospital. For you it was a matter of life and death. For your daughter, the telephone and the congregant were more important than she was.

And so we spoke, he about the difficulties of being brought up in a busy pastor's household, and I about the frustrations of attempting to orchestrate being a husband, a father, and a rabbi with a mission.

The plane ride ended very quickly; too quickly. He stood up with tears in his eyes. He embraced me. "You know," he said, "I think God put us together. I wasn't supposed to be sitting in coach. The first thing I'm going to do now, as soon as I get off the plane, is call my daddy. I understand him much better now." And I said to him, "I know that God put us together. I wasn't even supposed to be on this flight at all. I looked at you and I thought to myself, what I can possibly have in common with you? We don't have similar sartorial or literary tastes. I don't speak your kind of vocabulary, and, although I'm not proud of it, I never threw a football in my life. But what I learned from our encounter is that what unites us is more important than what divides us, that no matter the different cultural, ethnic or religious backgrounds we may each come from, we remain united in a very strong bond, the indelible bond of our common humanity."

The first lecture I gave at the Brandeis Institute was on the meaning of Shabbat, the meaning I discovered on that plane trip. The Bible tells us in its two accounts of the Decalogue that Shabbat is a reminder of the creation of the world and of the exodus from Egypt. Both of these reasons, creation and freedom, are given in the *Kiddush,* the sanctification of the wine at the advent of Shabbat.

I had never before understood the relationship between those two reasons. Now, since my encounter on the plane, I understood. If God is the Creator of the world, all of us are His creatures. If God is our Parent in Heaven, all of us are siblings. Our very creation, our brotherhood, unites us in a common destiny within which each of us is born, we know not quite why, and each of us is limited by our mortality, we know not quite for how long. Our common and united kinship with God guarantees the freedom of each of us, ensures the fact that each of us is an end unto himself and dare not be used – or misused – as a means to another's end, that every one of God's children has an inalienable right to be free and sovereign under God and God alone. And most of all I realized that no matter how unlikely it may superficially appear, I and every other human being on this planet are siblings, inextricably joined together by the spark of the same Divine God in each of us.

Chapter Sixty-Two

There Is No Atheist in a Foxhole

During my tenure at Lincoln Square I spent many summers in Israel and some summers in Miami Beach, Florida, because my wife's grandmother lived in Florida and she was not mobile. It was a good way to give her some *naḥat*, some pleasure from her daughter and grandchildren, and it was a fairly inexpensive vacation place. I met some wonderful people there and, as a family, we spent some lovely summers there.

One of the most special people I met was Rav Sender Gross, *z"l*, who had founded the Hebrew Academy of Miami. When he had come to Miami Beach, pre–air conditioning, there was virtually no opportunity for intensive Jewish education. He built up an educational empire – an elementary school, a high school, a *kollel*, as well as a shul that was well attended every Shabbat. Whatever *Yiddishkeit* there was, the overwhelming majority of it was thanks to Rav Sender Gross. We became very fast friends.

Having studied at Yeshiva Torah Vodaas, he had a different educational background than most of my Yeshiva University friends. He was a student of Rav Shraga Feivel Mendlowitz who called himself "Mr. Mendlowitz." (At Rav Mendlowitz's funeral, one of the major *maspidim*, eulogizers, said, "*Al tikre* Mister, *ela nister*," "Don't pronounce the word 'mister' but rather '*nister*,' 'hidden,' because he was a hidden saint, an individual of gifted mind and profound soul, who had an enormous influence on all of his students.) Rav Alexander Linchner, the founder of Kiryat No'ar, Boys Town, Jerusalem, was his son-in-law and student, as was my elementary school principal and teacher, Rav Mandel, and I have the impression that all of Rav Mendlowitz's close disciples devoted themselves to Jewish education.

One of the things that I heard from Rav Gross in the name of Rav Mendlowitz was a beautiful and unique interpretation of the words that begin our Rosh HaShana prayer of *Zikhronot*, or Remembrances: "*Ata zokher ma'asei olam, ufoked kol yetzurei kedem*," which he would translate, "You remember all the deeds from eternity, and bestow a function [*ufoked* sharing a root with *tafkid*] upon all of the creatures from yore." He would always stress the fact that each individual has a unique function to perform, and the most significant challenge facing each of us is to discover his or her specific function, taking into consideration the unique gifts that God has bestowed upon us, the period in which we live and the challenges with which we must cope.

When I was in Miami, my days were filled with studying, learning and writing. Rav Gross was zealously considerate of my time and he would never call me during the day. But we always met in the evening, he and his wife Shirley, and Vicky and I. We enjoyed many marvelous hours together discussing matters of education and matters of Torah, both of which were very precious to each of us. We spent just about every Shabbat together.

One morning he uncharacteristically called me, apologizing, but asking that we meet. He told me of the following moral problem with which he was faced.

When he had left Torah Vodaas and was newly married, he had had a terrible asthma attack, and it was obvious that he was seriously ill. The doctor, a specialist to whom he was sent, told him that if he would stay in New York, he had only a few months to live; but if he would move to Florida, which had a climate that was beneficial for asthma sufferers, he could have six months to a year. He and his wife moved immediately to Florida.

Although he felt he had received a death sentence, he realized that all of life is a terminal illness; no one gets out of it alive. The challenge is to maximize whatever God gives us, to try to make the most out of whatever time we have. Florida was then devoid of any real Jewish educational presence; although it was a popular winter resort, few families lived there full time. However, the situation seemed to be changing; so Sender decided that if God sent him to Florida, he would spend whatever time he had in building a day school. That must be his *tafkid,* his function, given his state of health and geographic location.

He worked indefatigably and, together with a dedicated group of *ba'alei batim* (non-rabbinical people involved in the community), created the Hebrew Academy, a high school and a *kollel.* The years went by, and thank God he continued to live, beyond the six months, beyond the year, beyond a decade, beyond two, even three decades.

So what was the problem that he wanted to discuss with me? The doctor, who had told him that a move to Miami would give him six to twelve months to live, had died, and his funeral was that morning. Rav Gross was questioning whether he ought to go to that funeral. On the one hand, he knew the individual and had been his patient for a time. On the other hand, how proper would it be to go to a funeral when he couldn't help having some feelings of joy that he had outlived the doctor who had given him such a short time to live?

My advice was that he should go to the funeral. I told him that I was certain his real focus would be on the tragedy of human mortality – and his thanks to the Almighty that he had been given a reprieve by God to create a Torah community where none had previously existed. After all, had the doctor not "sent" him to Miami, the entire educational infrastructure would never have been created.

Rav Gross passed away a number of years later, and this is how it happened. There was a school bus driver strike and Rav Sender Gross, although he was an older man and he was not very well, drove the school bus himself, picking up all the children in their appointed places to make sure that Torah study would not be canceled. Apparently the strain was too great. He had a heart attack and he died.

I was in New York when it happened. I flew to Florida, and I remember how strange I felt when I got off the plane. In my past trips to Florida I had always been mesmerized by the sheer beauty of the Miami skyline, the clouds forming magnificent mountains in the heavens, in varied colors and shapes, and the sun changing from yellow, to light red, to lavender, to blue-black. I was certain that nature in some way would react to Rav Sender Gross' death and that everything would look different, that the skyline would be sullied, that the sun would be paled, that nature itself would noticeably mourn the passing of Reb Sender. But the skyline remained in all of its pristine beauty. It was as if nature were mocking human tragedy, Torah's diminution...

I went to the funeral, I paid a *shiva* call and I flew back. And on the way back, I was rather despondent. I felt I had lost a friend, a mentor and a confidant. There was a woman sitting next to me and, although I'm usually fairly friendly, I didn't talk to her at all. I was lost in my own thoughts.

Dinner came. I had a kosher dinner. My seatmate had the regular dinner, which was steak, with which she ordered a glass of milk. As I began to eat my kosher food she initiated a conversation: "I suppose you think I'm not religious. I think I'm more religious than you are." I must admit I was rather taken aback at her unsolicited outburst. I said, "I didn't even think you were Jewish. I had no reason to think you were. I've just lost a special friend and I really wasn't thinking about you at all." She said to me, "Well, I'm very religious and I follow the Bible completely. And therefore I would not eat a kid in its mother's milk. But there's nothing wrong with my eating steak and drinking milk."

I tried to politely explain that the Jewish tradition includes an ancient interpretation of the biblical commands, which prohibits eating any meat and milk together, but that each of us has freedom of choice to do what he or she sees fit. To be honest, I could not emotionally enter into a long theological discussion at that point.

It turns out that this was the roughest ride that I've ever had on a plane in my life. A storm broke out. It felt as if lightning had actually hit the plane itself. We had to be rerouted. Children were crying; even some adults got nauseous. The woman turned to me, ashen faced. She asked if I was a rabbi, and when I said that I was, she asked if I would say Psalms with her. I did – and the Psalms calmed me as well. Then she blurted out, "If we land safely, I'll never eat non-kosher steak or have milk and meat at the same time again."

We reached our destination after a four-hour delay. By this time we were talking about our respective families. The weather conditions were much better and, shortly before landing, I invited her to spend a Shabbat with us. Suddenly her former, combative voice of our initial conversation came back. She said to me accusingly, "I guess you believe I don't have a Sabbath. I have a Sabbath. I'm a very proud Reform Jew and I don't have to go to your house for Sabbath. You can come to my house for Sabbath. And what I said about not eating steak with milk anymore – you realize I was only joking."

I wanted to change the subject, so in the last few minutes that we were together I told her the story of Rav Gross and how he had come to Miami Beach and how he had started a day school, and how important I thought day school education was. We exchanged addresses and phone numbers and I repeated my invitation for Shabbat.

I did not hear from her then, but about two years later I did receive a letter that was written on the stationery of a Reform day school outside of Miami Beach, of which she was the president. In the letter she wrote about how impressed she had been by our conversation, and how she realized that within Reform Judaism they needed more intensive Jewish studies, so she had started a day school within the Reform Movement. And, she added, the hot lunches served in the day school were kosher even according to my standards.

I felt that somehow Rav Gross had accomplished something important, even after his death.

Chapter Sixty-Three

"Promise Me the Plane Won't Crash"

At the conclusion of many summers, I have been privileged to lecture at the Hillel Summer Institute, which is a retreat for leadership students from universities throughout the world.

A number of years ago the retreat began on a Wednesday evening. Although I usually lecture for two full days, this time I could lecture, at the most, on Wednesday evening and Thursday in order to catch the Thursday night El Al flight back to Israel. I would be cutting it close to sunset on Friday but El Al generally tries very hard to leave on time.

Because I felt it really was important to teach the Hillel college youngsters, especially in light of the pro-Palestinian lobby at many campuses, I booked the later flight. I figured that if it were going to leave late, I just wouldn't get on it.

The plane appeared to be ready to leave on time. Everything worked out well and I was sitting in business class, very comfortably, looking forward to the plane ride. It was ten o'clock, the plane was supposed to start taxiing, but it wasn't moving. At about 10:10 there was an announcement on the loudspeaker, "Is there a doctor on board?"

A number of people got up. A few minutes later, the plane was still not moving. Then they announced, "Is there a psychiatrist or a psychologist on board?" A number of people got up and left their seats, but still the plane wasn't moving.

About 10:30, as I was beginning to get nervous, the pilot came over to me and said to me, "Aren't you the rabbi from Efrat?" A number of weeks before that plane ride I'd been on a television program on Channel 1 and he recognized me. The program was dedicated to the problem of parents coping with the loss of a child, specifically as a result of war or terrorist attacks. A psychiatrist and social worker were the professionals who were experts in how to cope with such a tragedy, and I joined them as the rabbinical professional.

The pilot recognized me, and he explained that there was a problem with one of the passengers. At first the crew thought that he was having a heart attack, but then they realized that he was having a very serious anxiety attack. "He wants to get off," said the pilot. "If he gets off the plane, locating his luggage could take anywhere from fifteen minutes to two hours, and the plane might not get to Tel Aviv before sundown. We would be very grateful if you could possibly do something to convince him to stay on the plane."

I left my seat. I quickly identified the individual in question sitting in coach, shaking almost convulsively, and perspiring profusely. He seemed to be in his late thirties or early forties, and he was saying to anyone who would listen to him, "I have to leave the plane." There was a gentleman sitting next to him. I asked if he would take my seat in business class, and he was understandably very happy to do so.

I took the now-empty seat and asked my new-found "patient" if he had always had a phobia of flying. He told me that it was only since the TWA crash, a short time before, that he had become so very frightened of flying. His wife's brother's son was having a bar mitzva in Jerusalem; his wife had gone the week before and he was supposed to have gone then as well. At the time, however, he could barely get into the taxi from his house to the airport, he had been so terrified. Now he had made it to the plane, but as he was speaking, his lips were chattering and every one of his pores was exuding perspiration. He said he simply had to leave the plane.

I asked him if he was religious. He said no, he was not devoutly religious, but he had gone to Hebrew school and he believed in God. I asked him if perhaps we might say Psalms together. He said he would certainly agree to that, as long as the plane didn't start to move. So we started saying Psalms, and I began with the twenty-third Psalm. "The Lord is my shepherd, I shall not want. Though I walk through the valley of the shadow of death, I shall not fear for You are with me." I said it in English and I said it in Hebrew, and then I said it in English again, and he said it together with me each time, in each language. And as we said it, he began to calm down. He stopped shaking and he stopped perspiring.

And then we said the twentieth Psalm, and he said to me, "If you'll stay with me the entire flight, I think I'll be able to remain on the plane." The pilot, sitting a few seats away from us, was all ears. He gave me a v-sign for "victory" and seemed very proud of himself for having elected me to resolve this problem. I had visions of a free season's pass to Business Class (or maybe even First) on El Al…

Announcements were made preparing the passengers for take-off. My new seatmate turned to me and said, "I'm going to say Psalms all night long. I find them very comforting. You'll say Psalms with me." Then I began getting nervous, because I'm not the most accomplished psalms reciter. I suggested that we intersperse the recitation with the study of Psalms, saying, "I would certainly enjoy reciting and studying Psalms together with you. It will make for a fascinating flight."

He agreed; it was amazing how calm he had become. And again, the announcement was made for the plane crew to be seated, to prepare for takeoff. He then turned to me and said, "I'm really willing to stay on the plane. But you have to promise me that nothing is going to happen." The pilot, who was still listening to all of this, mouthed to me in Hebrew, "*Tavtiaḥ lo*," "Promise him."

Now, until this moment I felt like the hero of the hour. But suddenly I felt myself in a quandary. How could I promise him? If the plane had already been in the air and there was no turning back, I could have promised just to make him feel better, because nothing could happen to change the course of the plane at that point. But it was still before takeoff. What right did I have to take away someone's free choice? After all, something *could* happen; I couldn't take the responsibility of his remaining on the flight – when he could have gotten off – on the strength of my empty promise.

I said to him that I didn't believe that anything would happen, that with God's help nothing would happen, that statistically it would seem that nothing would happen, that I've traveled very often on this particular route and, thank God, nothing had happened in the past, and that we take a chance every time we cross the street. Terrible things can always happen, but we can't live our lives in fear. He looked at me again, this time in disappointment. "You can't promise me?" And I had to say in all honesty, "I can't promise you." In a flash, he began trembling again, perspiring again, and promptly fainted in front of me.

The pilot didn't even look at me. In a few minutes an ambulance arrived. The paramedics tended to the patient and by the time he was taken off the plane, his eyes were already open and he did thank me. Miraculously, perhaps the only miracle that happened in this story, they found his luggage within twenty minutes. By 11:00 P.M. we were off, and happily the plane made very good time; I arrived in Efrat twenty-five minutes before candle-lighting time.

Over Shabbat dinner, we discussed the incident. My wife said I should have promised him and saved everyone at home in Efrat a great deal of anxiety. My children said I was absolutely right, and I felt in my heart of hearts that I was absolutely right as well. I lost a business seat because the gentleman who had taken my business seat didn't suggest giving it back to me, and I was too embarrassed about the whole incident to even ask for it. So I remained in coach, and suffered the fact that the pilot didn't even say goodbye. But I felt relieved that I hadn't removed from the anxious passenger his freedom of choice.

Chapter Sixty-Four

For the Sake of a Woman

As a platinum-card-carrying frequent traveler on El Al, I sometimes receive the privilege of an upgrade. One particular journey was especially memorable because I was upgraded to first class and had the privilege of sitting in close proximity to the Vizhnitzer Rebbe, one of the great Hasidic leaders of the preeminent Council of Torah Sages.

The Rebbe was seated in the front row next to his *gabbai*, two Hasidim were seated behind them, and I was in the third row together with Marlene Post, then president of Hadassah. Parallel to the Rebbe, across the aisle, was a middle-aged secular couple with two Hasidim behind them, and a younger secular couple across the aisle from me.

Everything seemed fine except for the fact that it was thirty minutes past takeoff time and the plane had not yet begun to move. I soon realized that the Rebbe was a bit agitated, and I deduced that it was because the woman across from him was directly in his sight line.

His *gabbai* very respectfully and very earnestly approached the middle-aged couple, first requesting and then literally begging them to please change seats with the Hasidim behind them. The husband seemed quite upset at the impertinence of the request. "After all," he said, "I reserved these seats six months ago and my wife and I are not going to move!"

The younger secular couple in the back loudly voiced their approval of his refusal to move. "These Hasidim hate women. Look at how we don't have stewardesses, only stewards because of them. Don't give in."

The *gabbai* seemed unruffled at the exchange and gently continued his entreaties. "Please, if you insist on not moving, we will have to leave the plane. Everyone will be delayed several hours because their luggage will have to be removed as well. Please understand that the Rebbe is a holy man and his request should be honored." This time the secular individual got rather hot under the collar. "Don't tell me who is holy and who is not holy! I'm holy because I served in the IDF and my children served in the IDF! I'm holier than your so-called rebbe!"

Tempers began to rage and I was afraid of an actual fist fight. I was witnessing a microcosm of the religious-secular tensions that characterize Israeli society. I had nothing to lose and decided to try my luck.

I approached the couple in the front row and introduced myself. They calmed down enough to speak to me most civilly, complimenting me on the fact that although I was observant, I did not appear to be "one of them." I confirmed that fact that indeed I was modern Orthodox and not Hasidic, but I then added, "However, there is one thing about Hasidim that you don't seem to understand. It's not that they hate women; much the opposite, they are very attracted to women. In fact," and with this I turned to the woman, "the Rebbe is apparently attracted to you. He feels he will not be able to concentrate properly on his studies if you will be in his line of vision."

"Do you really mean that the rebbe finds me attractive?" asked the woman, and then turning accusingly to her husband, "When was the last time you told me that you find me attractive?" The woman blushed and smiled. "You hear that?" she said to her husband. "The Rebbe is attracted to me. Of course I will move. It will be my pleasure."

I merited a kiss from the Rebbe and the plane departed forthwith. The stewards gave me a gift bottle of wine.

Chapter Sixty-Five

Tateh

This airplane story I cannot vouch for, since it didn't happen to me. It was sent to me in a letter signed only "Shmuel," asking me to publish it someday.

A friendly young rabbi who had come from South Africa was on a plane from Johannesburg to Jerusalem; he was working on relocating to Israel, to a Jewish Agency position. Next to him sat an elderly man who began to speak to him in Yiddish. The young rabbi had lived in Europe as a young child and grew up in a Yiddish environment; he was also used to hearing Yiddish from the *bubbes* and *zeides* (grandparents) in his congregation in South Africa. He loved the language and enjoyed every opportunity to speak it, and so he welcomed the idea of talking to this old man in Yiddish.

Then breakfast arrived, and breakfast on this South African airline consisted of sausages and scrambled eggs as its main staple. The non-kosher quality of the sausage could be smelled a mile away. To add insult to injury, the egg was a cheese omelet. The young rabbi had obviously ordered a kosher breakfast. He couldn't resist saying to the old man, with whom he had developed such a warm, Yiddish relationship, "Such a breakfast you're eating, *mit a zelcha treife* [such non-kosher] sausages?"

The old man looked at the rabbi almost accusingly. "You haven't gone through what I've gone through. You don't know what it means to have a son *arois gehapt fun dir*, snatched away from you in the Holocaust. Don't judge me and don't tell me what to eat. I'll eat whatever I want to eat, and I want to eat *treif* sausage!"

There was a bit of silent tension between them for a little while, but then they resumed a friendly conversation. The younger rabbi felt very much drawn to this old man. And when they left, they embraced each other. When the rabbi thought about it afterwards, he felt very sorry that he hadn't even taken the elderly man's full name or his telephone number. He hoped they would meet again soon…

A number of years went by. The rabbi was now living in Israel, working in the Jewish Agency. Part of his job involved leading trips to the Yad VaShem Holocaust museum. He had a special interest in Yad VaShem and was doing some research there as well. One particularly sunny afternoon, as the rabbi came out with his group of tourists from Yad VaShem's Children's Memorial, he saw his old Yiddish-speaking friend from the airplane, standing outside the museum.

He ran over to the old man and they immediately and naturally embraced each other. He said to him, "I never thought I would see you again; remember we were together in the plane?" And the old man said, "Of course I remember. I ate the sausages! You did not convince me not to eat the sausages. As a matter of fact, I still eat *treif* sausages." They both laughed. The young man then suggested, "Why don't you come in? I've just given a tour. I've finished with the group, but I can show you some very interesting things." The old man looked at him the same way he'd looked at him on the plane. "I told you," he said, "Don't tell me what to eat and don't tell me where to go. I never come to Yad VaShem. I don't have to see what's there. I lived through it, and it's too painful. I'll do what I want to do, and I'll go where I want to go. Here, I'm staying outside."

And the rabbi smiled back and he said, "I understand very well and I won't ask you to do whatever you don't want to do. But please, give me your name and your address. I wouldn't like us to lose contact again." And the old man gave the rabbi his name and his address in South Africa. The rabbi looked at the name and looked at the old man very closely. "You told me that your son was snatched from you. What did you mean?" "I meant that he was snatched from me. We had a neighbor and the neighbor was a Christian. When all of us were rounded up for the concentration camp, the neighbor said he would take my infant son and nothing would happen. I gave my son to him. I haven't seen my baby since. That's why I eat sausages. I'm angry at God."

The rabbi grabbed hold of the old man. "I grew up with the story of how I was miraculously saved from certain death by kind Christian neighbors. "Look closely at my face. I'm Shmuel. *Tateh,* I'm your son..."

The two now live in Israel. The old man lives with his son, daughter-in-law and grandchildren, and he no longer eats *treif* sausages.

Part VIII

Israel Bound, but Riding on a Donkey

Chapter Sixty-Six

Bumps on My Road to *Aliya*

I met my wife in Israel in 1961. Before we got married, we promised each other that we would live in Israel. But I promised her parents that she would first graduate Barnard. Meanwhile, I was teaching Torah to eager students without yeshiva background at Yeshiva University in their James Striar School. Lincoln Square Synagogue was becoming known internationally since the apartment synagogue had turned into a beautiful travertine-faced center of Torah study in the heart of Manhattan's cultural Lincoln Center for the Performing Arts, and our family was growing. Life was exciting and productive on the West Side of Manhattan due to the outreach nature of our synagogue and my teaching at Yeshiva University. Additionally, our intimate involvement in the movement for Soviet Jewry provided an idealistic focus to our Diaspora existence – but our geographical distance from Israel day-to-day left us with a sense of loss and frustration.

Because I had come home later than expected from Russia (due to my brief excursion in the Soviet prison), I landed in New York in 1970, only two days before Rosh HaShana. The new synagogue building was being completed, and I went to look at it for a kind of final inspection a few hours before the onset of the New Year. The associate rabbi, my beloved friend and partner, Rav Herschel Cohen, very proudly showed me around so I could see the finishing touches. The sanctuary was still in a raw state; not yet completed, but nevertheless ready enough for people to pray there.

There was a young worker setting the stained-glass windows over the *Aron Kodesh* (Holy Ark). I said in Hebrew to Rav Cohen, "Please explain to the *goy* [Gentile] that within the next half hour he has to stop and clean up because people will start coming in for *Minḥa*." To my intense embarrassment, the young man called down, also in Hebrew, "I understood every word you said because I'm an Israeli; obviously I'm not a *goy*, but a Jew." I felt like sinking into the floor.

However, I did respond to him, "I'm very sorry, but I walked into the sanctuary and there was a whole box of *kippot* [skullcaps] at the door. I couldn't imagine that a Jew would be working around the *Aron Kodesh* and wouldn't take one of those *kippot*."

So he said to me, "I understand where you're coming from, but you have to understand where I'm coming from. I'm an Israeli from a non-religious kibbutz. I never really felt Jewish in Israel. I felt Israeli. Now, for the first time, especially working on the synagogue, I do feel certain Jewish stirrings – but it would never have dawned on me to put on a *kippa*!"

I asked him if he was invited anywhere for Rosh HaShana. When he said he hadn't been, I invited him to my home that evening, and the next day, and the whole Rosh HaShana holiday, and he was with us for all of the holidays of that season. He ended up studying at Yeshiva University and he's now a religious educator in Israel.

This incident, on the heels of my Russian experience, told me that there was work for me to do in Israel, and strengthened my resolve to make *aliya*. I felt to a great extent that once the synagogue was established, I had made my contribution to American Jewry. My family was growing – by then we were blessed with two girls and a boy – and I felt it was time to realize our dream to go to live in Israel.

But it was difficult for me to get a job, although I tried very hard. Just about every summer, my family and I would find some way to get to Israel;

I generally served as a counselor-teacher in an Israeli summer program for Americans. I utilized some of the precious time in Israel seeking year-round employment. Strangely enough, although in America I could have had virtually any position I wanted, in Israel I couldn't get any job at all!

To give but one example of my frustration, Rabbi S, a most respected educator in Beersheba, advertised a job for a high school *ram* (rabbi educator). I waited two hours for an interview – he was exceedingly busy – and, although when he did see me he was most gracious, I apparently didn't even impress him enough to be given the opportunity to give a model class. I was so disgruntled on my bus ride back to Jerusalem that I almost wept; I knew I would make an excellent *ram*.

By this time I had begun to develop the Ohr Torah High School in Riverdale, New York, which earned a marvelous reputation and attracted a very special student body.

Five years had passed since my disappointing rejection in Beersheba. Rabbi S had been quite successful and he was anxious to start a *yeshivat hesder*. To my great surprise, he called me in New York from Israel, made no reference at all to our previous encounter, complimented me on the good things he had heard about our Yeshiva High School, and asked if he could address our students with an aim toward inspiring some of them to attend his new *yeshivat hesder* for their post–high school, Israel experience. I was a bit surprised, and even annoyed, but I agreed.

He spoke to the students after prayers one morning, and in the opening words of his remarks, he praised me most generously. When I had a private breakfast with him afterwards, I could not control myself. "Rabbi S, if you hadn't said anything, *I* wouldn't say anything. But how could you have praised me so effusively? If you really thought I could make a contribution, you would have accepted me as one of your high school educators." I immediately felt sorry that I had spoken as I did, because he turned bright red. "I was hoping you had forgotten. Let me be very honest with you. You came to my office in Beersheba. Maybe you were twenty-five but you looked like you were fifteen and you didn't have a beard. And in Israel it just doesn't go without a beard." Suddenly I understood why I couldn't get a job in Israel. How foolish! If only someone had told me; after all, it is much easier to grow a beard – it takes much less time and effort – than it is to become an accomplished teacher.

I found it strange and superficial to judge an individual on the basis of a mere external appendage – and besides, the only two things my unbelievably generous wife ever asked of me were not to drive and not to grow a beard. The least I could do was acquiesce to her minimal requests. If Israel didn't want me without a beard, I guess I might have to stay in America for now. But I didn't give up on *aliya*.

I was especially anxious to move to Israel the summer after the shul was opened; I had successfully brought the Lincoln Square Synagogue to a desired plateau, and felt I could make *aliya* without a guilty conscience. There was a respected figure in Mafdal (National Religious Party) circles, Rabbi W, who was responsible for synagogues in Jerusalem and the Negev under the Ministry of Religion. He saw me in the street one Shabbat afternoon in Jerusalem, and said, out of the blue, "I would like to meet with you. I think I have a perfect job for you." Arad was just then starting up as a "development town," and he asked if I would like to be the rabbi of Arad. I got very excited about the idea and discussed it with my wife. Vicky had not quite thought in terms of Arad when she thought of Israel, but as the primary Zionist in the family, she immediately agreed – as long as the job came with a regular salary (she was also the prime realist of the family).

When I met with him and was actually offered the position, I excitedly concluded the interview without even thinking to ask him about the salary. Vicky was reservedly happy for us, but she correctly said that we couldn't make any concrete plans without knowing what my remuneration would be. I knew she was right and I immediately returned to his office. "My wife wants to know what the salary is," I sheepishly said. He seemed to look at me with surprise, even dismay, at my bringing up such a topic. "*HaRav Riskin*, you get an apartment. There's a regular salary from the Ministry of Religion. Whatever it is, no one in Israel starves. *Smokh alai* – trust me. But remember, you must begin right after Sukkot."

I went back to my wife greatly relieved: "Don't worry, there's a standard salary, everything seems fine, after all, Israeli rabbis generally have big families." We spoke almost the whole night. We were both very excited. We decided that it would be impossible financially for us as a family to go back to America for the High Holy Days and then to come back to Israel. I had always refused to sign any contract with Lincoln Square; I told them up-front that the first opportunity that came up, I would go to Israel. So I just had to draft a letter to the president of the synagogue informing him of our decision.

I spent a good deal of time that night carefully crafting the letter, writing that my family would remain in Israel, that I would come back to the shul for Rosh HaShana, Yom Kippur and Sukkot, and then I would rejoin my family in Arad, where I had been offered the position of rabbi of the new, burgeoning city.

The next morning, with the letter in my pocket, I went to pray at the Kotel to say a special prayer of thanksgiving. After that I planned to mail the letter. On my way back from the Kotel I met someone I knew and respected, a venerable rabbi almost twenty years my senior, Rav Kellman. Of course I greeted him very warmly. I was bursting to tell someone that I was staying in Israel, and I thought that when he asked how I was, I would tell him my good news. But he said to me first, "Congratulations are in order! I'm staying in Israel, and I have a rabbinical position." I said, "That's wonderful, where?" He said, "In Arad." A bit taken aback, I asked, "Who gave you the position?" Well, of course it was the same rabbi who had promised that very position to me less than twenty-four hours ago!

I was nonplussed. I didn't say a word to him. Thank God I hadn't mailed the letter. I went straight to the rabbi's office. "I want to know exactly how much I'll be making and I want to sign a precise contract with you." He seemed insulted. "Rav Riskin, what is troubling you all of a sudden? There's no need for a contract between us. *Smokh alai* – trust me." I responded angrily, "I just met Rav Kellman and he told me that he got the position as the rabbi of Arad. Neither of us is a Sepharadi so you can't claim the necessity of two rabbis!" The rabbi in charge of synagogues in Jerusalem and the Negev didn't so much as flutter an eyelid. He said to me, "Listen, we have no budget yet from the Ministry of Religion for any rabbi in Arad, not for you, and not for Rav Kellman. However, I went to your synagogue and I went to his synagogue. I know how your congregants love and admire you and I know how his congregants love and admire him. You'll say you want to move to Israel. The congregation will say, 'Take a Sabbatical first and see how you like it,' which is logical.

A rabbi on Sabbatical generally receives fifty percent of an American salary from his congregation. With fifty percent of a salary from America you'll do very well in Israel. You'll both come; you'll both have a fifty-percent salary from America. You'll both work as the rabbis of Arad. At the end of the year we'll see who will stay. Chances are that one of you will want to go back anyway, and by that time I'm sure we'll be able to work out a regular salary for the one who stays. *Smokh alai,* trust me."

At that point I felt that there was nothing else for me to say – and no opportunity for me in Israel. Almost heartbroken, I went back to America, resigned to make my life in *galut,* the Diaspora. I immediately began redoubling my efforts in the American Ohr Torah Schools. Even though I thought at the time that I would never realize my dream of *aliya,* I cannot say that I wasn't fulfilled as a rabbi and educator in New York. But something was missing. I felt I was letting God down. I wasn't really responding to the great miracle of the generation…

Chapter Sixty-Seven

Paving the Way for the Messiah via Two Kibbutzim

And then, in 1975, a conference was held at Kibbutz Lavi. It was a special convocation to which five rabbis were invited from America, along with the leaders of the religious kibbutz movement. Each of us coming from the United States was to give a lecture – Rabbis Saul Berman, Yitz Greenberg, Norman Lamm, Shubert Spero, Walter Wurtzberger, and myself.

Now, I don't really believe in coincidences. I think coincidences are God's way of letting us know that He's really in charge. I often feel that life is a string of coincidences, or opportunities for decisions, and everything depends on the right decision. At any rate, it was a wonderful conference. Each of the American guests was to spend Shabbat on a kibbutz where he would present his paper; I was invited by the *merakez hameshek*, the administrator, of Kibbutz Lavi.

Lavi had a rabbi, Rav Moshe Levinger, who today serves as the head of a yeshiva in Hebron. I didn't know the protocol in Israel and I certainly didn't know the protocol among kibbutzim. In America, however, a rabbi invites another rabbi to come to his pulpit; no guest rabbi would accept an invitation from the president or the chairman of the board of a synagogue that has a resident rabbi. I felt that if the kibbutz rabbi himself didn't invite me, maybe he didn't want me. I therefore responded to the *merakez hameshek*, that I would prefer to go to a kibbutz that didn't have a rabbi at all. He suggested Kibbutz Ein Tzurim, and that changed my whole life.

I experienced a remarkable Shabbat in an idealistic atmosphere, with very special individuals who have become life-long friends. After I gave a *devar Torah* in shul and a number of lectures, they invited me to come back that summer with my entire family as a scholar-in-residence.

I stayed at the home of Yehuda and Zahava Noiman. Yehuda Noiman is a remarkable person who studied in the Petaḥ Tikva Yeshiva with Rav Shach. He is an erudite Talmudic scholar and a deeply committed Zionist who fought in all the wars of Israel. At the time of my visit, he would spend eight hours a day working and a further eight hours a day studying. We struck up a very close relationship that we still maintain to this day. I spent an unforgettable Shabbat – and a long Motza'ei Shabbat (Saturday night) in which I received a crash course on modern Zionist history, especially of Gush Etzion, where this particular kibbutz had originated in the early 1940s.

Then something else happened that I felt was another message from God. There was a bookseller in Me'ah She'arim, Reb Shmuel, from whom I would purchase *sefarim* (books) during my summers in Israel; he would give me the whole of that winter to pay him, in installments. When I came back from Kibbutz Ein Tzurim, to spend another week in Jerusalem, I knocked on his door (he sold books from his home). More often than not, he would open the door with a grunt, "Uh." This was not due to lack of manners. You see, Reb Shmuel believed that we sin far more with what comes out of our mouths than what goes into our mouths. And therefore he would very often take upon himself a *ta'anit dibbur*, a fast from speaking. So if he would grunt in his greeting, I understood that he was fasting. "Uh, uh" – two grunts meant he had a good book for me. "Uh, uh, uh," – meant *yekar hametziot*, a very excellent book at a bargain price. So I was expecting a grunt. This time, however, he opened the door, embraced me, and was quite verbose, voluble, affable: "Reb Shlomo, how are you?" I said, "Reb Shmuel, how come you're so gregarious?" He looked at me smilingly, saying, "Haven't you heard?" And he grabbed my hand: "The Messiah is in Jerusalem."

Okay, I smiled to humor him, and he gave me some very special *sefarim*. I left, but I felt a growing sensation in my gut, in my soul, that I couldn't quite explain. I went to the Kotel, where I prayed *Minḥa* and *Ma'ariv*. I felt as though I were waiting for something – or someone. The next morning I went back for *Shaharit*. I don't usually do that, but I felt that if the Messiah was indeed in Jerusalem, he would show himself first at the Kotel.

I found it difficult to leave the Kotel. That night after dark I listened to all the news reports, figuring that maybe I would hear an announcement that the Messiah was here. Finally that evening, I had to take my plane back to New York. I knocked on the door of Reb Shmuel's home. He was surprised to see me. "I already supplied you with *sefarim*," he said.

I said to him, "I don't understand, you told me that the Messiah is in Jerusalem. I went to the Kotel for every prayer service since I saw you. I looked, I waited: no Messiah." He looked at me and smiled. He said, "Reb Shlomo, Reb Shlomo, *ir macht a groisen taus* – you're making a very big mistake. You think we have to look for the Messiah. You think we have to wait for the Messiah. But it's the opposite. The Messiah is looking for us. The Messiah is waiting for you."

I went out shaken. I felt the Messiah really was in Jerusalem, but whether or not he would be revealed depended on us, and I was part of the "us."

* * *

I went to Ein Tzurim that summer with my whole family and we had a wonderful time. Since respect in kibbutz society is definitely related to work (*avoda*), at least as much as Torah, I volunteered to work – with the cows. I chose that particular branch of kibbutz "employment" since milking the cows on the 3:30 A.M. shift was one of the most unpopular duties on the schedule; I felt that if I volunteered for that, I would be freed from working at any other time during the day. Since I wanted a block of time each day for study and writing, this particular duty suited my schedule perfectly.

I grew to love and anticipate my two nocturnal hours in the *refet* (cowshed). The silent walk under the star-filled skies, the closeness to the cows who would look up at me trustingly as I adjusted the milking implements, the proximity to nature above me and beside me, and the sense afterwards that I had succeeded completely in properly performing a specific task that had a beginning and an end, gave me a sense of exhilaration that was deeply satisfying. Often, my then four-year-old son, Hillel, would ask me to wake him up and bring him along. The first time he came, he was full of questions: about the cows, the source of the milk, the little calves nearby. Suddenly his face lit up: "Abba, you mean cows have milk just like Imma has milk, and Imma cows feed their babies just like Imma feeds Yoni? You mean Hashem made a world where Immas can always feed their little babies who can't get food for themselves?" Suddenly I sensed, along with my son, the magnificent harmony of the world, the connection between heaven and earth, the goodness of God within every aspect of a perfect, interrelated and interdependent creation, the all within the All. And for me it was not by accident that I felt this profound unity with all of creation especially in Israel!

It was also that first summer on Kibbutz Ein Tzurim that I met a most extraordinary individual: Moshe Moshkovitz, known to all as "Moshko." He came from Gush Etzion, actually from Moshav Masuot Yitzḥak. There had been four settlements in Gush Etzion in the 1940s. When the massacre by the Jordanian Legion took place and the four settlements fell, very few people survived. He was one of them because he had been sent on a special mission to Cyprus just before the attack.

The survivors were taken into Jordanian captivity. When they were released nine months later, the State of Israel had already been declared and they reestablished three of the four fallen settlements in the Ashkelon/Ashdod region – Ein Tzurim, Masuot and Revadim. Moshko was the *rosh hamo'etza* (municipal head), the "mayor," of that area and he was very well connected politically. He was one of the important advisors to the Minister of the Interior at that time, Yosef Burg.

Moshko sat in one of my classes. Afterwards he said, "What are you doing in America? We need you in Israel." I said that my life's dream was *aliya*, but that I had not been able to find a job in Israel, though not through lack of trying.

He told me that he had attended my synagogue in Lincoln Square, and that he thought I could make a very important contribution to Israel. He invited me to go on a short trip with him so that he could better explain his idea to me.

He took me in his car to an empty hill that was to someday become Efrat. He looked at me and said, "You know, they once asked Dizengoff, the first mayor of Tel Aviv, how one could become the mayor of a city in Israel. Dizengoff responded, 'In Israel, if you want to become the mayor of a city, you have to build the city.' Golda Meir wrote into Israel's law books that a city could be established in this location, with the condition that it be a city founded by new immigrants from countries of plenty like America and South Africa [*sic*], educated immigrants who were coming out of choice, rather than escaping from poverty or persecution. Let us be partners. You find the new immigrants and I will take care of the Israeli bureaucracy. And you'll see: in a short time, a city will stand on this spot, a city in which I will be the mayor and you will be the chief rabbi."

We shook hands, and I *davened Minḥa* on that spot. I believed it could happen. My dream of *aliya* had been fully resurrected.

Chapter Sixty-Eight

The Opportunity of Change, the Sanctity of Renewal

I returned to America with my family, and at the instigation of a close student and friend, Dr. Ralph (Menaḥem) Marcus, we started an organization called Reishit Geula – the Beginning of the Redemption. Those who joined came from the ranks of the members of the Lincoln Square Synagogue, as well as the many hundreds who came to Torah lectures every week – 195 families made a $1,500 deposit for an eventual home in Efrat.

Moshko, of course, as the head of the Israel-based *Ḥevra LePituaḥ Arei Yehuda*, the Development Company of the Cities of Judah, continued to lobby his considerable political connections in Israel. Meanwhile, every summer I returned to Kibbutz Ein Tzurim as scholar-in-residence, and would bike from Ein Tzurim to Masuot Yitzḥak to see Moshko every day. As we began to see progress, I would visit Israel and Moshko in the winter as well.

During this period there were many disappointments in addition to minor victories. The most important issue to be dealt with was the exact legal status of the land on which we wished to build Efrat. If there were Arabs who could in any way prove ownership of the land – and the Land Authority Registry (*Tabu*) had the names, going back many years, of anyone who had assumed ownership – then the Israeli Government, as well as I, personally, would not consider building there.

The Supreme Court of Israel dealt with this issue from 1977–81, carefully checking every Arab claim and investigating the status of every inch of land. In the meantime, my family would spend each summer on the kibbutz, intensifying our relationship with the Noimans, gaining greater fluency in Hebrew and feeling more and more a part of Hebrew-speaking Israeli society.

At one point in the late 1970s, I was visited in New York by Ḥayyim Nadivi, a close friend of Moshko's, who had a responsible position directing religious settlements. He offered me a hill in Sha'ar HaGai, which he said was a much "surer bet" than Efrat. I said I would much rather take my chances with a city between Hebron and Jerusalem than a city between Tel Aviv and Jerusalem. After all, Abraham and Sarah started out in Hebron and Jewish history will culminate with the Messiah in Jerusalem.

And then another one of those special stories "happened" that only intensified my desire to "wait it out" for Efrat. Ein Tzurim was fast becoming our home-away-from-home, our *beit abba* in Israel. There was a kibbutz member (Mivtzari was his name, but everyone called him "Moshavnik") who prayed in the same row as Yehuda Noiman and me in the kibbutz synagogue. His father, who had lived in Kfar Hasidim near Haifa, died, and I joined a whole delegation from the kibbutz to attend the funeral. The funeral cortège was to proceed from the Yeshiva in Kfar Hasidim to the cemetery nearby, and the kibbutzniks arrived while the *tahara* – the purification of the body – was taking place inside the yeshiva. Two distinct groups were now waiting for this body to be brought out and for the eulogies to begin: the kibbutzniks, dressed in shorts, colored short-sleeved shirts and sandals; and the yeshiva students, garbed in black pants and white shirts. It was as if the two groups had an invisible *meḥitza* between them.

The rosh yeshiva, Rav Elya Mishkovsky, came out, viewed the assembly from the higher yeshiva portico, and seemed to have noticed my friend Yehuda Noiman. He actually then addressed him in Yiddish, "Yudke? Yudke *iluy*?" (Yudke is a Yiddish affectionate diminutive for Yehuda; *iluy* is Hebrew for "prodigy.") Yehuda, whom I knew as a rather shy and humble individual, turned red, blushed deeply, and responded in Hebrew, "Yes, Reb Elya, that's what they called me in the yeshiva of Rav Shach in Petaḥ Tikva, where we studied together." The rosh yeshiva's eyes narrowed. He asked, in Yiddish, "But what happened to you. I know you left the Yeshiva, but how did Rav Shach allow you to leave? You, too, could have been a rosh yeshiva." Yehuda answered in Hebrew, and by this time everyone, from both groups, was listening to the conversation intently. "Rav Shach sent me many letters urging me to stay." Reb Elya, the rosh yeshiva, seemed to rise to his full height, literally looking down at my friend, and said strongly (but not harshly) in Yiddish – perhaps more to his students than to my friend: "And those letters of our Rebbe will serve as a prosecuting attorney when you stand before the throne of God after a hundred and twenty years."

I felt very sorry for Yehuda. I didn't think my laid-back, self-effacing friend would give any answer at all. But he responded immediately, decisively, and in Hebrew, "And the kibbutz that I helped build, and the guns that I used in the wars that I fought, and the souls of the many Israeli Jews whose lives I protected – they will be my defense attorneys. And they will win the day and exonerate me before God."

The rosh yeshiva took a step backward. He realized that he had lost that first round, and apparently decided not to continue the debate. Again he said in Yiddish, but this time with a smile on his face and in his voice, "*Bist nuch dee zelbe yudke, dee zelbe iluy.*" "You remained the same Yudke, the same prodigy." My friend didn't let it rest. He responded in Hebrew, "No, Reb Elya, I didn't remain the same Yudke that I was in the Yeshiva. I changed. I saw the changes in history. I saw what our generation demanded. I think I even saw what God expected of me. I looked around myself at the ravages of the Holocaust. I understood that our era demanded that the kibbutz, and the battlegrounds of war, had to serve as the infrastructure for the establishment of the Jewish State, the first Jewish State in close to two thousand years. I didn't remain the same because Jewish history didn't remain the same. You remained the same. You didn't change."

The funeral began. But obviously the encounter was very important to me and all I could think of was the first commandment in the Torah, "*Haḥodesh hazeh lakhem Rosh Ḥodashim,* This renewal of the moon shall be for you a festival of the Beginning of the Months" (Exodus 12:2). Look at the moon, mark the changes of the moon, praise the God of Nature who brings forth the bright sliver of the new moon from a blackened, darkened sky, and realize that our God is a God of change and renewal, that our God wants us to change as times change, as needs change, as history changes. "*Binu shenot dor vador,* Understand the changes in each generation" (Deuteronomy 32:7).

God is the God of history. "I will be what I will be, *Ye-Ho-Va.*" He will bring about change. "The old must be renewed and the new must be sanctified." That's what Rav Kook taught. That's what Yehuda Noiman was expressing.

And that's why, even though it took time, it was worth working toward and waiting for Efrat, the bridge between Hebron and Jerusalem, past and future, tradition and redemption.

Perhaps five years later, shortly after we made our *aliya* to Israel, we joined the Noiman family at the IDF swearing-in ceremony of their younger son, Ḥanan, for the Golani Brigade. While we were still living in New York, their older son, Nadav, had been killed mountain climbing in the northern region of Israel, between Rosh HaShana and Yom Kippur, preparing himself for the army. I had flown in to spend a day of mourning with our friends, but of course I could only feel a very small part of their intense pain. Now, several years later as Ḥanan was shouting out, "I swear," in fealty to the State of Israel he was pledging to defend, I could see tears coursing down Yehuda's face. This was most uncharacteristic because kibbutzniks in general, and Yehuda in particular, are not known for expressing feelings. I whispered, "You must be thinking of Nadav." "No," he said, "not really. Of course I never stop thinking of Nadav, no matter whatever else I may be doing, or thinking, or studying or speaking. But at this moment I am thinking of Ḥanan and the great privilege that is his. After all, ours is the first generation after almost two thousand years of exile that is privileged to defend ourselves against our enemies, that can forge our destiny with our own hands. These are tears of joy, tears of pride…"

Chapter Sixty-Nine

The Lubavitcher Rebbe, Begin and Herzl Join Hands to Rescue Efrat

It was February of 1980, and I was scheduled to perform a wedding that Sunday night and then – the following morning – to board an El Al plane for Israel, where, after five long years of planning and lobbying, the laying of the cornerstone of Efrat would take place. But on that very Sunday evening of the wedding, I had also been invited by Rav Groner and Rav Krinsky to attend a very special *"farbrengen"* (Hasidic joyous gathering) at 770 Eastern Parkway, for the thirtieth anniversary of the Lubavitcher Rebbe, Rav Menaḥem Mendel Schneerson's *nesiut* (presidency) as the leader of Chabad. I had sought a blessing for Efrat from the Rebbe several months prior to that gala occasion, but unfortunately his health had not permitted a meeting. His two *gabbai'im* hoped that it might be possible for me to open a few moments of conversation with the Rebbe at the gala event itself.

I arrived at the hall at 770 Eastern Parkway, which was teeming with people, shortly before midnight, directly from my wedding in Queens and just as my teacher and mentor, Rav J.B. Soloveitchik, was taking his leave. The Rav and the Rebbe had a close and long-standing relationship, harking back to when they were students together at the University of Berlin. I heard the Rebbe refer to the Rav as *lamdan hador* (the most learned scholar of the generation), and then I was ushered to a seat in close proximity to the dais, not far from where the Rav had previously been sitting. I felt that the Rebbe looked directly into my eyes as he raised a glass of wine in my direction, mouthing the traditional *leḥayyim* (to life) blessing, but I'm certain that many others thought that he was gazing directly at them as well. I thrilled to the Rebbe's rendition of *Tzama Lekha Nafshi* ("My soul yearns for You, O Lord"). I understood that personal conversation with the Rebbe would be impossible and rose to attention when, after several hours, the Rebbe began to exit the hall.

As it turned out, the Rebbe passed directly in front of me. This time he really did look into my eyes, and said in Yiddish, "Rav Riskin, the Rebbe has you in his prayers every day." I felt discombobulated, overcome with emotion, and blurted out that I was on the way to Israel for the laying of the cornerstone of Efrat and would greatly appreciate the Rebbe's blessing. "May the Lord prosper your ways," the Rebbe said. He then continued a few steps, turned back in my direction, and repeated, "May the Lord prosper your ways." (*Hashem yatzliaḥ et derakhekha*).

Without going home first, I made my way to the airport feeling as though I could fly to Israel even without an airplane, merely on the wings of the Rebbe's twice-expressed blessing. When I arrived at Ben Gurion, however, I was shocked to find Moshko waiting for me at the airport, something he had never done before. "I came to tell you to turn around, go back to New York," he said sadly. "I tried to reach you but couldn't [this was 1980, before the age of cell-phones; I had truly been unreachable from the time of the wedding in Queens to the time I arrived in Tel Aviv]. A yeshiva student in Hebron, named Yehoshua Saloma, was murdered last week, and the Knesset (Israeli Cabinet) ordered a moratorium on all new settlements. I'm sorry, but there won't be a cornerstone-laying ceremony, not this week, and perhaps – with this loss of momentum – not at all!"

I told him of the Rebbe's blessing – actually the Rebbe's two blessings – and although I'm not officially a Hasid, I felt confident that there would definitely be a cornerstone-laying ceremony for Efrat and that I wasn't returning to New York without one. Moshko looked at me as though I had fallen on my head, but offered me a ride in his car to Kibbutz Ein Tzurim. On the way, I asked who could possibly overrule the Cabinet decision. Only the prime minister, Menaḥem Begin, he said. And how could we get to the prime minister? After thinking for a while, Moshko said that the member of Knesset closest to Menaḥem Begin who would be sympathetic to the cause of Efrat was Rav Ḥayyim Druckman, but he was recuperating from a recent heart attack. Nevertheless, Moshko pulled into the next gas station, started to dial Rav Druckman's number, and almost apologetically mentioned to me, "I guess the Rebbe's blessing got to me, too."

Rav Druckman understood the urgency of the situation; a significant delay could abort our entire project. He promised to leave his sick bed, meet with the prime minister and attempt to secure a meeting for us as soon as possible. That evening we got the word: a meeting would take place with the prime minister that Thursday morning at his Knesset office.

I asked my wife and a number of our big financial supporters to fly in for what I hoped would be a momentous meeting. The prime minister welcomed us most graciously, but said that unfortunately, his hands were tied; the Cabinet had taken a unanimous vote to freeze all new settlement building. I told him how we had been planning Efrat for five years, since 1976, and that 195 families had given a significant down payment for a home in Efrat. I gave him the list of all the families and their New York addresses. The prime minister had tears in his eyes, and then he looked at me very closely. "You are familiar to me," he said. "Did we meet in Rav Soloveitchik's apartment? Did we not speak of how my father broke the lock on the door of the synagogue in Brisk in order to eulogize Theodore Herzl? Let the student of the grandson of the Brisker Rav benefit from the prophecy of Theodore Herzl and build his settlement." He asked his aide, Yeḥiel Kadishai, to get him a copy of Theodor Herzl's classic work, *The Jewish State*, which was apparently close at hand in the Knesset. After only a few moments of leafing through the pages, he read aloud Herzl's vision that once the State became a reality, "every congregation will settle in Israel, each congregation with its rabbi." In an emotion-charged voice, he said, "You are fulfilling Herzl's prophecy. How can I stop your progress? I will overrule the decision of the Cabinet. This Sunday you may have the cornerstone-laying ceremony, but with only two government ministers in attendance and without any publicity whatsoever."

I embraced him in gratitude. Somehow, "with no publicity whatsoever," there were more than three thousand people who came to the event. Somehow the Rebbe must have let them know...

Part IX

Coming Home 1983–Present

Chapter Seventy

Central Park West Bank and a Promise Fulfilled

When I first came to Efrat, it was with a great deal of excitement. I'd been in Lincoln Square Synagogue for nineteen years, and the community watched me leave with mixed feelings. Quite honestly, most of the leadership of the synagogue was certain that I'd be back in a year. I said that I was leaving the shul for *aliya* to Israel; they said that I was taking a year's leave of absence. They specifically hired an interim rabbi for one year only.

Nevertheless, they feted me with numerous tributes. There were a number of farewell parties, the most moving of which was at Zalman Bernstein's Pound Ridge home, where they presented me with a *sefer Torah,* which I brought with me when I came on *aliya*. That *sefer Torah* has since been in almost every new synagogue in Efrat, until each congregation received its own, and then I would loan it to the next newest synagogue (at the time of this writing, there are thirty-four synagogues with regular Shabbat services in Efrat). Soon I hope to be able to bring the *sefer Torah* back to my own home, where I have an *Aron Kodesh* waiting for it – but, truth to tell, I'd rather see Efrat synagogues continue to multiply.

The time of my *aliya* was very romantic and very exciting – until I actually arrived in Efrat and reality set in. The streets weren't paved, there were no private telephones – only one public telephone that generally didn't work – and during that first very rough winter we were often without heat, or electricity, or without either of the two.

Add to that the fact that within a few months I realized that I had no clear means of earning a livelihood for my wife and four children. The rabbinate in Efrat would be an elected position – and in order to teach I would have to first pass a special exam on all of *Shas* and *Poskim* (the whole of Talmudic and Responsa Literature) administered by a Council of the Chief Rabbinate. Ohr Torah Institutions opened when I arrived in Efrat (Elul, 1983) with one high school, Neveh Shmuel, which had twenty students. The only salary I actually received in hand was as the Rav of the *Beit Sefer*, the elementary school, which had only two grades: that job paid one-third of a rather modest full-time salary. For the first year, I was still being paid by Lincoln Square Synagogue for a year's leave of absence, but the year was quickly passing.

My family was still young, and I would get up in the middle of the night in a cold sweat, thinking that maybe I had made a terrible mistake. It was the kind of thing that was difficult for me to admit even to my wife. The fact was that we had sold our apartment in New York – even though the real estate experts (including my father-in-law) told us to rent it because Manhattan real estate was on the threshold of a boom – precisely because we didn't want an easy escape-hatch for a return to America. My fear was that I had no satisfactory job in sight in Israel, and no place to return to in New York.

We were renting a rather modest apartment in Efrat at that time. We had begun to build a home in Efrat when we still lived in New York, but the contractor had initially promised me that it wouldn't cost more than $100,000, which I could barely manage. In the meantime, upon arrival, we received a bill for $120,000 just for the skeleton alone, along with the explanation that there had been many price changes from the time that he had made the promise; now the completion of the house would cost $300,000. There was no way that I could afford such a price, and although I had made certain that the families I brought to Efrat were protected by legal counsel, I had never gotten a lawyer for myself. I began to panic, beset as I was by what appeared to be insurmountable problems.

Parenthetically, I would say that my wife was much more steadfast in her commitment to *aliya* than I was. Vicky said that even if she had to wash floors ("do *sponja*") we had come to Israel to stay! If Efrat didn't work out, there would be someplace else that would, and I needn't worry. But I was still very concerned and felt my responsibility for my family very deeply.

In the midst of all these difficult thoughts there was a knock on the door of our apartment. It was Yoni Ben-Ari, who was then in charge of security of the young community. "*Kevod HaRav*" (respected Rabbi), he said. "Take this Uzi. You have guard duty between two and six o'clock tomorrow morning."

My wife whispered to my older children, "If Abba is protecting us, maybe we should spend the night in Jerusalem."

Yoni understood, both from my wife's comment and by the way I looked at the Uzi, that I didn't quite know what to do with it. "You don't know how to shoot an Uzi?" he asked.

I said, "Listen Yoni, I don't think I've ever killed a mosquito in my life. How should I know how to shoot an Uzi?" He took me out to what passes for a forest in Efrat, an area of many trees that I affectionately call Central Park West Bank, and within short order I learned how to use an Uzi.

Sure enough, from 2:00 A.M. to 6:00 A.M. I had guard duty. My partner was a very fine young man who still lives in Efrat with his family. He came from Holland. We walked the outer periphery of inhabited Efrat at that time in about fifteen minutes. He spoke a flawless Hebrew, and he had come to many of the classes that I'd already begun to give as soon as I'd moved in.

We walked in the stillness of the night, completing a full circle every quarter of an hour. He asked me about my life prior to *aliya*, and I, of course, described what it was like being a rabbi in Lincoln Square, and the head of a number of yeshivot. I'm sure I described it nostalgically, even lovingly and yearningly, because as I mentioned, I was beginning to think that maybe I'd made a mistake by burning my bridges behind me.

Then I asked him about his life before his *aliya*. He told me the following: "Believe it or not, I was a Christian. I went to church every Sunday with my parents and brother. But on June 7, 1967, when I was a young high-school boy, nineteen years ago, I read something that changed my life. It was on the front page of the Dutch daily newspaper, a most laudatory story of the amazing Israeli victory in the Six Day War. From that moment on I became invested and involved – body and soul – in the State of Israel. I responded viscerally to the victory, to the salvation from enemy danger and destruction, to the gutsiness of a nation that emerged from the ashes of the Holocaust to recreate itself.

"When I had to write a senior paper for graduation the last year of high school, I chose to write on the burgeoning State of Israel. There was a compulsory draft in Holland, and everyone who is in the Dutch army is expected to talk to a clergyman of some kind. I found myself filling out the form with the request to talk to a rabbi, and I began learning how to read Hebrew.

"At home, one weekend, I was learning the Grace after Meals. The rabbi had given me a prayer book. And as I was trying to make out the words, I saw my mother mouthing the words in Hebrew. I was shocked, and when I asked how she knew this prayer, she smiled and explained that before the war she had worked as an *au pair* for a religious Jewish family. This seemingly inconsequential piece of information seemed to strengthen my resolve to learn even more about Judaism.

"Came the Yom Kippur War, and there was a call for volunteers to help on the farms. I volunteered. After all, the kibbutzniks were all fighting on the front lines of battle, and the fruits and vegetables needed to be gathered and harvested. Three Christian friends and I were sent to a non-religious kibbutz in the Galil. I was sparked and excited. I fell in love with the land. I fell in love with the people. I have a good ear for music and therefore picked up Hebrew very easily. I read a great deal about Jewish history, Jewish philosophy and Jewish religion. I decided then that I wanted to keep kosher, so I became a vegetarian. I also wanted to keep the Sabbath, and someone from the non-religious kibbutz suggested that maybe I should go to a special *ulpan*, a school for converts. There was one in Kfar Etzion, a kibbutz right near Efrat [this was before there ever was an Efrat].

"I went to Kibbutz Kfar Etzion and joined the school for converts. After an intensive period of study, I was assigned a date to go to the *mikveh,* to immerse and to convert. I felt that the time had come to tell my parents. After all, conversion was a rather momentous decision for a nineteen-year-old to make by himself.

"I called home and told my parents that I had an important matter to discuss with them. They immediately sent me a plane ticket, and after a vegetarian dinner with them, I announced that I wanted to convert to Judaism and live my life in Israel.

"My mother broke out in a cold sweat and fainted. When she was revived, she said to me, 'You don't have to convert. You're Jewish because I'm Jewish. I'm the daughter of the *ḥazan,* the cantor, of the main shul in the town where my parents were murdered in front of my eyes. Before the Nazis shot my father dead, he cried out "*Shema Yisrael Adonai Eloheinu Adonai Eḥad,*" but to no avail. While being transported in the crowded, smelly cattle-car to Theresienstadt concentration camp, I felt that if one Holocaust was occurring, a second was even more likely, and I did not want my grandchildren, my great-grandchildren, to suffer as I was suffering. I took an oath that if I ever got out of that hell-hole, it would be as a Christian, and not as a Jew.

'I got out, I don't know how or why. I had no one to answer to because all of my blood relatives were murdered in the Holocaust, so I became a Christian. The only one until this point who knew of my Jewish background was your father. But if you wish to rejoin the religion of my parents and grandparents, may the God in whom I can no longer believe, bless you and keep you.'"

In the stillness of the night, doing guard duty in the young city of Efrat, all I could think of was a four-thousand-year-old promise that Moses gave to the Jewish people in God's name. Yes, you will be exiled. Yes, you will be persecuted. Yes, you will be scattered to the four corners of the world. Nevertheless, "Even if you are scattered to the ends of the heavens, from there the Lord your God will gather you, and from there will He take you up... and return you to the land of your fathers" (Deuteronomy 30:4–5).

The promise is being fulfilled. It is being fulfilled in our generation.

Gone were all my questions. I understood that Israel was not only my final destination, but it was the destiny of my family and my people. I understood as deeply as anyone could understand that no matter the unpaved streets, the lack of heat or electricity, the financial insecurity – I had finally come home.

My faith was truly confirmed that momentous night of my guard duty. The fulfillment of God's covenant, the security of the Jewish people, the ultimate perfection of the world and world peace, will emanate from Israel and Jerusalem.

If we've come so far, since the Holocaust, to have realized Moses' prophecy, we will come to the next stage, to realize the vision of our prophets, that "From Zion shall come forth Torah and the word of God from Jerusalem… Nation will not lift up sword against nation and humanity will not learn war anymore…" (Isaiah 2; Micah 4).

POST SCRIPT:

I had the privilege not long ago of performing the wedding of the eldest son of my guard-duty partner. Avishai is a pilot in the IDF, an Air Force career man, his *tzitzit* blending in with his pilot's uniform. Unfortunately, his paternal grandmother couldn't make it to the wedding. Throughout the ceremony, however, I could hear her saying, "I was wrong; my father was right when he said the *Shema*. If he sees this wedding from his place on high – and I believe he does – he is whispering '*Moshiach tzeiten*,' these are nothing less than the days of the Messiah…"

Chapter Seventy-One

The Birth of Ohr Torah Israel: God Is My Partner in Institutional Fundraising

From time immemorial, Jewish institutions have required – and received – necessary financial help from generous donors. There were even names of donors on important places in the Holy Temple. And generally speaking, anyone who is involved in creating and directing Torah institutions must also take responsibility for acquiring the necessary financing for them. As Efrat has grown, so have the Ohr Torah Stone high schools, colleges and graduate schools, and so have my financial obligations.

Strangely enough, I have come to find the fund-raising aspect of my responsibilities deeply satisfying. When people give you their money they also give you their trust; as a result, mutually caring relationships emerge with donors, and I often feel that I have developed an international community of close friends who are among the most committed and generous Jews in the world.

I have heard many individuals say that the one thing they cannot do is ask for money. I must say that the one thing I find it easy to ask for is money – primarily because I don't believe that money in itself has intrinsic value, whereas Torah, and especially Torah education, has unlimited value. In effect, therefore, I am facilitating the opportunity for an individual to take what is a mere medium of exchange – in itself devoid of value – and transform it, exchange it, for the most significant and valuable commodity in a Jew's life.

My mother always explained why I eventually found the funds for my projects. She said it was a function of the fact that I myself have neither an understanding of nor an appreciation for money. Hence, I have no difficulty in asking for comparatively large sums, and getting them from those with means. My mother certainly had a point; to this day I don't know how much money I earn, nor do I have a checkbook that I sign. My wife has managed the family finances from the day we were married, and others in my organizations have the day-to-day responsibility of the proper allocation of funds.

I then read a story that supported my mother's contention. Rav Yosef Yozel was an outstanding disciple of Rav Yisrael Salanter (1800–1870), founder of the *Musar* (Ethicist) movement. He began the first Nevardok Yeshiva that, in addition to Talmudic learning, attempted to train students to be indifferent to human attitudes and expectations, but to be extremely punctilious in trying to fulfill Divine attitudes and expectations. There were 180 Nevardok yeshivot in Europe between the World Wars; only one survived the Holocaust.

One of Rav Yosef Yozel's students displayed neither competence nor interest in learning, so he was asked to leave the yeshiva. The student was accepted to another Talmudical academy, where he stayed without much accomplishment for two years, after which he became greatly successful in business. Rav Yosef Yozel went to visit this former student, and came away with one million rubles, a large enough contribution to enable him to build a new Nevardok yeshiva in a neighboring town.

The other yeshiva dean, the one who had admitted this former student to his yeshiva after he had been expelled by Rav Yozel, excitedly made an appointment to see this now wealthy businessman. He thoroughly expected that if Rav Yosef Yozel had gotten one million rubles, he would receive at least double that amount. After all, he had taken him in to his yeshiva! You can imagine his surprise and chagrin when he was given only eighteen rubles; he asked for an explanation, unable to conceal his disappointment in the lack of gratitude this student was displaying.

"I will gladly tell you why," said the former student. "When Rav Yosef Yozel came into my home, he didn't even remove his muddied shoes. He paid no attention to my expensive furniture or precious artistic pieces. Rather he immediately began impressing upon me the need for another yeshiva to stem the tide of assimilation that was a result of the *Haskala* (Enlightenment) that was overtaking European Jewry.

"I must admit that I fell under his spell. As he spoke, only the yeshiva assumed importance; my wealth lost all the glitter and allure and I gladly gave him a million rubles.

"You, on the other hand, entered my doorway, looked wide-eyed at all my home furnishings, and immediately removed your shoes so as not to sully my carpet. You appeared to be walking on eggshells, and you kept referring to me as 'Reb Shimon.' Now you and I both know that my knowledge of Torah would not engender your respect; it must be my money. And when I saw the appreciation and wonder in your eyes as they feasted upon my material objects, I, too, began to value my money and fancy lifestyle even more than before. Therefore, when under your influence, I couldn't bring myself to part with any more than eighteen rubles…"

There is also another and even more important reason for success in fund-raising. It's called *siyata dishmaya*, help from Heaven. I truly believe that if you are honestly trying to do God's work as a very junior partner, the Senior Partner in Heaven will never let you down. There is a Sabbath afternoon song (*zemira*) based upon a Talmudic guarantee (Babylonian Talmud, Tractate *Shabbat*) whose refrain repeats: "Borrow from Me, My children…" God is speaking to would-be donors and suggesting that they give money to charity even when they don't have the money; God will pay them back. I take this guarantee seriously, and so I never have compunctions about borrowing from the bank to build a yeshiva, or about mortgaging my own home to meet payroll. And so far, I have never been disappointed.

The fact is that my earliest successful experiences at Lincoln

Square Synagogue encouraged and inspired me to embark on even greater projects. I've already related how we acquired a prime piece of property, initially valued at $250,000 in 1963, for a $5,000 down-payment. When we embarked on a building campaign for an edifice, which was to cost $1,250,000, the professional fundraising organization we hired made a market study and concluded that we would never be able to raise $250,000. The fact that the developing neighborhood was "arty," avant-garde, intellectual and areligious would seem to vindicate the market study's claim. They declined our request to become their clients.

I refused to give up. I went to see Jack Resnick, a prominent real estate developer in the area, who – although he was not an Orthodox Jew – had given me $1,000 toward that $5,000 down-payment I needed a few years previously. I told him about the market study and sought his advice.

"Do you believe that you can succeed?" he asked me.

"I certainly do," I replied. "Doesn't the fact that our apartment is now filled to overflowing with more than a hundred worshipers each Shabbat and the same number for Wednesday evening classes – most of whom were non-religious only a year ago – prove the market study wrong?"

He smiled. "I'm a businessman," he said. "I believe in people who believe in their product. Here is a $10,000 check for your new building."

That gift convinced the board to go ahead with the project even without professional fund-raisers. And, as our sages of the Talmud teach us, "If one attempts to purify, he is helped from Above." We raised not only the $1,250,000 for the building, we also raised a deeply observant Jewish community in that "intellectual, avant-garde, areligious" community on the West Side of Manhattan, with close to a thousand Shabbat worshipers and 1,600 attending Torah classes each week.

* * *

There is an even more remarkable fund-raising *siyata dishmaya* story, this one bound up with the origins of Ohr Torah Stone Institutions in Israel.

I was still living in America, but planning to make *aliya* to Efrat within the year. I would spend the morning at the American Ohr Torah Schools, then in Queens, and, at about three o'clock in the afternoon, I would go to Lincoln Square Synagogue for the rest of the day.

I got a call one afternoon, and the caller was speaking to me in Yiddish, weeping between his words. It was hard for me to ascertain precisely what was bothering him. Finally, the story emerged that his only son, who was a yeshiva high school graduate, had fallen in love with a Gentile from Italy, and was about to marry her. And he said, "Only you can save my son's life and my life. My wife wears a *sheitel* [wig worn by women for religious purposes]. We observe everything in our home. For me to have a son marrying out of the faith is the end of the world."

The elderly gentleman insisted on continuing his tale in person and he came to see me. He seemed to be in his seventies, wearing an old gray hat, a rumpled gray suit and a spotted gray tie. He told me that his son came to my Wednesday-evening lectures and had even quoted many of my ideas. He begged me, with tears in his eyes, to save the situation. I said I would try to talk to his son; I called the young man out of the blue, and he agreed to meet with me.

The young man looked little older than a teenager. He told me that, indeed, he was about to marry an Italian Gentile woman, but that he had not been religious for a long time. Religion didn't concern him too much, although he did enjoy listening to my lectures, he said. When I pressed him about his yeshiva high school experience, he certainly did not lead me to believe that it was negative. His memories from his parents' home were also positive. So, I decided to play very harsh therapy with him. "I'm sure the woman is a lovely person, who certainly is not to blame. But you are a Jew who has had many generations of Jewishness reinforced within you by a religious home and a superb religious education. If your children are not Jewish – since the religion of the children follows that of the mother – you, as an only child, will be destroying the Jewishness of all the generations that came before you. You are committing a form of Jewish homicide." He began to weep: "What can I do? I love her." When I ascertained that conversion was out of the question, I took a deep breath and said, "Forget that I'm a rabbi for a minute. She's going back to Italy; go back with her. Live with her if you must, but don't marry her. Don't form a lasting relationship, at least not yet. After all, you're very young. Tell her you're simply too young to get married."

He took my advice.

Time passed. About a week before we were to make *aliya* I was at school. The phone rang. I heard the Yiddish voice of the man with the gray hat and the gray suit and the gray tie. He said to me, "Rabbi, I have to see you right away. It's a *sha'as hakosher,* an opportune time." When he arrived, he explained: "Rabbi, this is the moment that I've been waiting for. My son had an appendicitis attack in Italy. He was flown from Italy to New York and he's in Roosevelt Hospital on Ninth Avenue, not far from Lincoln Square Synagogue. He's just come out of the recovery room; he's very weak. If you just say the right word, you'll get him to give up the non-Jew."

So I went to Roosevelt Hospital. I was told at the desk that this young man had already been transferred to his room, but as I neared the room, I heard shouts and loud screams. Somewhat alarmed, I walked into the hospital room and what greeted my eyes was the chalk-white patient and two women, one considerably older than the other, locked in what appeared to be a wrestling match. A *sheitel* was on the floor, which apparently fell or was pushed off the head of the older woman.

When things returned to normal, the story began to emerge. The young man's mother had rushed to the hospital to be with her son, and was quite surprised to find the Italian Gentile in the room. The mother must have asked the girlfriend to leave, to which the young woman had responded, "I have more right to be here than you. We live together." The two women began shouting at one another, and the shouts turned to blows. The Gentile woman was very much hurt that her "significant other" hadn't taken her side in the altercation; she left as soon as I arrived. The young man, who was post-op, looking very wan and pale, took my hand and said, "Rabbi, thank you for coming. This was the ugliest scene I've ever witnessed in my life. I can never look at that woman again after she lifted her hand against my mother. Our relationship is over."

* * *

Shortly after this incident, we moved to Israel; as you shall soon see, it was an important segue between my life in America and my new life in Efrat.

I very much wanted to pursue an active life in Israel where I was desperate to make a contribution – I had neither the disposition nor the financial wherewithal to retire (I was only forty-three years old) – and since Gush Etzion at that time had many youngsters but no high school, I laid the groundwork for the Neveh Shmuel High School of Ohr Torah while I was still in New York. It was initially situated in the synagogue building of Elazar, across the road from Efrat, since Efrat had no vacant buildings at the time. As soon as we received the funds for a building, which we received from Fred and Susan Ehrman, we moved "Neveh Shmuel" to Efrat. The then Minister of Education, Zevulun Hammer, *z"l*, and Zevulun Orlev, his Director General, were most encouraging, waiving much bureaucracy to pave the way for the opening of the school. I felt good about arriving in Israel with a yeshiva in which to be involved.

I had appointed a director general, David Freund, and thought everything was going well. The school was up and running, we had twenty students, a rosh yeshiva (Rav Shimon Golan), a principal (Meir Krauss), and a *ram* (Rav Shuki Reich). I was also teaching, but felt that I needed that first year to become acclimated to Israel and Israeli students before assuming a major teaching role.

Then, suddenly, four months into that first school year, my director general told me that we were $500,000 in arrears. The bank, unlike American banks, had allowed our debts to accumulate. I had naively thought that the Ministry of Education took care of all the bills, so had I understood from my talks with Zevulun Hammer. However, what was true of a school with hundreds of students is not true of a start-up school of twenty students. When I discovered the depth of my naivety, I panicked.

I went to America with a very clear goal. I had to come back with $500,000, or I'd have to close the school almost before it began. Perhaps I'd even be forced back to America with my tail between my legs because of the students who would be without a school, and the individuals who had been hired and could not be paid. I was given an office at Lincoln Square Synagogue and a telephone. I had to raise money in a hurry, and I began to call people. I quickly discovered that many congregants were resentful, even angry, over my leaving, and had no real desire to help me. I began to fear that my future in Israel was behind me.

To add to my discomfort, there was only one public telephone in Efrat at the time. My whole family, wife and four children, would stand outside the phone on Friday when I would call home and try to bless my children trans-Atlantically. At least every other week the phone was out of order. It was a very cold winter, replete with sleet, rain and snow, and, of course, barely an intermittent supply of heat and electricity. My youngest son, Yoni, once got on the phone with me and asked me to come home. "If you were home, Abba, I'm sure the house would be warm. I'm freezing." You can imagine how torn I was, but I felt that I could not return to Efrat a failure. Our entire *aliya*, our very future, was at stake.

When I had left America, there was one individual who had promised me that he would never let me down. He was one of the only congregants who greatly encouraged my going to Israel. It was Daniel S. Abraham, the creator of Slim-Fast®. I telephoned him. He was very busy and didn't always answer his phone calls. I finally went to his office and sat in front of his door until he came out and almost fell over me. When I told him my story and I reminded him of his promise, he made out a $250,000 check to me on the spot. I felt heartened to continue my quest for the rest.

But after that, I would get $18, maybe $100 from other individuals. I hardly earned enough to cover the bare necessities that I needed to live every day. I was living in my in-laws' home at 200 Central Park South, so my expenses were minimal, but I was at my wits' end. I started going through the Rolodex of Lincoln Square Synagogue, name by name.

In the midst of all of this I got a call. I recognized the distinctive Yiddish voice of my friend with the gray suit. He said to me in Yiddish that he needed to see me, that everything with his son was fine, and that he wanted to thank me in person for having broken up the relationship between his son and the Italian Gentile. I told him that his thanks were not necessary, that I had had nothing to do with it; it was God. The young man had seen his mother struck by this woman, and he could never have any feelings for her again. Nevertheless, his father insisted he wanted to see me. I agreed to meet him at the synagogue the next day at 1:00 P.M.

Meantime, from 9:00 the next morning, I was sequestered in my office, making calls and getting nowhere. At about 3:30 I left the office to go to the men's room, and saw my friend with the gray suit sitting there. I had completely forgotten about the appointment; I had no secretary to tell me that he had come. I was extremely embarrassed, even mortified, at having kept him waiting for two and a half hours! He had been too refined to knock on my office door.

I apologized profusely and told him that I was under tremendous pressure. First he said to me that he wanted to thank me. Again I told him that it was God he ought to thank, that I hadn't done anything. And then he had a request. His son was about to marry a Jewish woman from a wonderful family. Would I please officiate at the marriage? The wedding was to be three months hence.

I tried to explain my situation. "Listen, I don't even know where I'm going to be living, or what I'm going to be doing in three months' time. Everything is up in the air right now. I'm under extreme financial strain. I can't guarantee anything. I can't commit myself to anything."

He said to me, "Rabbi, I understand. At least allow me to show you how much I appreciate what you did; it was much more than what you think you did. Let me give you a gift." I said, "No, no I don't take any gifts for myself." "Then let me give you a gift for the yeshiva," he said.

I thought to myself, what is he going to give me, $18, $25? Let him rather buy a new tie! "I really don't need anything," I said. He took out his checkbook and he said to me, "Rabbi, if I give you $350,000, will you officiate at my son's wedding in a few months?"

That individual has since given several million dollars to us. And that was when I realized that when you're trying to do something for the sake of Heaven, Heaven helps.

Chapter Seventy-Two

Horodenke Hasidim Picket – Ohr Torah Gains a *Beit Midrash*

A good friend and emissary of Chabad, Rav Ḥayyim Farrow, invited me to lecture at a Jewish Center he had established in Manchester, England, in the winter of 1996. I planned for a week of lectures and meetings in London, and set aside Tuesday for Manchester. Rav Ḥayyim took me by train from London, we arrived in Manchester shortly before sunset, and went for the afternoon prayers to the most conveniently located synagogue, the *shtiebl* of the Horodenke Hasidim (about whom I had heard nothing prior to my trip). During the repetition of the *Amida,* I noticed a large notice on the wall forbidding any God-fearing Jew to be contaminated by a particular lecturer coming to town. Curious as to the identity of the object of this "*pashkevil*" (best translated as "damning indictment") and wondering who the British "heretic of the month" happened to be, I inched closer to the notice in order to read its contents. You can imagine my shock to discover that the *pashkevil* referred to me!

A close reading of the indictment revealed that my heresy lay in an article on Moses that I had published in my weekly *Jerusalem Post* column. I had suggested that, while Moses succeeded more than any other human being in relaying the will of the Divine to all generations in the form of the five Books of Moses, which were in actuality the word of the living God (Maimonides says in the *Guide for the Perplexed* that Moses' active intellect perceived and actually kissed the Divine Active Intellect), he failed as a politician; he failed in his duty to convince the Israelites to conquer and settle the land of Israel. Apparently the Hasidim (or the Rebbe, or both) believed it heretical to critique Moses in any form whatsoever.

I quickly looked around and realized that no one recognized me. I showed Rav Farrow the *pashkevil*; he was as surprised as I was, but he was certain that none of the Horodenke Hasidim would have come to the lecture in any case. And as far as his (and my) natural audience was concerned, they paid no mind to what the Horodenke thought anyway.

After a quiet dinner with Rav Farrow, we set out at the appointed time for the lecture hall – only to hear loud shouts and the stamping of feet emanating from the direction of the Jewish Center. We were shocked to see about fifty Hasidim loudly picketing the lecture, urging that nobody attend, and claiming that, at the very least, they would disrupt the proceedings. The police had been summoned, more than five hundred attendees packed the hall as a result of the ruckus (we certainly hadn't expected more than two hundred), and reporters from the *Manchester Evening News* and the *Jewish Chronicle* were getting interviews and anxiously awaiting the lecture – and the real action – to begin.

The police kept the picketers outside maintaining a semblance of order and quiet. I gave the lecture to what appeared to be a most appreciative audience without making reference to the outside overflow, and when I went to pray in another synagogue in Manchester the following morning, I was given a standing ovation by the congregants. The *Jewish Chronicle* made a front page story of the incident.

But the truly important aspect of my treatment at the hands of the Horodenke took place that Shabbat in London, and especially that

Saturday night. One of our Ohr Torah Stone institutions, Yeshivat Torat Yosef, had just moved campuses and was in desperate need of a study hall (*beit midrash*), which would cost $350,000. I had planned the England trip in the hope of receiving a significant portion of the funds, since many of our students traditionally came (and still come) from England. Unfortunately that was a difficult financial period for British Jewry, and even Clive Marks – who was one of my most beloved friends and among the most generous of my benefactors – would not even see me. "I know how precious your time is, Rabbi, and this time I won't be able to give you any donation at all." I felt that Manchester had only been the icing on a cake that had collapsed in the oven; I resolved to make the best of my visit from a Torah teaching perspective, and forget about the fundraising aspect.

That Shabbat I was scholar-in-residence in Ner Yisrael, the Hendon synagogue of my good friend and colleague, Rav Alan Kimchi. You can imagine my surprise upon seeing Clive Marks in the front row on Shabbat morning, since Ner Yisrael was not his synagogue. "I made arrangements to pray with you," he said. "When my rabbi is being attacked, his friends must stand with him. Please come to my home this evening." That Saturday night Adrienne and Clive Marks handed me a check for $350,000 to pay for the *beit midrash*. I sent a thank-you letter to the Horodenke Rebbe.

Chapter Seventy-Three

The Lubavitcher Rebbe Still Keeps Watch: A Rabbinical Seminary Is Born

I had been living in Israel for two years and seen the establishment of the Neveh Shmuel High School for young men in Efrat and the Neveh Channah High School for young women on Yellow Hill of Gush Etzion under the banner of Ohr Torah, a name I had brought with me from the West Side of Manhattan, Riverdale and Queens (Manhattan Day School Ohr Torah, and the Ohr Torah High Schools). I was also directing and teaching in a special *kollel* in Jerusalem set up by the Rothschild Foundation (then headed by Arthur Fried and Moshe Berlin) to train young rabbinical students for rabbinical positions in South America.

One rainy Thursday afternoon – after an especially busy day at the end of a frustratingly busy week – I took my half-hour break between *kollel* classes at a nearby restaurant, Leah's, on Keren Kayemet, less than two blocks from the *kollel* on Al Ḥarizi. I felt I needed to clear my head over a cup of hot soup and a brief period of isolation.

No sooner had I begun my soup than a spry, elderly, pleasant-faced woman came over to my table, introduced herself as a newly-established member of Lincoln Square Synagogue, and gently asked if I would mind her joining me for some soup and conversation. To be quite frank, I felt like saying that I really required a few quiet minutes alone – and had I done so, (God forbid), the subsequent history of my career in Israel may well have been far less fulfilling and exciting.

She told me that she was very enamored by what she had discovered at Lincoln Square Synagogue – an outreach center that attempted to reach and teach every Jew from whatever place on the religious-observance spectrum he or she happened to be – and that she, Gwendolyn Straus, would like to see more synagogues in that very same spirit and with that very same mission, all over America and even all over the world.

And since she was looking for a fitting manner in which to honor her husband's memory, she had decided that during her current trip to Israel (she had come with Amit Women, an organization in which she had been very active over the years), she would make an effort to track me down and suggest that I inaugurate the Joseph Straus Rabbinical Seminary to train outreach rabbis. She was ready to make an initial million-dollar commitment to get this project off the ground.

You can well imagine my grateful surprise – especially since I had almost aborted this historic meeting before it took place. Mrs. Straus and I took a trip to Efrat the next day, where we rented a space in the shopping center that served as the initial *beit midrash* for our rabbinical seminary. Mrs. Gwen Straus and I had our initial meeting in 1985. Now, twenty-five years later, we have some 350 rabbis and educators in synagogues and Jewish schools all over the world!

* * *

It was 1988, building the settlements was officially prohibited, and we at Ohr Torah had to find a new home for our rabbinical seminary, yeshiva *beit midrash* and dormitory since we had greatly outgrown our rental quarters in Efrat. There was a triangle of about sixty-five dunam of empty land adjacent to Kibbutz Migdal Oz, just a ten-minute walk from my home. We borrowed a million dollars from the bank, worked on the infrastructure, and brought in old caravans to serve as a dormitory, classrooms, and a *beit midrash* that filled up immediately. But how could I ever repay the bank?

I had planned a trip to Australia just at that time, built around a lecture to a large group of women on "love and marriage" sponsored by Stera Gutnick, the most intelligent, committed and charming wife of Rav Yosef Gutnick, special Australian emissary to Israel of the Lubavitcher Rebbe. Rav Yosef, emanating from a prominent rabbinical Australian family, had done enormously well financially, mining gold and diamonds after having received a blessing from the Rebbe. He built a magnificent *beit midrash*-synagogue-library in Melbourne, physically modeled after the building at 770 Eastern Parkway (Lubavitch headquarters), put up a kosher hotel with gourmet kosher food and a swimming pool not far from the synagogue, and had become a world-renowned philanthropist for worthy Jewish causes throughout Israel and the Diaspora.

Rav Yosef invited me to dinner at the hotel before my lecture. "I'm sure you didn't come to Australia to swim in our pool and eat in our hotel. What can I do for your institutions?" he asked. This was the first time I had met him so I believed I ought to begin slowly. "I am developing an outreach rabbinical seminary," I said. "Twenty-five thousand dollars a year would sponsor one rabbi. Three hundred and fifty thousand dollars would enable us to build a permanent *beit midrash*. And one million dollars would endow the land, with a naming opportunity for the entire rabbinical village we are developing.

Rav Gutnick suggested we adjourn our discussion until breakfast the following morning; in the meantime he would be the only "rooster" in attendance at my lecture with the special permission given to the husband of the organizer.

The next morning at breakfast he said that he had decided on the million and that he would like to name the village after his deceased mother, Kiryat Shoshana. After expressing my gratitude, I could not help but add, "I'm not a fool. I think my lecture was good, but it certainly wasn't worth a million dollars. What made you decide?"

He told me that he had made a call that previous night to Rav Yehuda Krinsky, his *meḥutan* (in-law), who was one of the two closest aides to the Lubavitcher Rebbe. He had heard from Rav Krinsky that the Rebbe had given me a special blessing for the rabbinical seminary, that it would "produce rabbis the world over who would be modern on the outside and Chabad on the inside." And, given such a blessing from the Rebbe, "the greater my investment, the greater will be the return for world Jewry." Apparently, the Rebbe continued to work overtime for the fulfillment of his blessing.

Chapter Seventy-Four

Ohr Torah Receives a Last Name

Irving Stone, CEO of American Greeting Corporation, Cleveland, Ohio, was a world-class philanthropist who had a very clearly defined philosophy of giving: his first priority was Jewish education, without which there was no hope of Jewish continuity; his second priority was compassionate loving kindness, for hospitals that tended to the sick and old-age homes that tended to the aged; his third priority was Israel, the blazing eternal light at the end of the very dark tunnel that had blacked out with the Holocaust, the *alt-neu* homeland that testified like nothing else to the eternity of our people.

At first I would come to his office for a once-yearly visit, meet with Morry Weiss, Irving's son-in-law and heir apparent, spend a few precious moments with Irving discussing an issue in Jewish education that had grabbed him at the time, and receive an $18,000 check for Ohr Torah.

But then, in the year 2000, when our schools were beginning to truly blossom and develop the foundation for a "Yeshiva University" in Israel – with six high schools, a burgeoning university program, a women's college, graduate school and yeshivat hesder, and a rabbinical seminary for men – Morry felt that the time was ripe for me to request a major gift to set us on our way. He said that this was an especially opportune moment, since one of Irving's major charitable institutions had just disappointed him very deeply; he discovered that the million dollars he had given for an educational institution had in reality gone into a family real estate business. He refused to sue that institution – since the last thing he wanted to do was cause a desecration of God's name by revealing the scandal – but he was certainly ready for a change in charitable allegiances. Morry further suggested that I prepare a booklet with a picture, brief educational description and budget outline, and number of students in each of our institutions, as well as an overall list of the Board of Directors and sources of funding. I would then be ready to approach Irving for a major gift – and I ought, at the same time, to think about a premises-naming opportunity that I could offer him.

The preparation of this booklet, which was really done by our Director of Development, David Katz, proved to be a real labor of love. I didn't begin our educational enterprise with a master plan; as and when I saw the necessity for each institution, we established it. I myself had never stopped to actually look at our then total of twelve (now twenty) separate institutions on nine campuses in Efrat, Gush Etzion and Jerusalem; and I had never stopped long enough to make an overall assessment of the unique contribution Ohr Torah was making, especially on the Israeli scene. Moreover, two of our major institutions are educating Diaspora students studying in Israel, and the rabbis and educators we produce are ministering all over the world.

I met with Irving in a truly fired-up mood myself, filled with gratitude to the Almighty for having caused so many wonderful things to happen; in Yiddish the expression goes, "An individual must act, but it's God who actually activates, makes things happen" ("*a mentsh muz tuhn, uber der Eibishte tut uff*"). After going through the kaleidoscopic view of Ohr Torah, I told Irving that for a two-million-dollar immediate pledge, and then a longer term, five-million-dollar pledge, I would like to give our institution a last name: Ohr Torah Stone.

He smiled – and then laughed. "A Torah institution must have a name with significant meaning, like Torah Vodaas (Torah and Knowledge), or Yeshivat Rabbeinu Yitzḥak Elḥanan, after a great rav. You don't name a Torah institution after a donor."

"I believe you are a great man," I said sincerely, because I truly meant it. "But let me ask you something. The tablets of the Ten Commandments are called by the Bible 'tablets of stone' (לוחות אבן). Why? Is it not because stone comes from the earth, and although 'generations come and generations go, the earth lasts forever' (Ecclesiastes 1:4)? And the Ten Commandments, the ethical underpinning of God's laws, express an absolute morality that must always last, transcending the trends and vagaries of different cultures and eras! And what is the real value of Torah education? It transmits absolute values and a unique lifestyle from parent to child, from generation to generation. The Hebrew word for stone is *even* (אבן); *av* and *ben*, parent and child, contracted together in one word. Can you think of a more meaningful name than Ohr Torah Stone?"

We embraced, and I saw tears in Irving's eyes. Thanks to him, our institutions received a most meaningful last name!

Chapter Seventy-Five

Changing Fate into Destiny: Make Schools That Make a Difference

I have a good friend, a highly respected man, Rav Moshe Ebstein, who started the Hebrew Institute for the Deaf, the first yeshiva (initially in Borough Park, and now with a second branch in Benei Berak) to teach Torah to deaf children. I asked him how he came to start such an institution, and here is the answer he gave me.

"When I was a young boy, I was sent to a Siberian labor camp, together with my *ḥeder* rebbe. I never got a chance to even say goodbye to my parents; I was taken from school, and put on a truck.

"I was certainly frightened, but being with my rebbe – though he was no more than sixteen or seventeen himself – mitigated my fear. We bunked together and worked together.

"I don't want to tell you the details of life in the camp; it was too horrific for words. But I do want to tell you about Shabbos there, especially the very first Shabbos.

"We worked every day from before sunrise until way after dark. The work was backbreaking. There were no 'time outs' for a bit of respite, not even to relieve oneself. Guards were constantly on the lookout for anyone who slackened his work pace; the immediate punishment was to be shot dead.

"We received lunch at midday. It was two pieces of stale, dry black bread, and a tin bowl of tasteless gruel that passed for soup. My rebbe worked alongside of me, and encouraged me to continue whenever I felt like giving up and giving in to my muscle-aching tiredness.

"Then the first Friday arrived. When 'lunch' came, my rebbe told me to eat only the soup and to put the bread in my pocket. As the sun started to set, my rebbe began to chant in a low voice '*Lekha Dodi*.' At the conclusion of the prayers I heard his *Kiddush* over the bread – and then we sang *zemirot* and he regaled me with beautiful stories from the Midrash and commentaries on the Torah reading.

"For the hours of Shabbos I was transported, far removed from the stinking camp. I could see my family's Shabbos table. I could taste my mother's *gefilte* fish, *kneidlach* and *cholent*. I could feel my father's caress, I could sense the Divine Presence. You know, those Sabbaths in the camp were among the most beautiful I have ever experienced in my life.

"Many years later, after I was liberated, I came to America, got married and had my first child. I was devastated to learn that my beautiful *bekhor*, first-born, was deaf, and then so was his brother. Apparently it was a hereditary congenital deafness.

"At first I was filled with bitter despair and self-pity. What did God want from me, and from my poor blameless sons?

"But then I remembered my rebbe in Siberia, and how he transformed a louse-filled, backbreaking, labor-camp Shabbos into a transcending religious experience, how he took sour lemons and turned them into sweet lemonade, how he changed fate into destiny.

"And I started the first yeshiva for the deaf."

I attempted to learn from Rav Ebstein not only the importance of changing fate into destiny, but also that a significant institute of Torah must attempt to make a real difference in society, must help perfect our world.

Chapter Seventy-Six

A Rebbe's Warning, a Donor's Support

This tale begins in 1981, two years before we moved to Efrat. I had just received from Ktav Publishing the first copy off the press of my interpretation of the Passover *Haggada,* the very first "*sefer*" I had put out; I immediately called Rav Soloveitchik and got on a plane to Boston, anxious to present my rebbe with my *bikkurim* (first fruits).

We spent at least an hour and a half together, at the end of which I revealed my plans to make *aliya* to Efrat and requested a "blessing." "I'm not a Hasidic rebbe," demurred the Rav, but he nevertheless took my hand, saying, "May the Lord prosper your ways." I returned home grateful and humbled by God's gifts.

The next morning the telephone woke me up at 6:00 A.M. To my great surprise it was Rav Soloveitchik, apologetically asking if I could please come to Boston to see him that day. I felt an incipient panic attack, certain that he had found fault with the *Haggada* and kicking myself for not having shown it to him pre-publication. During the trip that I took that morning, my heart was literally in my mouth; when I entered the Rav's Brookline residence, however, I realized that his concern was not at all with my interpretation. "I was up all night worrying about you," he said. "I don't believe you should go to Israel. I know you; you have original and creative ideas, and you have a most promising future in America. In Israel they can be primitive; they are liable to swallow you and spit you out" (this last phrase he said in Yiddish). And he then began to relate, with the help of yellowed newspaper articles he had saved, the difficult time the more *ḥaredi* religious establishment, as well as their press, had given him when he had been a candidate for the Chief Rabbinate of Tel Aviv in 1935.

The truth is that I was both touched and relieved by his words; touched deeply by how much this giant of his generation could care about one of his many students, and relieved that I wouldn't have to impound my publication. Listening to him, I saw how deeply he had been hurt, and was hurt still, by the unfair critique that had been leveled against him, and I was ashamed that my request for a blessing had immediately caused his wounds to surface.

Nevertheless, I was fairly certain that my much lowlier station in Israeli society as well as my anonymous pedigree would never evoke the arrows of competitive jealousy and ideological disagreement that his desire to be chief rabbi had engendered.

"Rebbe, are you giving me good advice or a *pesak halakha*?" I timidly whispered. The Rav laughed, said that he knew that I would go ahead with my plans despite his words, but that he felt it important to warn me. I thanked him sincerely, saying that, in any case, my *aliya* was at least two years away.

The fact is that my rebbe's concern was indeed almost prophetic. My first job in Israel was directing a program sponsored by the Rothschild Foundation to train young rabbinical students one afternoon a week for two years for a future position as rabbi in a South American community. They were to receive their halakhic expertise from their sundry yeshivot, the spectrum ranging from Ponevezh to Kerem B'Yavneh; my task was to see that they were professionally prepared to create and foster a community, including public speaking, pedagogic skills in formal and informal education, *kiruv* (outreach), psychological counseling, political expertise in dealing with the board (*junta*) of *ba'alei batim*, fundraising and communal institution building.

Within my purview was also arranging practical classes in the art of circumcision and ritual slaughtering for those with the will and potential to provide those crucial services, especially in communities far from "the beaten path."

My experience in teaching these intelligent, motivated and idealistic young men quickly taught me that while they were far advanced in their Talmudic and halakhic knowledge, their proficiency in the Bible – and in applying the biblical portions of the week to meaningful sermons and short addresses to couples under the marriage canopy or for a bar/bat mitzva – was sadly lacking. Since, in addition to the *Shulḥan Arukh*, a rabbi's stock-in-trade is the Bible, I asked the world's foremost Torah scholar and pedagogue, Professor Neḥama Leibowitz (who was then in her eighties), to give a Bible class to our rabbinical students; she accepted with alacrity.

Unfortunately, I had to dismiss one particular faculty member who had not been adequately preparing his classes and whose students were voting with their feet. He had close relationships with the leadership of Ponevezh Yeshiva, and the rumor mill began to leak news of an impending *ḥerem* (religious sanctions) against our rabbinical program because of a "prominent female teacher" on our faculty. I immediately went to two respected religious authorities to request a ruling regarding the *kashrut* of Professor Neḥama Leibowitz teaching our rabbis: Rav Shlomo Zalman Auerbach (a respected and saintly decisor of the *ḥaredi* world) and Rav Avraham Shapiro (Dean of Yeshivat Merkaz HaRav Kook and Ashkenazi Chief Rabbi of Israel). Both of these sages used the same expression, with Rav Shapiro signing a letter to that effect: Neḥama Leibowitz is an "*isha keshera*," a capable and trustworthy transmitter of our *Mesora* for the teaching of the Written Law, and her advanced age makes it permissible for her to teach the much younger rabbinical students. With these rulings I thought the issue had come to an end.

But the very next issue of the Lithuanian *ḥaredi* newspaper *Yated Ne'eman* thought otherwise: the front-page headline read, "Mr. Riskin, get your pig's feet off the ramparts of Jerusalem and return to your home in New York." The article continued to discuss at length the great transgression of having a woman teach male students, pointed out several "heresies" in things I had written and ordered God-fearing students and faculty to leave the institution immediately, ominously concluding, "Whoever steps foot in that institution will suffer a bitter end."

A much more concise letter, signed by two great representatives of the *ḥaredi* world, concurred with the sanctions against our institution without going into the gory details.

About half the student body and a number of faculty members (those hailing from *ḥaredi* institutions), resigned from our program. I thought my first job in Israel had ended almost before it began, and Rav Soloveitchik's warnings seemed to have been prophetic.

To my grateful and ecstatic surprise, Arthur Fried, then Director of the Rothschild Foundation, which funded the entire rabbinical training project, asked to meet with me. He gave me complete and unqualified support, assuring me that the course of study would continue unabated, and new replacement faculty would be hired, no matter how depleted the student body might be.

Unfortunately, the fallout was not very pleasant. The Yemenite Rav who was teaching the art of ritual slaughtering was warned that if he so much as entered the building in which our program was being taught, his legs would be broken; we sent the students to learn ritual slaughter in his home. I called one of the *ḥaredi gedolim* in dismay. I asked if he knew me. I asked him how he could levy sanctions without even checking out the situation first-hand. I told him I wouldn't invalidate a chicken without first seeing the chicken. The old man wept on the phone, begging me to understand that "he was frightened of the *Yated Ne'eman*." I was devastated, suddenly having discovered in Israel the phenomenon of "Torarism," the terrorism of Torah in a specific extremist-*ḥaredi* circle.

The year concluded, Neḥama Leibowitz continued to teach, but the issue abated nevertheless. The following year the students and faculty members who had left requested to be taken back; I refused to do so, but our enrollment still doubled in size, and I received some very large spontaneous donations from sources who had never supported me before. I learned from the unfortunate incident that if you refuse to be intimidated, and stick to your guns in matters of principle, the fanatics will be silenced in their opposition.

Chapter Seventy-Seven

Rav Moshe Feinstein Saves My Rabbinate

I was very privileged to have had a real relationship with three of the greatest religious personalities of the last century: Rav J.B. Soloveitchik, my rebbe *muvhak* (mentor), who was *lamdan hador* (the leading Talmudic scholar of the generation); the Lubavitcher Rebbe, Rav Menaḥem Mendel Schneerson, who was *manhig hador* (literally, the shepherd-leader of the generation), who took responsibility for the Jews even in the farthest recesses of the globe, like South Africa, Australia and the Soviet Union; and Rav Moshe Feinstein, who was *posek ledor* (decisor of the generation). When I began receiving difficult questions from the *ba'al teshuva* Lincoln Square Synagogue community, questions of a Kohen married to a divorcee and issues of *mamzerut*, Rav Soloveitchik introduced me by telephone to his relative, Rav Moshe Feinstein. "The world calls me the Rav and him the Rosh Yeshiva, whereas the opposite is the truth: he was a *shtadt rav* [city rabbi] in Europe whereas I always lived within the four walls of halakha and the *beit midrash*. And it is our *mesora* [tradition] that it is specifically the communal rav who is in daily touch with the multitudes of Jews and their problems, who must be their *posek*."

And so it came to be that almost every Friday morning for the better part of a year I would travel to the very modest FDR Drive apartment of Rav Moshe and ask him my questions. It is simply amazing to consider that this small Jew, with bright eyes and an open, cheerful countenance, who considered halakhic questions from all over the globe, would answer the door himself, bring me tea and cake, and appear as if I and my question were the only concern he had in the world. One of the first issues I brought before him was a very difficult case:

A man from the Israeli Mossad, one of those who served on the "hit team" to avenge the murders of the Munich athletes, had entered a romantic relationship with a religious European divorcee. She had been married for a very short time; her husband had previously undergone an operation to cure impotence (a malady of which she had no prior knowledge), their marriage had never been consummated, but she had received a "*get*" nevertheless. Now she had fallen in love with this secular Israeli who had become a Sabbath observer as a result of his relationship with her. The problem, however, was that the Israeli was a Kohen, and a Kohen is biblically forbidden from marrying a divorcee.

Rav Moshe explained that, although the woman's previous marriage was annulled since her ignorance of her husband's physical condition made it a marriage under false pretense (she even had a gynecologist's letter attesting to the fact that she was still a virgin), once she received a bona fide *get* (bill of divorcement), the major halakhic decisor Rav Moshe Isserless insists that she is a divorcee.

Rav Moshe then suggested that I ascertain two more facts of information. Did the Israeli have a father or grandfather, a paternal uncle or great-uncle who were Sabbath observers? Only if he knows he is a Kohen from a relative who is truly observant and may be considered a valid witness in a Court of Jewish Law, is he to be disqualified from marrying a divorcee. The many peregrinations of the Jews from land to sea, from exile to Holocaust, wakened the presumptions of family lineage – including the *Kehuna* – to the extent that Rav Moshe required a Sabbath-observing confirmation of the Israeli's *Kehuna* status. We found such a family witness.

Finally, Rav Moshe suggested that I check into where the Israeli's mother had gone to university – and whether she had engaged in a sexual liaison with a Gentile male prior to her marriage. As it turned out, she had attended the University of Berlin, and she produced two witnesses who gave me signed letters that she had lived with a Gentile man off-campus during her time at university. When I brought these letters to Rav Moshe, the sage ruled that since she had lived with a Gentile prior to her marriage to a Kohen, the child of her marriage to the Kohen was not to be considered a Kohen and would be permitted to marry a divorcee!

During this period of investigation into the Israeli's *Kehuna* status, however, life was continuing to change for all of us; the divorcee's father suffered a serious heart attack that required a recuperation period without the excitement of a wedding, and my family and I had made *aliya* to Efrat. It took about two years after Rav Moshe's ruling for the wedding to finally take place – and I, the newly elected Rav of Efrat, performed the ceremony in a hotel in Jerusalem. What I hadn't realized, however, was just how efficient the computer system in Israel was – and barely a month after the wedding I received a letter from the Chief Rabbi's office informing me that I had performed a marriage between a registered Kohen and a registered divorcee, and that Rav Avraham Shapiro wished to see me immediately. Since I didn't want to meet with Rav Shapiro without a signed statement from Rav Moshe, and since I had been planning a trip to America for the following week in any case, I made the appointment with the chief rabbi after my return from overseas.

There was one serious complication, however; Rav Moshe was very seriously ill in Roosevelt Hospital, and was absolutely forbidden any visitors except for close family members. His grandson, Rav Mordekhai Tendler, who was with his grandfather day and night, promised me that as soon as there was a change for the better, he would let me in. On the Friday afternoon prior to my Saturday night return flight to Israel, I got the call saying that Rav Moshe could see me from his hospital bed within that hour.

Rav Moshe was physically a short man; lying in the hospital bed he seemed absolutely tiny. As I neared the bed, but before he noticed my presence, I could see his face grimacing in pain. But his eyes were clear, and there were neither creases on his forehead nor wrinkles on his cheeks.

He looked like a pure, innocent child, with a beautiful, other-worldly translucence showing through his features. I immediately thought of the rays of splendor on Moses' face when he descended from Sinai.

He smiled at me when he saw me, asked about my family, enquired after the success of our *aliya* and requested that I pray for him at the Kotel, "which is the closest place to the Lord." And then, when I began to ask if he remembered the matter I had brought before him concerning the Kohen and his divorcee, he immediately interrupted me. "Of course I remember," he said, and recounted their names! "And of course I'll put it in writing." He asked his grandson for writing material and penned a two-line response on a two-by-four card above his scrawled signature.

There were tears in my eyes; my "case" was one of hundreds that Rav Moshe had dealt with during the past two years, and during this last period his body had been ravaged with illness and pain. Through it all, he still remembered the names of the people I asked him about. And not only because he had a phenomenal memory (he once told me that until the age of sixty, he had never tasted forgetfulness). It was mostly because he cared, cared sincerely and desperately, about the Jewish people, about the individuals for whom he had been asked to render religio-legal decisions. He was like the High Priest of old who carried the twelve tribes on his shoulders and on his breast, who took responsibility for and deeply loved the tribes of Israel.

As I walked backwards out of the hospital room, keeping his receding figure in my sightline as long as possible, I was reminded of the child-like visage of the winged cherubs through whom the Divine spoke in the Sanctuary. "If your teacher is like an angel of the Lord of hosts, then you may ask Torah of his mouth."

POST SCRIPT:

Another response I received from Rav Moshe further revealed the depth of his love for the Jewish people. One of my very good students at Yeshiva University's James Striar School went on to become a *sofer stam* (scribe of Torah scrolls and *tefillin* and *mezuza* parchments) for the Satmar community, of which he became a prominent member; nevertheless, he continued to call and see me regularly, and even ate in my home. This *sofer* made an appointment to see me, armed with scientific and botanical material from journals and encyclopedias. In short, his problem concerned the resin used to blacken *tefillin* straps and *batim* (little "houses" that enclose the four parchment portions of the Bible). Every important aspect of the *tefillin* must be made from kosher material, "objects that are permissible to be put in your mouth." Since the resin we use comes from the bark of a tree indigenous to Israel, Rav Shmuel Salant, Chief Rabbi of Jerusalem more than one hundred years ago, permitted its use for *tefillin*. However, my former student had unmistakable scientific evidence that the resin actually emanated not from the bark of the tree but rather from worms that inhabit the bark of the tree – and worms are living, crawling, impure, and therefore non-kosher creatures.

The first thing I did was order for myself a new pair of *tefillin* with a different and purely vegetable source for the resin – and those *tefillin* cost me $900 some thirty-five years ago. The second thing I did was to bring the issue before Rav Moshe. Is it my obligation to alert my Lincoln Square Synagogue to the issue – and at least attempt to educate our community to the necessity of acquiring new *tefillin*? And perhaps I ought to go beyond my community and into the Yeshiva University community, the Orthodox Union community, the Rabbinical Council of America community?

Rav Moshe took my material and read it with great concentration and intensity. His response to my earlier questions each week had either been immediate – citing sources of chapter and verse by heart along with his ruling – or almost immediate, as he would first apologetically check one or more of the sources before presenting his response. This time he asked me to return the following Friday for his answer.

When I came back the next week, his rebbetzin opened the door, and I could see Rav Moshe pacing back and forth. "You certainly worried my husband with your question last week," said the rebbetzin. "He's been thinking and pacing steadily almost since you left him." As soon as Rav Moshe saw me, he stopped pacing, and his entire manner expressed a resolute decision. "I'm glad you brought this matter to my attention," he said. "I don't want you to say anything further about it, or to do anything further about it. We dare not invalidate the *tefillin* of the entire Jewish people for these last hundreds of years; we dare not bring disrepute upon Rav Shmuel Salant. Our parents and grandparents have prayed with kosher *tefillin*; God would never have allowed them to do otherwise. *Mir tuhr nit paselin die tefillin fun klal yisrael* – we dare not invalidate the *tefillin* of the entire Jewish people…"

On one of those Friday mornings, after answering my questions, Rav Moshe asked if I would be good enough to accompany him to the *beit midrash* of his Talmudical Academy, Mesivta Tiferet Yerushalayim, since he needed a *minyan*, and wasn't certain – since Friday was the day off – that there would be one without me. He took with him a brown paper bag in which he placed a quarter of a bottle of whiskey (it was J&B), a small honey cake, and some plastic utensils, plates and cups that had apparently been previously prepared by the rebbetzin.

We arrived shortly after twelve noon, and there were seven boys just on their way out. Rav Moshe asked if they would please find one more young man, since he wanted to make a *siyyum* (completion of a tractate of Talmud).

He quickly read and explained the last lines of the tractate, recited the *hadran* prayers and the *Kaddish* (which required a *minyan*), and invited the assembled group to partake of the schnapps and cake; he was making a *siyyum* on *Shas* (all the tractates of the Babylonian Talmud). I blurted out without thinking, "Is this the first time the Rosh Yeshiva is completing *Shas*?" Rav Moshe seemed to blush in embarrassment. "*Nein*, no, ordinarily I don't make an issue of a *siyyum*, but this is the hundredth time…" The next morning I began to study *Daf Yomi*.

Chapter Seventy-Eight

A Second Crisis, with Rav Mordekhai Eliyahu to the Rescue

I had been in Israel a little more than a decade; I had passed the Chief Rabbinate examination to qualify as a City Rabbi as well as the examination to be a Marriage Recorder (*Roshem Nisuin*), and was busily involved in ministering to the ever-growing municipality of Efrat and developing the Ohr Torah Stone Institutions, especially our Straus Rabbinical Seminary. And then I received a telephone call from an American student who had retained his relationship with me for close to twenty years. He had returned to his Jewish roots (become a "born-again" Jew) while still in a secular high school through the YU Seminar Program, and had been an excellent Talmud student in my class at the James Striar School. I remembered that when I had taught him he was living with his single-parent mother; his father, of Eastern European background, had cast off his Judaism as well as his family, and was living with a divorcee in a California commune dedicated to the New Age, "hippy" concepts of love that flourished in the sixties.

The former student began the conversation with "good news and bad news." The good news: his father and his "significant other" had left the commune and moved to Eilat, and then to Tel Aviv and now to Jerusalem; as the world turns, they had both returned to Orthodox Judaism, which had given my student a great deal of "*naḥat*." Moreover, his father had rediscovered and reclaimed his Kohen pedigree status; his father was also praying, "*duchaning*" (reciting the Priestly Blessing) and studying *Daf Yomi* every morning at the Kotel with a group that had become his *ḥevra* (group of close friends).

The bad news: his father wanted to legalize his relationship with the "significant other," but a Kohen is forbidden marrying a divorcee. By now his father was an old, sick man, suffering from an advanced stage of diabetes; his "significant other" was a registered nurse who took care of him as a labor of love. Totally devoid of financial resources, his father had no other option for medical or household help, other than the woman he had been living with all this time.

I met with the elderly couple; it turned out that the father's *Kehuna* pedigree was questionable at best, since neither his father nor grandfather had been Sabbath-observing Jews; that there was only one living paternal uncle who knew nothing of a priestly lineage within the family; and that the "significant other's" former marriage and divorce had not been in accordance with Jewish law. Since the Kohen was not a Kohen and the divorcee was not a divorcee, I married the couple "*Kedat Moshe VeYisrael*" in a friend's apartment in Jerusalem.

The next month an ultra-Orthodox Jerusalem tabloid, *Yom HaShishi*, featured a front-page headline: "Rav of Efrat marries a Kohen to a divorcee" with a full page story about how I circumvented the halakha. Needless to say, no one had contacted me from the newspaper for my side of the story – and when I questioned the columnist as to the ethical correctness of such a clear breach of the laws against slander, she told me that she had received a halakhic decision from "a great authority" that it was a mitzva to reveal the incident as she had published it. Since no one in "my world" – and certainly no one in Efrat – reads *Yom HaShishi*, I decided to drop the issue without comment.

That following week, during my regular round of teaching, I called my wife from Midreshet Lindenbaum at 10:00 P.M. Tuesday night. She told me that a Hebrew-speaking gentleman had called shortly before my call, and had left a home number for me to call him back, merely saying that it was Mordekhai Eliyahu who wanted to speak to me. "Could it possibly be the Rav Mordekhai Eliyahu *shlita*, the Rishon LeTziyon and a great religious luminary of our generation? I immediately called back – and it was indeed the Rishon LeTziyon. "I hear that the extremists are shedding your blood," he said. "And I've only heard good things about you, especially from my son Ben, who prayed in your former synagogue in New York when he was studying at Columbia Law School. Everyone who knows you understands you would never marry a Kohen to a divorcee. Please make an appointment to see me."

I was touched to the core that this great Torah scholar would take the time to speak to me about an ugly newspaper article. I met with him, laid the case out before him, suggested that he meet with the couple, and offered to undo the marriage if he thought I had acted inappropriately. Rav Eliyahu did meet with the couple; he then gave me a letter stating clearly that he had reviewed the issue at my suggestion, and had found my having married them to have been halakhically correct and humanistically required. He even permitted me to publish the letter in *Yom HaShishi* or any other place if I desired to do so. I opted not to publish it – it would only serve to remind those readers of the initial charge against me, and they would very likely forget the letter of vindication.

I did show Rav Mordekhai Eliyahu's letter to the editor of *Yom HaShishi*. To his credit, he had the magazine feature a four-page, picture spread about me, Efrat and the Ohr Torah Stone Institutions, emphasizing the positive side of my accomplishments in Israel, with God's help. Hopefully the latter praise would cause the earlier slander to be forgotten.

Chapter Seventy-Nine

Women Advocates for Divorce Courts, Women Officers in the IDF

Rav Mordekhai Eliyahu, as well as his rebbetzin and his son Ben, proved most helpful in what I consider to be one of my most important projects in Israel, the Monica Dennis Goldberg School for Women Advocates and Yad L'Isha within Midreshet Lindenbaum. I did my doctoral work at New York University under Professor Larry Shiffman on the "Rights of Women to Sue for Divorce in Jewish Law," a subject that intrigued me in terms of the ability of the Oral Law to match practical halakha with changing times (in this case, the much improved position both socially and economically of the single woman, and therefore, the post-biblical, late-Talmudical phenomenon of a woman who may well be desirous of a divorce if not treated properly by her husband), as well as the contrast between the development of Talmudic law and the non-development of Sharia law in the Muslim world.

Nevertheless, I also discovered (in 1986) that the percentage of women in Israel that were "chained" to impossible-to-endure marital situations was higher than anywhere else in the world. Since Israeli law does not offer the possibility of a secular divorce, so that each secular Israeli Jewish woman has to appear before the religious Israeli court for a *get,* and since there was no possibility of women *"to'anot"* (advocates trained in Jewish law of personal status as it appears in Tractates *Ketubot, Gittin* and *Kiddushin,* and the Code of *Even HaEzer*) promoting women's rights before the Religious Court judges, I understood why the *get* problem for Israeli women was so severe.

After a lengthy conversation with Dr. Nurit Fried, Bible teacher par excellence and a leading voice on behalf of women's rights within Jewish law, she agreed to direct a school for women advocates on the highest of levels under the banner of Ohr Torah Stone. Dr. Fried assembled a marvelous faculty – especially in the area of the laws of personal status – and ran several ads in the Israeli press urging interested women to come for an interview as well as an examination on an "unseen" passage of the Talmud that the applicant would have to explicate. Every ad had to stipulate the fact that there was no guaranty that the three-year course of study would enable the successful graduate to appear before a Religious Court on behalf of a client; at that point in time, by Knesset rule as well as Chief Rabbinate insistence, only male advocates were allowed to function within the Religious Courtroom for Divorce. In addition, Dr. Fried and I had no idea how many Israeli women could pass an exam on an unseen Talmudic passage; with the exception of Midreshet Lindenbaum and the Israeli universities, Talmudic study was basically a closed book for women in Israeli schools. But, somewhat quixotically, we were resolved to send out a trial balloon.

Much to our pleasant surprise, more than a hundred applicants – from ages twenty to eighty, hailing from Haifa to Beersheba – vying for twenty-five spaces, arrived for the interview and exam. The overwhelming majority of these women had studied Talmud surreptitiously with a father, husband or son; all of them were excited about participating in our venture, with or without an eventual professional degree.

We carefully chose our first class, and immediately began working on official recognition for our program. Knesset Member Yael Dayan, who had always been an avid and vocal spokesperson for women's rights, quickly got the Knesset to rescind their previous law and allow women advocates to appear before Religious Court judges. But that was the easy part; how could we move the Chief Rabbinate?

At that point, Rav Mordekhai Eliyahu, the Rishon LeTziyon, was the Sepharadi Chief Rabbi in charge of the Religious Court. I knew one of his sons, Ben, who was a highly respected lawyer and was soon to be appointed Director General of the Ministry of Housing; he had come to Lincoln Square Synagogue while I had been rabbi there when he was attending Columbia Law School, and he and his father had helped me in the past. I invited Ben to lunch in Jerusalem.

After speaking about many different things, I finally came to the point: how might I be able to convince the Rishon LeTziyon to allow women advocates to come before the Religious Court judges in matters of divorce? He thought a few minutes, and then replied, "Since this is a women's matter, I suggest you first speak to my mother." Since it is hardly proper protocol to request a meeting with the chief Rebbetzin, he suggested I arrange a meeting with his father for late in the evening, arrive early and speak to his mother.

A week later I arrived at the modest Kanfei Nesharim apartment at 9:30 P.M. for a 10:00 P.M. appointment. Rav Eliyahu was busy with someone else in his office, his Rebbetzin offered me coffee, and as she was preparing it in the kitchen, I followed after her and blurted out the importance of a woman advocate pleading the case for women's rights of divorce to the judges. She turned to me, looking deeply into my eyes: "It's more than that. A woman often has a sexual problem with her husband that she lacks even the proper vocabulary to explain to three bearded judges. It's important that women have the opportunity of having another knowledgeable woman plead their cause. Rav Riskin, I'm sure there are urgent matters for you to take care of in Efrat. Allow me some time to speak to my husband privately." A week later I met with Rav Mordekhai Eliyahu in his office; he approved the option of women advocates!

* * *

There was only one hurdle left. By the time our women were ready to graduate – and the twenty-five who made it to the end of the third year had all passed their exams with flying colors (they took the same exams as their male counterparts) – there were two new Chief Rabbis, Rav Yisrael Meir Lau and Rav Bakshi Doron. Nurit Fried and I accompanied the twenty-five to the joint graduation, the certificates were given out by Rav Bakshi – but when he came to the first woman on his list of graduates, he closed the proceedings and concluded the graduation. Needless to say, we were devastated... and neither Rav Lau nor Rav Bakshi was willing to discuss the issue with me.

I had no other recourse but to go to the Supreme Court, claiming unfair gender discrimination. We won the case – three out of three judges. To the credit of the chief rabbis, they both attended our own Midreshet Lindenbaum, first graduation some six months later.

Rav Lau spoke, and he graciously admitted that he had been mistaken, and that – in the Tel Aviv Religious Court – the women advocates had raised the entire level of the proceedings. And so a significant cause was won on behalf of women's rights in halakha.

The success of this project inspired me to go one giant step forward and establish the Hadas Yeshivat Hesder for Women. Even before I left America, my beloved friends Belda and Marcel Lindenbaum were anxious to establish a women's college in Israel that would combine Torah study and army service for religious graduates of *ulpanot* (high schools for the religious Zionist community). The religious establishment, including the Chief Rabbinate, had always been opposed to religious women serving in the IDF. National Service, mostly involving working in poor development towns, was considered to be the desirable alternative for religious young women. This, however, would not enable them to continue formal Torah study, nor would they be serving in the most prestigious institution of modern Israel, the IDF. Their religious male counterparts did serve, through a special "arrangement" between the army and the yeshivot. But as far as the women were concerned, the Israeli religious establishment declared that it would be "preferable for a religious woman to die rather than serve in the IDF" (many women did serve nevertheless, but without religious sanction).

Our Midreshet Lindenbaum enjoyed a wonderful reputation for attracting the most intellectually gifted students from the Diaspora (the United States, South America, Europe and Australia) as well as from

Israel. I met with the proper IDF representatives, and they agreed with alacrity that our young women would receive modest uniforms (according to my specifications), would live together in their base under a female commanding officer, would be able to receive Torah classes every two weeks wherever they were stationed (we would obviously provide the educator), and could even conduct *Shabbatonim* for their entire base once a month at the army's expense. Moreover, our young women would be given the opportunity to serve in the Educational Corps, the Intelligence Corps, and even the Secret Service if they qualified. In addition, the women would study for extended periods at Midreshet Lindenbaum during their years of IDF service.

We announced enrollment and received an overwhelming response. A few weeks later, I was in the car driving to Efrat after returning from a trip to England, when the 6:00 A.M. news reported a meeting taking place that afternoon of all principals of *ulpanot* in order to condemn the proposed Yeshivat Hesder for Women and to revoke rabbinical ordination from the Chief Rabbi of Efrat. The news item concluded saying that the Chief Rabbi of Efrat had been contacted for comment, but was out of the country. Needless to say, I, myself, showed up for the meeting. After I was charged with going against the decisions of the Chief Rabbinate, I was given the right of reply. I explained the details of my understanding with the IDF, stressed the fact that since the arrangement that I had brokered had never happened before, the previous opposition of the Chief Rabbinate to women in the IDF could not have applied to our school, and I gently reminded them that since it was not they who awarded me my *semikha* (rabbinical ordination), neither was it within their power to revoke it. I then thanked them for their courtesy and left.

Our program continues to prosper with hundreds of students. We proudly boast of sixty religious women who are IDF commanding officers and a 100 percent record of religious retention. My proudest moments of vindication are when a director of one of the *ulpanot* present at that meeting calls to ask for "*protektzia*" (preferential treatment, or favoritism) to get his daughter or granddaughter into our program. I also consider it a great compliment that two "sister" programs developed in our wake.

Chapter Eighty

A Rabbi without a Beard

How important is it for a rabbi to have a beard?

Initially, I couldn't even get a job as a *ram* (rabbi educator) in a yeshiva in Israel because I didn't have a beard, although nobody told me that was why I couldn't pass an interview. Had I known then what the reason was, perhaps I would have grown a beard early on in my career. The more the beard becomes an issue however, the more adamant I become not to grow one.

The fact is, I was almost refused even the possibility of taking the required test to apply for a city rabbinate in Israel because I didn't have a beard – and to this day I am the only city rabbi in Israel who is generally clean shaven.

Indeed, the Bible does command, "You shall not destroy the corners of your beard" (Leviticus 19:27), and, although our Talmudic sages interpret this to mean that it is forbidden to shave with a razor blade on the skin from which a beard usually sprouts, and rabbinic interpretation generally permits shaving with an electric shaver, most rabbis, certainly in Israel, do sport at least a goatee.

Nevertheless, for personal reasons I have chosen not to wear a beard, mostly because my wife has asked this of me, and secondly because I am mindful of a Yiddish vignette in which the Keeper of the Gates to Paradise asks one would-be entrant: "Jew, where is the beard you should have?" but nevertheless lets him in. Later the Gate-Keeper blocks another customer anxious for entrance with the words: "Beard, where is the Jew you should be?"

But there is also a deeper, more serious reason. When the Lubavitcher Rebbe gave me a blessing for Efrat, he told me to create rabbis who were modern on the outside and "Chabad" on the inside, advising that my personal, religious and educational contribution could best be made looking modern on the outside, which I understood to mean not sporting a beard.

From its very inception, Efrat was slated to be a city and it began, indeed, as a separate municipality; hence the rabbi of Efrat – or anyone who was interested in being elected for the position of rabbi of Efrat – had to be certified as a City Rabbi. That meant that my rabbinical ordinations from Rav J.B. Soloveitchik of Yeshiva University, Rav Avraham Shapiro of Merkaz HaRav (also the Chief Rabbi of Israel at the time of my *aliya*), and Rav Shlomo Goren were not sufficient. I had to take a test on *Shas* and *Poskim* administered by three of the most respected rabbis of Jerusalem, Rav Kolitz, Rav Meshash, and Rav Yisraeli. Only after passing this test would I be allowed to serve as a rabbi in a city in Israel.

I arrived at Heikhal Shlomo very early the morning of my exam, after a fitful and restless night reviewing several of the more salient topics of Talmudical discourse. What added significantly to my nervousness was the fact that several rabbis who arrived after me were tested before me – and before long it was already 12:30 P.M. and there seemed no prospects for me to be tested before the venerable sages left for the day.

In an agitated and angry state of mind, I entered Rav Avraham Shapiro's office without knocking. "Why am I being discriminated against? I demand to know the reason!" I shouted. He called into the examination room, "What about Riskin?" and then told me straight: "You have no beard; they aren't interested in your becoming a City Rabbi in Israel." After my remonstrations, he called in again: "You don't have to pass him, but you do have to test him." I then heard my name called; I entered the room fearful and trembling – with my deflated ego just about non-existent.

The atmosphere in the room was cold as ice; no one greeted me or asked about my prior rabbinical career. (I had after all been the rabbi of a major New York synagogue for nineteen years, an Associate Professor of Talmud and Bible at Yeshiva University, and the founder of academically praised, Torah-oriented high schools for young men and women). They made me feel like a penny asking for change. For the first time in my life – at the age of forty-four – I felt like an outsider, like an individual who desperately wanted to join a fraternity but whose application was being rejected, not because he lacked proper credentials, but because he was from a foreign country. I was in turmoil; I felt as if my whole self-definition was being challenged and denied.

Then they began to ask questions.

The first few were difficult, but because I had dealt with the issues (*eruvin* and *mikvaot*) during the early months of Efrat, I responded properly. The sages seemed less adversarial; the atmosphere in the room seemed to lighten. Then they asked questions about Shabbat and Festival laws – which I handled with comparative ease. I knew, however, that realistically they would eventually find something I did not know. My mouth and my throat constricted.

And then God came to my rescue. They asked if a woman finds her husband distasteful, can she sue for divorce? Well, my doctoral dissertation had been on Divorce Law and I had written a book on the Jewish woman's right to divorce. I made a quick calculation that in thirty minutes the rabbis would conclude the exam and go for lunch; my best strategy would be to speak for as much of the remaining time as I could. So I launched into a learned discourse about the question, citing the relevant passages from the Jerusalem, as well as the Babylonian Talmud, the Geonim, Rishonim, Responsa literature and halakhic decisions. I concluded by citing a Rabbinical Court decision in a recent case germane to the issue, in which Rav Yisraeli – one of my examiners – had given a minority dissenting ruling; I cited a document found in the Cairo Geniza by Mordekhai Friedman that completely vindicated Rav Yisraeli's position.

Rav Yisraeli rose – and visibly moved – kissed me on the forehead. Rav Meshash cried out, "Done! Over. He's passed!" As I left the room, elated and thankful to God, Rav Yisraeli gently asked, "But why don't you have a beard?" I gave him the truest response of all. "*Shalom bayit.* My wife asked only two things of me: that I not drive and that I not wear a beard." The venerable sages seemed satisfied.

Chapter Eighty-One

A Beard without a Rabbi

Early on in our married life my wife presented me with a Purim gift of a remarkably realistic-looking beard, one that seemed to be "made for my face" and provided me with an instant Purim costume. Initially, in Lincoln Square, Manhattan, and for the last two decades in Efrat, I would proudly appear at all Purim celebrations – from the various *Megilla* readings to the sundry Purim "*shpiels*" and "*leḥayyims*" – with my special Purim beard. "At least once a year we have a real rabbi," my cooperative congregants would remark.

At the conclusion of Purim I would lovingly pack away my beard, together with my precious scribe-written Esther scroll and specially crafted wooden *grogger* (noisemaker) for the next year's Purim festivities.

There was one Purim, no different from the previous ones, during which I was a "bearded" rabbi. After the traditional yeshiva "*shpiel*," which generally made fun of my less hirsute appearances during the other 364 days of the year as well as a number of other characteristics of mine, I went to a bar mitzva celebration rather far from Efrat on the coastal plain of Israel.

One of the teenage waiters, Lior by name, was bedecked with purple hair in honor of Purim and seemed fascinated by my beard. After

I had given my *devar Torah* blessing to the bar mitzva whilst wearing my beard, Lior asked to borrow it while he continued to do his serving of the food, to which I gladly consented. When I was about to leave, he asked if he might keep it, "After all," he explained, "I used to go to day school (yeshiva) and was very religious after my bar mitzva. Although I'm not religious any more, I do have religious stirrings." I spontaneously, although not too magnanimously responded that I would gladly give him the beard if he would agree to pray each morning with *tefillin*. "I can't make such a commitment," he said. I told him of my sentimental attachment to this particular beard, but promised that I would make every effort to send him a similar specimen. He returned the beard and we exchanged telephone numbers.

From the bar mitzva I went on to Bikkur Ḥolim hospital in Jerusalem, where I had a patient to visit, Tzofia Levy, the administrative secretary of our high school.

Obviously I entered the hospital in my beard, because I especially wanted to cheer up the patient. While I was there, I used the public telephone to check on a student who had seemed well on the way to inebriation that morning at the *shpiel*. I then went on to Tel Aviv, where I was scheduled to appear at a fiftieth birthday celebration and Purim party. As we were leaving the outskirts of Jerusalem, I discovered that I had misplaced my beard – apparently at the hospital. I called from my car to try to locate it, but neither the patient nor the nurse near the public telephone could give me a clue as to the whereabouts of my missing beard. I became reconciled to my loss. I even felt I deserved to lose it because I hadn't been sufficiently generous to Lior!

The next morning, while sitting in my office, I received a telephone call from someone whose voice I did not recognize. "Rabbi, this is the waiter, Lior. Remember me? Well, you don't have to bring me a beard. An amazing coincidence happened. You see, my grandfather is recovering from surgery in Bikkur Ḥolim hospital in Jerusalem. I went to see him yesterday afternoon after work. On my way out I stopped off to call my girlfriend, and right next to the public telephone was a fake beard that is a dead ringer for the one you lent me. I kind of see it as a sign from God. I put on *tefillin* this morning, and I plan to continue to do so every day of my life."

I put down the receiver with tears in my eyes. Coincidence? Miracle? Or perhaps just the power of a beard.

Oh, and my wife has since found another beard – not quite like the one I left behind, but one that allows me to look like a "real Rav," at least once a year. By the following Purim, I was back in full costume – and hopefully Lior was still putting on *tefillin*.

Chapter Eighty-Two

His Most Precious Possession

Within the context of visiting our rabbinical and educational graduates throughout the world – as well as under the rubric of our fundraising needs – I accepted an invitation to dedicate a synagogue in the newly built Moriah School in Sydney, Australia. The eminent philanthropist Frank Lowy financed the building, and I shall never forget the talk he gave at that occasion.

He explained that he was not a particularly observant Jew, but that, nevertheless, he had decided to honor the memory of his father by building a school synagogue, and he told us why.

A number of years earlier, one of his sons had gone to Phoenix, Arizona, with an organized tour group to celebrate Passover. His son had heard his name, "David Lowy," called out over the hotel loudspeaker notifying him that he had a message, but when he arrived at the reception desk, he found that it was another participant named David Lowy, a much older gentleman, who was the intended recipient of the message.

The two David Lowys began to talk, and it turned out that the young man's grandfather, Frank Lowy's father, and this elderly David

Lowy, came from the same Polish *shtetl*. Even more surprising, the older gentleman asked his young namesake if he had ever known his grandfather's date of death, and exactly how he had died.

"We were landsmen, your grandfather and I, distant relatives but close friends. We were sent together to Auschwitz. We stood next to each other in line, when each of us had to place whatever possessions he was carrying on a conveyer belt, as a prelude to undressing and receiving the uniform Auschwitz garb. I'll never forget the date. Each of us had packed a last-minute suitcase or valise filled with precious possessions: jewelry, cash, photographs, books…

"Your grandfather clutched a small brown bag that he did not place on the conveyer belt, despite the Nazi orders. The Nazi guard faced your grandfather menacingly, shot a few bullets into the air, and pointed to the conveyer belt. Your grandfather parted with his bag, continued to march with us, but – as soon as the Nazi turned the other way – lunged backwards to retrieve his package. The Nazi guard, as if he had eyes in the back of his head, turned around and shot your grandfather dead. The bag lay open at his feet. Inside was a pair of *tefillin*…"

Chapter Eighty-Three

Their Most Precious Mitzva

In the fall of 2002, I made a trip to Manipur, in the northeast of India in order to establish contact with a group of Jews (some five thousand strong) who call themselves Bnei Menashe, claiming to be descendants of the lost tribe of Menashe. Their appearance is Indo-Chinese and, mostly as a result of the indefatigable efforts of Rav Eliyahu Aviḥayil, are in large measure observant Jews. They do not have a Torah scroll, but they do have a lengthy narrative, in the dialect of Mizo, which relates the history of Israel from the Garden of Eden to the Monarchs in Jerusalem. Their elders know this history-song by heart, and despite their isolation from the rest of Israel, they have staunchly remained committed to those rituals they preserved, like slaughtering a lamb on the fourteenth day of Nisan and painting its blood on their door-posts. They stubbornly held on to their Judaism despite their wanderings and even in the face of much persecution. They also have a tradition of circumcision – which they perform with sharp flints, as did the biblical Tzippora when she circumcised her son. The large area in India where they live has familiar names for streets and stores, like Zion Square and Jerusalem Plaza. The Mayor of Manipur proudly reported that yes, they are all descendants from the tribe of Menashe; some even trace their lineage to the daughters of Zelophehad. But a charismatic Christian missionary in the late nineteenth century converted them all to Christianity with the exception of five or six thousand Jews who remained steadfast and proud Jews to the end.

And so in a synagogue in Manipur, India, overlooking the magnificent mountains, not far from Bangladesh, and to the tune of an Indian chant that seemed to contain ancient rhythms and secrets of eternity, I was privileged to witness a Shabbat circumcision, which took twenty-two minutes to perform. The father had a beatific smile throughout the ceremony; the sun's last rays seemed to rest on the baby's forehead, forming rays of splendor reminiscent of Moses' glow when he descended from Mt. Sinai. I was asked to intone the blessings, and I did so with pride and palpitations.

I am also proud to relate that father and son – together with the rest of their Bnei Menashe family – made their way to Israel, the land of the miracle of the ingathering of the exiles.

Chapter Eighty-Four

When It Is a Mitzva to Gamble

Ohr Torah Stone's Joseph Straus Rabbinical Seminary sends out rabbis to congregations all over Israel and the world. About a decade ago we dispatched a young Sepharadi student, Raḥamim Cohen, to a small Moroccan *moshav* (cooperative settlement) outside of Safed.

Soon after his arrival in the *moshav*, he contacted me, asking if I could send him several thousand shekels as a donation from my *tzedaka* (charity) discretionary fund, no questions asked. I assumed he needed the money for his moving expenses and immediately fulfilled his request.

About two years later, in the course of an extended field trip to visit some of the rabbis whom we had dispatched within Israel, I was invited by Rav Raḥamim to give a class to his congregants between *Minḥa* and *Ma'ariv*, to have dinner with his family, and then to see his proudest accomplishment.

After dinner he took me to the Youth Center he had fashioned – three large caravans strung together, with hundreds of teenagers in attendance. Some were playing Ping-Pong, billiards and knock-hockey; others were listening to music, several were reading or doing homework in an impressively well-stocked library corner, and many were simply talking and hanging out in what appeared to be a wholesome and healthy environment. "This is what I accomplished with the three thousand shekels you sent me," he proudly exclaimed.

I looked at him quizzically. It certainly cost many times the NIS 3,000 to have outfitted such a well-stocked game room, to say nothing of the salaries for the two or three youth counselors I met engaging the various groups of youngsters.

Rav Raḥamim explained that when he had arrived at the *moshav*, he met very pious and scholarly grandparents, traditional but less observant parents, and disinterested rebellious grandchildren. The game room of the three caravans we had just visited had previously been stocked with card tables, roulette wheels, and even a bar with drinks. That had been the nightly, teenage hangout spot.

Raḥamim understood that if he was to make a dent in the *moshav* religiously, he had to reach out to these teenagers. He also understood that he had to reach them "in the place they were at."

So he asked me for NIS 3,000, "no questions asked," because he wanted to use the money for gambling purposes. He played cards with them, even shot the breeze with them over a beer, won their confidence and slowly convinced them to seek other forms of entertainment.

He developed a Youth Self-Governing Council that eventually petitioned the governing body of the *mo'etza* (local municipality) to furnish a new kind of game room. Eventually, the *mo'etza* put up half the funds, and the young people themselves raised the other half.

"I guess in this case it was a mitzva to gamble," concluded Raḥamim, with which I certainly concurred.

Chapter Eighty-Five

God Loves the Prisoner, Too

When I first came to Efrat and had much more free time, a rabbinical friend of mine, who visited prisons regularly, urged me to visit Ma'asiyahu, one of the prisons outside of Jerusalem. "You're into *kiruv* [bringing Jews back to tradition], right? In Israel, you'll have no happier hunting ground than the prisons."

I was taken a little aback. I teach Torah. Who in prison would be interested in learning Torah? "They're Jewish prisoners. Their hearts are open and their souls are sensitized. The potential is indescribable," said my friend. So during my first year in Efrat, I went at least once a month to Ma'asiyahu. Let me describe my first experience, which was for me an unforgettable one.

It was a Thursday afternoon, right before *Parashat Shemot* (December/January), when I arrived in Ma'asiyahu in heavy rain. It was the first time I had ever entered the portals of a prison without being the prisoner myself (in Russia, and before that, in New York, after I chained myself to the entrance of the United Nations building in an effort to secure emigration rights for the Jews of the Soviet Union. Subsequently, in June 1995, I was in two Israeli prisons for protesting against Prime Minister Rabin's plan to sign Oslo II. I once even thought of writing an article, "Prisons I Have Known: A Comparative Study," but I decided against it for fear it would hamper my grandchildren's chances for good *shiddukhim*).

I saw two notices on the walls. One was for a John Wayne movie, and the other for my talk on *Parashat HaShavua*, the weekly Torah portion. I thought to myself, this is a no-brainer; if I were an inmate, I would certainly go to the John Wayne movie.

To my surprise, when I walked by the room where the movie was screened, I saw that there were very few people in it. But my lecture room, which was the same size as the movie hall, was more than filled to capacity.

I was quite shocked that so many prisoners chose to learn Torah. I started to speak about Egyptian slavery and the birth of Moses – after all, that coming Shabbat we would read the opening portions of the book of Exodus in the synagogue.

I noticed unrest, a kind of rustling in the audience. Someone then jumped up and said, "*Kevod HaRav*, we were certain that you would speak about Joseph because we just finished reading the Joseph stories last Shabbat."

"Why are you so interested in Joseph?" I asked.

"Because Joseph was in prison and he got out," came the reply. "That's why there are so many people here. We want to know how to get out of prison and become rich and famous as well. Teach us – that's why we chose you over *Jun Vain*."

I understood.

So I told them about Joseph and about what it takes to be a great man, and how Joseph was really a *ba'al teshuva*, a penitent. Actually, as I spoke, I developed the interpretation, which I have come to believe is probably the truest of all the interpretations of the Joseph story. Why didn't Joseph speak to his father, at least get a message to his father that he was alive and well, especially after he became the Grand Vizier? He could easily have dispatched a messenger.

I suddenly realized that it was probably when Joseph was in the pit that he understood, for the first time, how much his brothers hated him. Until that time he had basked so much in the affection of his father, he had felt so loved by his father, that he was sure that he was loved by everyone. Otherwise, he never would have run around with his dreams, saying, "Hey fellows, listen to my dreams. Your sheaves of grain bow down to my sheaves of grain. The sun, the moon, the stars, all bow down to me." Only someone without self-awareness, who is certain that he is universally loved and admired, could have boasted of such things.

It was in the pit that Joseph had his rude awakening and realized how much he was hated. And it was also in the pit that he realized how much it was his father's fault because his father had given him the coat of many colors, and shown such blatant favoritism. I could picture Joseph saying in the pit, "I hate my brothers. I hate my father for causing the jealousy of my brothers by displaying such outright favoritism toward me. I will never contact my father's house again."

So Joseph tries very hard to forget his past. He does the three things that, according to the Midrash, no Jew who wants to be aware of his Jewishness must ever do: the Jew must never change his name, his garb or his language. Joseph changed his garb; he wore the *ravid zahav*, the golden cloak, a symbol of Egyptian aristocracy. He spoke Egyptian, not Hebrew. The Bible tells us that even when the brothers came before Joseph and spoke Hebrew, there was an interpreter between them and the Grand Vizier. And when Joseph marries Osnat bat Potifera, who was the daughter of the priest of On, the sun god, he becomes the Egyptian's Egyptian! Apparently, Joseph does a pretty good job of forgetting his past. He even names his eldest son Menashe (literally forgetfulness), "because God has enabled me to forget my father's house and all my toil." Yes, he still has his morality, and he still speaks of *Elokim*, but that is the universal name for God. He doesn't speak of *Yod-Keh-Vav-Keh*, the more personal Abrahamic name for the God of Abraham, Isaac and Jacob-Israel.

When the brothers arrive to purchase food, Joseph is at first filled with loathing and revenge, and puts them all in a pit dungeon. But then he thinks about it, and he can't sleep all night. He is suddenly brought back to his childhood in his father's house, a part of his life he had tried to forget. And he thinks about his little brother, Benjamin, for whom he has so many suppressed feelings of love. Benjamin was his whole brother; they shared the same mother, Rachel. And Benjamin had played no part in selling Joseph into slavery, in casting him into the pit – Benjamin had been too young, had stayed behind with his father. So Joseph, all night, dreams while awake, dreams of seeing, once again, his beloved brother, the son of Rachel, the brother who had always venerated him, looked up to him as a model – Benjamin.

The next day the Grand Vizier sends all the brothers back home except for one who is kept hostage, as collateral. The others are commanded to return with Benjamin…

Benjamin comes to Egypt and Joseph, unable to mask his feelings for this brother, shows special favoritism to him, giving him more food than everyone else. Then, through a ruse, a very expensive wine goblet is placed in Benjamin's knapsack. Joseph claims that Benjamin is the thief, and that Benjamin has to remain in Egypt as his slave. Joseph is apparently planning to reveal himself only to Benjamin, so that he and Benjamin will live in Egypt together happily ever after, two brothers reunited.

But then Yehuda steps into the fray, and Yehuda describes their grieving father, and what it will mean if there is yet a second blow to old Father Jacob. And suddenly Joseph's mind is filled with repressed memories of Shabbat and festival meals. He remembers pleasant hours of study with his father, of hearing about the covenant, and the Jewish vision and ideal of a world of peace, and the songs his father would sing to him in praise of God and in praise of nature. Yes his father hadn't managed the family properly, but it is difficult to successfully manage so many teenage sons; after all, his sin was one of *too much* love for Joseph, not too little. Joseph breaks down, reveals himself to his brothers, and he emerges as the consummate penitent, a genuine *ba'al teshuva*.

That's what I told them in prison.

I cannot tell you how moved they seemed to be, how appreciative they were of my message, of the possibility of *teshuva* for Joseph and for each of them as well.

And then it was time for *Ma'ariv*, the evening service. The individual who led the prayers prayed with such sweetness, with such sensitivity, with such concentration, with such energy, that I thought it was *Ne'ila* (the concluding prayer) on Yom Kippur rather than a regular weekday *Ma'ariv*.

Afterwards, I asked the prisoner sitting next to me, "Who was that cantor who led the prayers? How could he pray with such feeling? He certainly is not one of the prisoners."

"He certainly is," was the reply. "Why don't you talk to him about it?"

I asked to meet with him, and he spoke to me willingly and freely. Yes, he said, he was in prison for life, unless he could be paroled in some way. He told me one of the most amazing stories I've ever heard, a story of true *teshuva*. He had come from a not untypical Moroccan Jewish family that moved to Israel, with the older generation deeply devout and the younger generation "wild and free." He did many things, he said. He stole, he had many women and he drank. He had tasted almost every imaginable sin. And then he got married. He served in the army, got out of the army, and became a night watchman. He and his wife had a little baby girl. His father barely spoke to him because he didn't live a religious lifestyle. To tell the truth, he wasn't even faithful to his wife. But he loved his wife, and he especially loved his daughter.

And once in the middle of the night, while on the job, he didn't feel well. He came home unexpectedly at 2:30 in the morning. He found his wife in bed with his best friend, who lived across the hall.

He told me he went absolutely out of his mind. His whole world fell apart. The moment that he saw his wife and her lover in bed together, and his little baby daughter between them, he was overcome with blind rage. He took the gun issued to him as a night watchman and meant to shoot his wife's lover, but by mistake killed his own baby daughter. When he realized what he had done, he screamed out for the police, fainted and awoke to a kind of apathetic, almost catatonic existence of self-revulsion.

His wife sent a proxy to receive a divorce. She never wanted to look at him again. Now, not only his father, but his mother also stopped talking to him. The only one who visited him in prison was his lawyer.

He felt himself sink even further into a deep, black hole. He tried to commit suicide, but failed; he was guarded heavily in prison. And then a rabbi, a Sepharadi *ḥakham* (sage), came to see him. And the *ḥakham* said three things to him. The first thing he told him was the definition of God. "God is our Parent in Heaven who loves us unconditionally. One of God's names is *Raḥum*, the Compassionate One, which comes from the root word *reḥem*, a womb. Watch a mother diaper her baby, the fruit of her womb; watch how she accepts her baby, despite its mess, how she kisses the baby even as she cleans him. That's how God loves us. And secondly, even when no one else will talk to us, God will always hear us out. All we have to do is open the prayer book and pray, and God is right there visiting us. And if you stand with a prayer book five minutes longer than the greatest, most righteous rabbi in the world, God will have five more minutes for you than he has for that great righteous rabbi." And the third thing he said was, "This world is only temporary. The other world is permanent. The life after death is eternal. This world is only preparatory. And you can prepare yourself for the eternal world anywhere, even in prison."

And so, when he was finally given a prison sentence, he became a *ba'al teshuva*. He now spends a number of hours each day studying the sacred texts. He especially loves prayer because, though he knows and understands why his parents and friends may never visit him, whenever he opens the prayer book, God will be right there at his side. And he tries to do the best he can, to be the best person he can be to prepare himself as well as possible.

This is what I learned in Ma'asiyahu: that God is an unconditionally loving Parent in Heaven, that whenever we turn to Him, He's always there to listen to us, and that this temporary world is only a passageway of preparation for life eternal.

Chapter Eighty-Six

Miracle at Efrat's Shopping Center

It was a sunny, warm, busy, bustling Friday morning in Efrat. The shopping center, usually teeming with customers on Friday for the pre-Shabbat purchases, was even more crowded that Friday because it was also only a few days before Purim: people had to stock up for *mishlo'aḥ manot* (Purim gifts for friends), for the Purim *se'uda* (meal), and for the masquerade costumes. There was also a circumcision ceremony with a breakfast celebration at the Lev Efrat synagogue, only meters away from the shopping center. All in all, it was an excitedly happy Friday morning. No one would have anticipated the danger lurking within, the destruction a Palestinian was proposing and that God was already disposing…

Early that morning, "L," an *oleh* (immigrant) from Chicago, rose with the sun for his daily jog. But on this morning he awoke with a gnawing headache. He decided to skip the jog and – after his regular morning preparations – visit the shopping center near his former home on Pomegranate Hill (*Rimon*) to do some shopping for Purim. He had just completed a beautiful home in Olive Hill (*Zayit*), but the amenities in his newer community could not yet compare to the well-established stores to which he had become accustomed.

That same morning, Mrs. Beulah Wagner set out with her neighbor, Aharon Rosenberg, who drove her the short distance to and from the shopping center each week. Her husband was ill with Parkinson's disease, she was an older woman herself, and she could no longer manage to take care of the groceries alone. Aharon Rosenberg told her that this Friday he could only take her to the shopping center; he had a pressing appointment in Jerusalem for which he had to leave immediately. Luckily, when they arrived at the supermarket, L was just leaving. L had formerly been Beulah's neighbor and they all greeted each other warmly. She asked if L wouldn't mind delaying his departure for about half an hour, and could then drive her home with her groceries. L had already given up on his jog, so he was glad to accommodate Beulah's request; he said he would wait outside the supermarket and take in some early sun.

As L stood absentmindedly enjoying the scene of a blooming Efrat, he suddenly noticed something very strange. The Palestinian who had just finished building his house, and with whom he had drunk many cups of coffee while exchanging pleasantries about their respective families, was about to enter the supermarket. L wondered what this Palestinian builder was doing in Efrat that Friday morning. It was the first day of a Muslim three-day festival, *Eid al-Adha,* when Palestinian families enjoy a feast of lamb together. And besides, the Palestinian was uncharacteristically wearing sunglasses and a large raincoat – and it was a warm, sunny, clear spring day! Could it be that the man he knew and worked with and had grown to like was in actuality a terrorist?

L put his hand in the pocket where he always carried his pistol and quickly followed the Palestinian into the supermarket. He almost froze as he saw the Palestinian place his hand in his raincoat and heard a click; mercifully nothing had detonated. As the Palestinian was about to place his hand a second time in his raincoat, L took out his pistol and used it against someone for the first time in his life. He took careful aim and shot the would-be terrorist in the head. And as the Palestinian fell to the floor, so did L – in a faint. That's when I was summoned, out from the circumcision to L who seemed in need of rabbinical pastoring. The police said there were enough explosives on the Palestinian's body to destroy the entire shopping center and the several hundred people within it… That Shabbat, Efrat celebrated our own special Purim miracle a few days early – with special praise and tribute to God as well as to L.

What if L hadn't awoken with a headache? What if Aharon Rosenberg hadn't had an appointment that morning? What if Beulah Wagner hadn't needed her former neighbor to wait for her outside of the shopping center that morning? Coincidences? What is a coincidence if not God letting us know He's really in control, albeit anonymously? What are a string of coincidences if not a miracle?

Chapter Eighty-Seven

For the Sake of a Hill in Efrat

In the summer of 1994, between Oslo Accords I and II, I came to believe that the Oslo agreement was indeed a Trojan horse, with Yasser Arafat and the Fatah taking the Kalashnikovs given to them by Prime Minister Rabin to use against Hamas, and firing them against us instead.

We, the people of Efrat, peacefully demonstrated against governmental policy by setting up a camp site on Givat HaDagan, Dagan Hill, an area that had initially been included in Municipal Efrat, but which the Oslo agreements precluded from settlement.

We were evicted from Dagan Hill, and I was imprisoned – first in the Russian Compound and then in Abu Kabir – despite our peacefulness and the sincere respect we showed to the IDF soldiers and police who evacuated us. (I have mentioned how prison was not new to me. Only in Israel, however, was I completely exonerated with an apology from both Prime Minister Rabin and Prime Minister Peres.) My twenty-four-hour incarceration led to demonstrations on my behalf in New York, Los Angeles and London, and with my release we were given permission to populate first Olive Hill (*Zayit*) and then Dagan Hill by Prime Minister Rabin himself.

* * *

During this period of intifadas, Ohr Torah Stone sponsored a *yeshivat hesder,* Yeshivat Siaḥ Yitzḥak, which is on Givat HaDagan, at the northern end of Efrat, right at the border with Bethlehem and El Hader. It was led by the sainted Rav Shimon Shagar, *z"l,* and Rav Yair Dreyfuss, well-known as *talmidei ḥakhamim* (Torah scholars) and forward-thinking and open-minded *rashei yeshiva.*

The yeshiva had gone through very difficult times because of its location. At the beginning of the Oslo War (September 2000) on the Thursday before Rosh HaShana, I received a frantic call from one of the students at the yeshiva. He said that there was terrible shooting coming from two directions, from Bethlehem and from El Hader. I called the *moked,* the local emergency station. The IDF immediately dispatched forty soldiers, and, soon thereafter, two tanks. (The tanks as well as the soldiers remained stationed near the yeshiva for two years.) The yeshiva endured constant trouble from our Palestinian neighbors.

The most difficult and inspiring hours came with the end of that Yom Kippur. I had just returned from the *Ne'ila* and *Ma'ariv* prayers at Neveh Shmuel and was about to say the *Havdala* prayer for my family, signaling the end of the holiday, when I received a call from one of the students, speaking from his cell phone. He said that there was terrible shooting in every direction. The IDF was trying to stop the attack, so far unsuccessfully. The *rashei yeshiva* were there, but the student had called to tell me that the situation was too dangerous for me to come to give a class. Contrary to what the student must have assumed, I wasn't scheduled to come, but after hearing what he told me, I knew I had to be there.

I arrived and this is what I saw: firebombs and bullets coming from the direction of El Hader as well as Bethlehem. The IDF had surrounded the yeshiva study hall – the *beit midrash* – and were shooting back. Everybody was on the floor of the *beit midrash,* which is actually an enlarged caravan. The IDF didn't want any of the yeshiva students to shoot back, although many of them were serving in the army as part of the *yeshivat hesder* program.

The shooting had apparently begun shortly before the end of *Ma'ariv*. That was a blessing, because everyone was in the *beit midrash*, which was the most protected structure. There were a goodly number of families associated with the yeshiva because married men, often with children, study there in the more advanced classes. Everyone, including the women and babies, had come to the study hall to hear the *shofar*-blowing at the end of *Ne'ila*, right before *Ma'ariv*. So all of the yeshiva and its extended family were together in the best place they could be under the circumstances. They were all lying on their stomachs on the floor of the *beit midrash* when I arrived.

At the same time, I got a frantic call from Rada, the principal of a very special school in El Hader called "The School of the Flower and the Hope" that goes from first grade through high school. Her father, Dr. Issa Hussein, had been the founder and director of the school until he was felled by a massive heart attack a short time prior to this incident. He was one of the most beloved Palestinians I have ever met, and one of the most idealistic about peace.

Our yeshiva, on the Dagan Hill, and this school in El Hader, are about a kilometer apart. There was a period when our yeshiva students were teaching the Palestinian pupils how to use computers, and they were teaching our students Arabic and the Koran. To a certain extent it was a golden period. We enjoyed a very good relationship with the Palestinian communities around Efrat, and especially with the School of the Flower and the Hope.

Rada, a young, intelligent, and very capable woman, took over the running of the school after her father died. Arafat was never much in favor of the school; in fact, he did whatever he could to cause it to fail. (It was too high-profile – especially with American donors – for him to totally close it down.) I did my best to encourage philanthropists to help because it was a marvelous example of Palestinian-Israeli cooperation.

So that Motza'ei Yom Kippur, Rada called me, almost hysterical. She assumed I was at home, and informed me that Radio Palestine was reporting some shooting emanating from the yeshiva into their El Hader school, and that the Efrat residents were vandalizing and destroying the school. She begged me to stop the people of Efrat from attacking this friendly institution.

I told her, "I'm here right now. I want you to know exactly what's happening. The school has been taken over by the fanatic Palestinians who are trying to get at us, at you and at me. They vandalized the school, and they're shooting from the school into our yeshiva. We're doing everything we can to stop the shooting. We have to shoot back, we have no other choice; our yeshiva students and their families are in terrible danger. There are no other people from Efrat present here except for myself, the IDF, and the students of the yeshiva. The artillery against us is coming from the Palestinian invaders of your school."

At that point some of the babies began to cry and one or two of the adults began to laugh hysterically on the *beit midrash* floor. There was a young man lying on his stomach – Yehoshua – who had a very good voice, and I asked him to begin to sing in order to calm everyone. He said he had a better idea, crawled out into the dormitory where he was staying, and crawled back with a guitar. He brought the guitar into the *beit midrash*. He started to play *Am Yisrael Ḥai, Od Avinu Ḥai,* a Shlomo Carlebach song from the Soviet Jewry movement. Everyone began to sing and clap, while on their stomachs on the floor of the *beit midrash*. Yehoshua continued to play songs of praise to God and songs of love of Israel. It was the most surrealistic and inspiring scene I have ever witnessed in my life. Up above, firebombs falling and bullets whizzing, while from the *beit midrash* floor, a *kumzitz* for an hour and twenty minutes.

The shooting from the other side finally died down, and the IDF ordered that the yeshiva be evacuated. Everyone was taken to our Ohr Torah retreat center. By now it was about 11:00 at night after Yom Kippur, and no one had broken the fast. My sister and I live next door to each other, right opposite the retreat center, on Te'ena Hill, about six kilometers from Dagan Hill. When the yeshiva families and students arrived, we opened the refrigerators in both of our homes and fed everybody.

The next morning, representatives of the yeshiva came to speak with me. They thanked me for making the retreat center available, but they said they had taken a vote, and decided they must return to Dagan Hill. It was their home. And besides, they said, if the yeshiva is forced to close, the Hill would be totally unpopulated and unprotected, and the Palestinians would move closer and start shooting at the center of

Efrat. Efrat and then Jerusalem. Dagan had to be populated and had to be defended. They were committed to staying.

I repeated what they had said to the IDF. The IDF understood the strategic importance of their decision. During the Sukkot vacation, the Defense Ministry put up *betonadot,* concrete slabs that are impervious to bullets, to surround the yeshiva and protect it.

The yeshiva has almost doubled in size since then, in spite of that very difficult period. Thank God, as of the time of this writing, there has been no need for tanks or special IDF protection on Dagan Hill, and we have received governmental permission for Jerusalem-stone-clad permanent housing.

Chapter Eighty-Eight

Pizzeria Efrat: Kosher Pizza, Holy People

Mordecai and Anne Goodman have been the proprietors of Pizzeria Efrat almost since Efrat began. They came to Israel via Lincoln Square Synagogue, although Anne grew up in Flatbush, Brooklyn, and Mordecai in Houston, Texas. They were blessed with nine children, the second son of whom was named Yosef (each of their seven sons is named for one of Israel's tribes).

I was privileged to have given Yosef his name at his circumcision, to have blessed him at his bar mitzva, to have observed his rambunctious, but good-natured, pranks that often got him into trouble, to have delighted in his success as an outstanding paratrooper in the Maglan Unit, and to have been warmed by his wide smile and strong embrace every time we met.

One fateful day, during a training maneuver, Yosef's parachute became intertwined with the parachute of his commanding officer; if he did nothing, chances were that both would be killed, but if he separated the parachutes, he would plunge to certain death while his CO, a veritable legend in the unit, would most probably live. In the split-second moment of decision, Yosef managed to disentangle the parachutes – he was given a hero's burial on Mount Herzl. The evening before the funeral, I spent many hours with the family. Mordecai hardly spoke a word, only adjuring me, as I left very late that night, "Rabbi, I don't want you to say at the eulogy that this is the price of *aliya*." I acceded to his request, but was perplexed as to its meaning. Was this not the ultimate sacrifice, the ultimate price of *aliya*?

One year later, Mordecai and Anne came to my home with a "*shayla*." Their third son, Yehuda, was about to enter the IDF, and wished to serve in Maglan. They, as parents of a soldier who had lost his life in the line of duty had to give their written permission. They didn't want to sign, Yehuda desperately wanted to continue his brother's path; what should they do? I hesitated, saw Anne's tears, but stated, "I do not believe we as parents have the right to make moral decisions for our children, or even to deny them their moral decisions." This time Mordecai was also crying. "Then we must sign," he said, as he and Anne left my home. I ran after them. "I believe what I told you was right. Nevertheless, if it was my son, I don't know if I myself would have the courage to sign."

The next night was our Yom HaZikaron (Remembrance Day) ceremony in Efrat. Mordecai asked me to come back to his house afterwards. I found a "party" in full swing, pizza and ice cream, a house filled with people, and films of Yosef on a screen. The entire Maglan unit was invited to welcome Yehuda, in the presence of the Goodman family and friends. I walked over to Mordecai: "You're a better man than I am, Gunga Din," I said. "No," he said; "our children are better than we are."

As I slowly and humbly walked home that evening, I finally think I understood Mordecai's request. Yosef's death was not the price of *aliya*; in a difficult but profound way, it was the privilege of *aliya*. Yosef had given up this world in order to secure a better world, a future world for Jews, a world of love and peace, a world of redemption. Yosef died protecting his people, his land, and his future. Yosef did not die as a victim, but as a victor – for the sake of Yom HaAtzma'ut. Yosef may have lost some of the temporal world, but he gained eternity.

Chapter Eighty-Nine

Amikam

Amikam was my son Yoni's best friend. He was a tall, husky teenager, full of fun, with a perennial smile and a constant willingness to initiate a good-natured prank. He was not a particularly devoted student, nor did he wear his religion on his sleeve. But he was a most enthusiastic singer of Shabbat and festival *zemirot*, the most dedicated, loving and beloved friend, the life of every party "*berosh tov*" (with a good head, as he used to smilingly say), and was regarded as the heart of his *ḥevra* circle of friends. On the day before the festival of Sukkot, 5756 (1996), during the course of his military service, Amikam was killed by a bullet shot by a Palestinian who turned against the Israelis guarding the settlement of Netzarim in Gush Katif.

Thousands of people, including hundreds and hundreds of teenagers, attended his funeral in Efrat. His parents maintained a heroic, quiet dignity, barely giving way to tears, quietly speaking of the tragic necessity of sacrifice for our homeland. I spoke as the rabbi of Efrat, and my son Yoni spoke as a friend; he and all of the *ḥevra* were still serving in the IDF. Yoni spoke without fear or bitterness, but with firm resolve on behalf of the group to redouble their efforts, to be even better soldiers – for the sake of Israel and Amikam – to make sure that he did not die in vain.

Though it has been many years since his passing, close to a hundred young adults still gather in his home for a Torah lecture in his memory on a regular basis. Many of the *ḥevra* have since married, and they have introduced the custom of an hour of singing before the *ḥuppa* in his memory. Two of the *ḥevra* who had removed their *kippot* in the army began wearing them again – in honor of Amikam, what he stood for and what he believed in. Israel is a country of great intensity – with life-and-death experiences touching everyone deeply.

The aftermath of Amikam's tragic death was the greatest tribute to his special life, so profoundly appreciated by a very special group of friends.

Chapter Ninety

Israel and Jerusalem Will Comfort Us

Tragically, the Palestinian intifadas and the suicide bomber attacks have taken the lives of too many people from Efrat – placing me (as the rabbi) in the very difficult and even impossible position of informing close relatives – at times aged parents, as well as young children – of the murder of their loved ones. The following incident – which occurred about a decade before my *aliya* – immeasurably helped me to come to grips with the enormous sacrifices our community is forced to make.

Toward the end of the Yom Kippur war, I received a call from the Israel Bonds office, asking that I guide a group of leading businessmen – some of whom had not previously donated to Israel – on a special tour of the country. I could plan out every detail of the itinerary for the five days of the tour as long as I understood that my goal was to try to get forty million dollars out of these forty individuals by the conclusion of the "mission."

I immediately agreed, especially because I felt very guilty about still living in America at the time, and yearned for an opportunity to do what I could for the struggling Jewish state. Among the participants were a few people whom I knew from before, most notably, Jerome Stern, then vice president of Lincoln Square Synagogue, a very beloved friend to this day and a devoted friend of Israel; Seymour Abrams, head of a bank in Chicago, who had become a devoted friend and a generous supporter; and Larry Phillips, then CEO of Van Heusen Shirts.

I traveled on the plane with a donated *sefer Torah* earmarked for a newly established community, and the fact that the wooden "*atzei ḥayyim*" (roller handles) kept moving dangerously close to the eyes of my seatmate (Harvey Kruger, soon to be President of the American Friends of the Hebrew University) got us off to a rather inauspicious start. We arrived at Ben Gurion just two days before the final cease-fire. We visited the Golan and we even brought back some war maps, which I still have. Obviously, we went to the hospital to visit those wounded in battle. It was a very full and emotionally wrenching trip.

Whilst on the plane to Israel, I had been shocked to see a particular notice of mourning in the *Jerusalem Post*. When I had first begun my career as the rabbi of Lincoln Square Synagogue, one of the earliest rabbinical functions I attended was a farewell brunch for Rav and Rebbetzin Schwartz, for their impending *aliya*. Rav Schwartz was a European rabbi living on the West Side, not really a practicing rabbi, but very well known and a Talmud scholar of note. He had lost his entire first family, wife and children, in the Holocaust, remarried in America and now had two sons, a teenager and a pre-bar mitzva.

In 1964, he and his family decided to move to Israel, and because he was so close to all of the rabbis, the Rabbinical Council of the West Side gave the Rav and Rebbetzin a farewell reception. I was a newcomer and I really barely knew them, but nevertheless I attended the brunch.

Later we were all shocked and saddened to hear that their eldest son had been killed in the Six Day War. And now, on the plane, on the way to Israel toward the end of the Yom Kippur War, I saw that their second son, their only remaining son, had been killed in action as well. I knew that I had to pay a condolence call. The notice had the day of the funeral as well, and I calculated that the day that we arrived in Israel would be the last full day of *shiva* (seven days of mourning).

I got everyone settled into their rooms in the King David Hotel. I then excused myself from the group and said that I would have to leave for a short time while they got organized and rested. The Schwartzes lived at 8 Shimoni Street in a small apartment, and there must have been close to a hundred people who had come to try to console. The Rav and Rebbetzin, who looked much, much older than I remembered them, were sitting on cushions on the floor. Everyone else was standing. The room was heavy with the press of the people and with an ominous and shrieking silence, a silence that seemed to scream out to the very heavens.

Jewish law dictates that when you pay a condolence call, the visitor is not supposed to speak first; the mourner is. The visitor must listen to what the mourner has to say and respond to whatever that happens to be. And if the mourners choose not to speak, then no one speaks. The Rav and his wife were sitting and not speaking, so no one was speaking. I stood in the back of the room for about twenty minutes. I didn't even know if Rav Schwartz remembered me at all.

Since I felt a responsibility for the group waiting for me back at the hotel, I began to leave, and, as I did so, I walked past Rav and Rebbetzin Schwartz, saying what one always says when one leaves a house of mourning: "*HaMakom yenaḥem etkhem betokh she'ar avelei Tziyon veYerushalayim*. May the Almighty comfort you among the rest of the mourners of Zion and Jerusalem."

Rav Schwartz looked up at me. "Rav Riskin, yes?"

"Yes," I replied.

"Rav Riskin," he said, "why is the subject of the prayer that you express to a mourner, '*HaMakom*?' '*HaMakom*' means place. Yes, in this context it's a synonym for God, because the whole world is God's place. But wouldn't it have made more sense for consolers to say '*HaShem yenaḥem etkhem*, 'May the God of compassion comfort you,' or 'May *Elokim*, the God of creation comfort you.' Why use '*HaMakom*?' the Place?

"I'll tell you why," he continued, "I understand it now for the first time. When my family was destroyed in the Holocaust, there was no comforting me; it was so senseless, so absurd. But now that I have lost my only remaining sons and have no chance for other children, I am sad, sad beyond even the ability to speak, but I am comforted nevertheless. At least this time my sons died so that the Jewish people could live. They died in defense of Israel. They died in defense of Yerushalayim. They died in defense of the Jewish future. *HaMakom,* the place: Jerusalem, Israel, the Jewish state. *HaMakom menaḥem oti,* the place comforts me among the mourners of Zion and Jerusalem."

I had entered the room in order to give comfort. I left the room having received it. And so very often, as a rabbi living and functioning in Israel, when close friends, beloved congregants, and students have been murdered in a war or a terrorist attack, I've repeated this magnificent interpretation and truth taught by Rav Schwartz. *HaMakom menaḥem otanu*: in our fateful times, the place does comfort us; Israel and Jerusalem, for whose sake our loved ones gave their lives, comfort us.

Chapter Ninety-One

"Tikkin Olam"

During the time when forty IDF soldiers were still stationed around Yeshivat Siaḥ Yitzḥak, I would give a class on Thursday afternoons and a number of the soldiers would generally come in to hear my *shiur.* There was one black soldier in IDF uniform who came into this particular class, sat in front and took voluminous notes. He didn't look like an Ethiopian; he looked like an African American.

After I finished the *shiur,* he quickly left the study hall. Curious as to his background, I ran out after him and introduced myself. He told me that his name was Dan and he came from Nigeria. I asked, "What are you doing here? How did you end up in the IDF? Why did you come?"

"*Tikkin olam*" he said.

It took me a little while to understand; he had meant to say *tikkun olam,* "to perfect the world." I said, "Please explain."

He told me that there were groups of Israelis, a kind of Israeli, post-army "peace corps" that were sent to third-world countries every year in order to share with them the latest developments in agriculture and medicine. Among the "peace corps" ambassadors who had come to Nigeria a few years before, had been a young man with a *kippa,* a leader in Bnei Akiva, with whom Dan had become friendly. (Dan explained that Dan was not his given name. He took it because he knew the black Ethiopian Jews traced their lineage back to the tribe of Dan.) Dan was drawn to this young man with the *kippa* and asked him many questions. In answer to Dan's query as to why Israelis would take one to two years out of their lives – after having concluded three to five years of army service – to help Nigerians, the Israeli explained the Jewish concept of *tikkun olam,* perfecting the world, and how that is the real mission of Judaism, why we had been elected by God in the first place, and the real purpose of our existence – and survival – as a nation.

After the delegation left, Dan corresponded with the Israeli. A year later Dan came to Israel, joined an *ulpan* for *giyur,* conversion, became Jewish and was drafted into the IDF. He had planned on enlisting anyway, he said, as a volunteer. He felt that only Israel was truly fighting terror in the world, so being in the IDF was part of "*tikkin*" *olam.*

I was amazed by his story. I invited him to join us for dinner in our home that Friday evening; I wanted my wife and my whole family to be inspired by him. He said he was on duty that Friday evening, but he would be able to visit the following week.

Dan never came to visit. He was killed in the line of duty that week, protecting Yeshivat Siaḥ Yitzḥak.

I went to the funeral at the military cemetery on Mount Herzl. I was told that his parents were notified, but that there had been no response. Of course he received an army funeral with full honors. I tore *keriya* (symbol of mourning), and said *Kaddish* for him that year.

About six weeks later, I was resting on Shabbat afternoon, and my wife, who zealously guards my Shabbat nap – since I usually speak in at least three synagogues on Shabbat morning, and then teach a long *Daf Yomi* class – apologetically woke me saying that she thought it was important that I greet our guests.

When I came down to the living room I saw two black people sitting on the living room sofa, unmistakably Dan's parents. They said, "Rabbi, we don't know why our son came to Israel. We don't know why our son became Jewish or why he joined the Israel Defense Forces. We don't know why our son had to die. Everyone tells us that you had a serious conversation with him before he was killed. Perhaps you can give us the answer."

I spoke with them for about three hours, until way after Shabbat had already ended. I told them about "*tikkin olam.*"

The next time I heard from them was about two years later, when I got a call from Dan's father. They had enrolled in an *ulpan* in Netanya. They had studied Hebrew and then they had studied for and implemented conversion. They had now decided to live in Israel. In fact, they had taken an apartment in Netanya and asked me to come for the *Ḥanukkat HaBayit,* the dedication of their new home. They invited me to put up the *mezuza,* and say a few words.

Of course I went. Whatever I said could not match what Dan's mother said. "I know all of you are questioning why we left Nigeria and why we're living in Israel. All of our friends and relatives ask the same question. We have decided to cast our lot with the Jewish people in the Jewish homeland. We have decided to stand alongside of all of you in your fight against terror. The reason is very simple: *tikkin olam.*"

Most of the time, if we are fortunate, children continue the narrative of their parents; in this instance, Dan's parents are continuing the narrative of their son, may his soul serve as a blessing.

Chapter Ninety-Two

Efrat's Palestinian Neighbors: What Unites Us

When I made *aliya* to Israel in 1983, a proud settler (*mitnaḥel*) to Efrat, Gush Etzion, reclaiming my legacy and believing incontrovertibly in my right to be here, I was also committed to being a good neighbor to the peaceful village Arabs in their homes near Efrat: Wadi El-Nis, Jorat Al-Shamaa, and Wadi Rahal. In fact, before we had been settled in for three months, I invited the *mukhtars* (Arab mayors) of the neighboring villages to my home for a late Monday afternoon, social get-together.

My wife strenuously objected – and we had one of the very rare disagreements in our married life together. She felt we were at war with the Arabs, and definitely did not want them in our home.

I insisted that unless we got to know them, the prejudice between us would only grow, and that it was my house as well to invite whomever I wished. My wife agreed – but she said that she would neither prepare for them nor serve them. I felt she was hitting below the belt because, as she knew so very well, I was incapable of adequately preparing even a cup of coffee. We finally compromised; my wife prepared everything, including baking cakes and cookies (there was no bakery in Efrat) – but left with the children for Jerusalem thirty minutes before the expected arrival of the *mukhtar*s.

Some half dozen Arab mayors arrived. I had received a briefing on proper Arab etiquette: begin with juices and colas, only serving coffee at the end of the meeting, since – for them – coffee was the signal that it was time to depart. I also understood that wine – as well as any inebriating beverage like whisky, liqueurs or beer – was absolutely forbidden to a Muslim.

The meeting was most cordial, and lasted for close to three hours. At the end of our get-together, one of the *mukhtar*s rose to thank me. "I wish to express gratitude to our host for attempting to meet us as people to people and neighbor to neighbor. I also want to give our thanks for the fine repast and home-baked cakes he prepared for us. But most of all, I wish to thank our host for his sensitivity to our feelings. There is no woman in sight; even his wife is not present. He must have understood that our Muslim tradition does not sanction the mixing of sexes at social gatherings."

* * *

Sue Tedman, a resident of Efrat, and a unique woman who has reached out especially to the women of Wadi Rahal, planned a song-fest in her home, with Arab and Efrati women singing and playing musical instruments for each other. I was asked by her to give greetings at the beginning of the evening.

Then I received a call from the *mukhtar* of Wadi Rahal, who sounded rather uncomfortable on the phone. He asked about my welfare, kept returning to the subject of the joint musical evening, asking if my busy schedule would actually enable me to attend the event. When I pressed him as to whether he had any objections to my giving greetings, he finally explained that the Koran forbids a man from hearing a female sing, and – conversely – a woman from singing in the presence of a man. Ah, I thought, *kol isha* (the prohibition against a male hearing a female singing), and I explained that I had no intention of remaining for the singing but only in giving introductory greetings before the song-fest would begin.

However, he still was not satisfied. "I do not wish to offend you," he said, "but the Koran forbids us from being someplace where people might even think that we had been present during the women's singing." Ah, I thought, the Talmudic concept of *marit ayin,* (not doing something that might be construed as wrongdoing), and I assured him that I would send greetings in absentia by a letter that would be read out by Sue Tedman.

Apparently, our religions have more in common than I realized.

* * *

Eid al-Adha is a joyous time for the Muslims, during which many traditional families slaughter a lamb as part of the three-day festival. Several of my American donor-supporters, aware of my desire to be a good neighbor to the peaceful Muslims living around Efrat, and mindful of the Talmudic adage that it is incumbent upon us "to support the poor Gentiles together with the poor Israelites, visit the sick Gentiles together with the sick Israelites, and bury the dead Gentiles together with the dead Israelites" (*Gittin* 61a), made a special *ḥesed* (kindness) fund available to me for the specific purpose of helping our Arab neighbors. Hence, I traditionally help the widows and orphans of Wadi El-Nis to purchase lambs for the festival of *Eid al-Adha.*

The *mukhtar* always calls to thank me in advance of the festival, and I remember the first time he invited me to participate in it with him. Since I obviously could not eat their meat or cooked foods, I opted to go for the last meal of the three days, which consists of fruits, nuts, tea and cold drinks. I took the opportunity to ask the *mukhtar* to explain the significance of the festival.

The *mukhtar* took a deep breath, threw his head back, closed his eyes and – with a smile on his face that expressed a most pleasant memory – began to speak, not only to me but to the entire assemblage, his family tribe, including his fourteen sons (from four wives) and their male children.

"We have a great-great-grandfather Ibrahim who lived in Hebron." (He pointed in the direction of Hebron and spoke of Ibrahim as though he had actually met him as a child.) "Ibrahim discovered Allah and served Him with all his heart and soul. And then one day Allah tested Ibrahim, to see if he really loved and feared Him. 'Take your son, your only son, the son whom you love, and sacrifice him to Me. Take Ishmael and sacrifice him to Me. Take Ishmael and sacrifice him.' Now you know, Rabbi, how much we love our sons. When my first son Ali was born, I came to be called Abu Ali. Our names change when we have a son because our sons are the very definition of ourselves. And Allah told Ibrahim to sacrifice his first son, Ishmael.

"And Ibrahim was ready to do it. He woke up early the next morning, and woke up Ishmael, and together they went to the sacrifice. And at the last moment, just as Ibrahim raised the knife, ready to slit Ishmael's throat, Allah said he didn't need to sacrifice him, he had already proved how much he [Ibrahim] loved Allah, and he could sacrifice a lamb instead. In thanks to Allah for showing such kindness to Ibrahim, and allowing Ishmael to live, every family slaughters a lamb and feasts for three days..."

* * *

It was 1986, and the first *Intifada*, Arab uprising against the Israelis, had begun. Arab adults as well as children were throwing stones at passing Israeli cars, breaking windshields, maiming the drivers, and causing many accidents and even deaths.

The IDF ruled that a protective fence be put up between Wadi El-Nis and Efrat. The *mukhtar* came to see me.

"We have a verse in the Koran," he said. "'A close neighbor is better than a far-away brother' [we have the same verse in our book of Proverbs]. We have been close neighbors whose love for each other has made us brothers. I beg of you, do not put up the fence. It would embarrass our friendship. I guarantee that there never will be a problem from Wadi El-Nis."

Our city council checked with the Israel Defense Forces, the IDF checked with Israeli Intelligence, and the order for us to put up a fence was removed. Until this day there has been no trouble from Wadi El-Nis – much the opposite, they have proven their friendship in many significant ways.

* * *

When my mother died, the *mukhtar* and a number of his sons and friends came to pay a condolence call. Just as they entered my home, a number of visitors were asking why there are twelve months of mourning for a parent and only thirty days of mourning for a child. Isn't the death of a child in a parent's lifetime a greater cause for mourning, since it goes against the natural order of things? Shouldn't mourning for a child be longer and not shorter than mourning for a parent?" I explained to the *mukhtar* the tenor of the discussion, and he immediately said, "It is the same in the Muslim tradition. We too mourn for a lost relative seven days (but in the evening, from sunset to midnight) sitting on the ground, and then for a month without celebrations for our parents. Why is it longer for parents than for children? You see, we love our children very much, but one has many children. We love our spouses, but one often marries again and can have a number of spouses. In my case, for example, I have four wives. But you and I will only have within our lifetime, one mother and one father; a mother and father are unique and irreplaceable."

Chapter Ninety-Three

Take Heed of an Enemy's Warning: What Divides Us

The Palestinians in Wadi El-Nis, Jorat Al-Shamaa and Wadi Rahal have no medical insurance, despite the millions of dollars the P.A. received from the European Union for this purpose. Our Efrat Emergency Medical Center accepts Palestinians as well as Israelis. Many of the doctors of Efrat (we have close to one hundred in our "Jewish city") tend to the Palestinians almost free of charge, we have raised considerable amounts of money to send Palestinians to Jerusalem hospitals when necessary, and our *Hatzala* (Emergency Ambulance Service) operates in the Palestinian villages as well as in Efrat.

We also shared expenses with the village of Wadi El-Nis to send Sami, son of Daoud, a young promising Palestinian, through medical school in Europe.

Upon his return to Wadi El-Nis as a fully-fledged doctor, I secured a $250,000 pledge from Daniel S. Abraham – a supporter of many Jewish and Palestinian causes and a dedicated advocate of peaceful relationships in the Middle East – for the establishment of an Emergency First-Stage Medical Clinic in Wadi El-Nis. The newly certified Palestinian doctor would initially see the medical patients, administer first aid, or whatever he deemed necessary and felt qualified to take on, and would send special cases either to Efrat, Bethlehem or Jerusalem.

We received this commitment in the autumn of 1992, the heyday of the Oslo agreements. One can imagine my surprise and disappointment to discover that the Palestinian National Commission – specifically Salah Ta'amri, who was responsible for the Arab villages in Judea – refused to allow Wadi El-Nis to accept the gift. After at least two dozen telephone calls, I managed to secure a meeting with Salah Ta'amri in his office in Bethlehem. And it was one of the most important educational experiences of my life.

Salah Ta'amri is a most articulate and educated Palestinian, who has a master's degree from one of the British universities and is married to the former Queen Dinah, the first wife of the late King Hussein of Jordan. He lives in a palatial residence not far from Tekoa, where I had visited with him in the past, and had found him open-minded and intelligent.

This meeting was a disaster. Walking up the staircase to his office, there were posters picturing Israelis cruelly beating Palestinians. He barely rose to greet me, curtly calling me an "ugly Israeli occupier." When I told him that my sole interest was a humanitarian one and that I would gladly give him the medical equipment to give to the Palestinians in his name, he said it was too late because they would know it came from me. "But Palestinians will die without this medical opportunity," I argued. "In war, people die," he responded. "But I thought we were moving toward peace," I remonstrated. "Then you are a fool," he said. "With you, we are always at war. Until you leave Efrat, Jerusalem and Tel Aviv."

I was truly in shock. You see, I had read a book called *Mine Enemy* written by Aharon Barnea, a well-known Israeli writer and correspondent, together with his wife Amalia, about their friendship with Salah Ta'amri and his wife Dinah. The two men first met when Salah gave himself up to the Israelis at the beginning of the Lebanon War (1982). Ta'amri had become a "Judaeophile," widely read in Jewish history and philosophy, and believed that there must be a political compromise, a sharing of land brokered by the two sides. He was freed in a prisoner exchange, and had certainly expected that his fundamental position had not changed. I therefore told him that I had read the book, and asked why he now seemed to be so adamant about the necessity of warfare between Israel and Palestine.

"If you really want to know, I'll tell you. I believed in a peace based on compromise with Israel when I thought Israel would win. I changed my mind; I now believe that we will win in an armed battle. I changed my mind shortly before the prisoner exchange. I was exercising in the prison courtyard when I saw the Israeli guard eating pita and falafel. 'How can you eat what you are eating?' I asked him. 'I'll eat whatever I want,' he responded. 'I am still the guard and you are still the prisoner! I tell you what to eat. You don't tell me what to eat.' 'But today is the third day of Passover,' I told him. 'Your Bible forbids you eating pita bread on Passover.' 'I couldn't give a damn what a book written four thousand years ago has to say about anything,' said the guard. At that moment, I felt I had experienced an epiphany.

"If the Israelis don't care what the Bible says about Passover, they won't care about the Land of Israel either. If they are not connected to the Bible, they will not be connected to the land. They will not be willing to sacrifice for the land. This is a bad neighborhood for you Israelis."

I looked at Salah Ta'amri squarely in the eye. "You are wrong," I said to him, "dead wrong. You underestimate the Israeli and you underestimate the God of Israel. We have not just come to Israel. We have finally come home. And we will win. Our God of love and peace will emerge victorious over your God of power and *jihad*. We will win for our children's sake, we will win for God's sake, we will win for the free world's sake…

"And you know what? We will win for your sake and for the sake of a Palestinian people, most of whom want peace like we do. In our tradition, you see, in our Bible, Ishmael eventually rejoins the family of Abraham, and we finally live in this war-torn land together in peace."

Salah Ta'amri's words also contributed to one of the most important projects of Ohr Torah Stone – Yaḥad, committed to the promotion of Jewish unity and continuity within secular Israel, disseminating Jewish culture through the community centers. For nights after my meeting with Salah Ta'amri, I couldn't sleep. Is it true that the new Israelis are disengaged from their Biblical roots, are detached from the Jewish narrative and the Jewish mission, and are therefore apathetic even about educating their children toward a Jewish future, even about fighting for Israel? Have we finally returned to our homeland after two thousand years only to trade it in for Uganda, or even worse, for New York or California? And if so, how can we re-ignite them once again with a sense of Jewish purpose, of Israel's destiny? In the Diaspora we do it by producing dedicated and gifted synagogue rabbis and day-school educators (Straus Rabbinical School and Beren Educators Seminary has 350 graduates inspiring and engaging previously disaffected Jews all over the globe). But what about Israel where, due to the politicized nature of the religious establishment, the secular Jew has an allergy to synagogue and is disconnected from religious education? And then it came to me: just about every Israeli belongs to his local *matnas*, Jewish community center.

We started with radio ads: "Are you curious about Yom Kippur, but you won't step foot into a synagogue? Come to your local *matnas*, to a free explanatory service, an hour and fifteen minutes *Kol Nidrei*, an hour and fifteen minutes *Ne'ila*. All of your questions are welcome." The first year, 220 Israelis came; by the seventh year, more than 95,000 Israelis who called themselves secular piled into at least 240 community centers with the help of Rav Melchior, the Tzohar organization and the Bachrach family. Today, with the help of Robert M. Beren we have eighteen *Matnasim* with full time Jewish Culture Facilitators engaging Israelis to explore the treasure trove of their tradition with amazing success, and we will not stop until all four-hundred-plus community centers are so directed.

No, Salah Ta'amri, the Israelis do care, desperately, about their common narrative, about their unique destiny to bring compassionate righteousness, moral justice and a secure peace to the world. It only requires the right venue to draw the desire out of them.

Chapter Ninety-Four

Let the Messiah Decide

One of the great signs – indeed, miracles – of this very fateful and momentous period of "the beginning of the sprouting of our redemption" – in addition to the return of our Jewish national sovereignty over Israel after two millennia of persecution and pogrom, the ingathering of our exiles, especially the lost tribe of Dan from Ethiopia and the lost tribe of Menashe from Northern India, and our ability to resuscitate the Hebrew language and make the desert bloom – is the rapprochement between Christians and Jews after almost two thousand years of enmity, anti-Semitism and the calumny of deicide. And our new-found friends could not have appeared one moment too soon. Today the fundamentalist Muslim ideology seems to be the major vocal expression of the more than one billion Muslims, rapidly multiplying from Europe to the third world by their high birth rate and active conversions, threatening to extirpate Israel from the Middle East and rule the world through *jihad*. It hardly seems plausible that fewer than thirteen million Jews can stop the fanatically driven, militaristic advance of these heinous heirs to Nazi Germany.

And precisely now, significant leadership within Catholic, Protestant, and especially Evangelical Christianity – representing one and a half billion people – is suddenly proffering the hand of friendship, asking our forgiveness for the church anti-Semitism that set the stage for the European Holocaust, rejecting replacement theology and supersessionism, calling us their elder brother and the recipients of the root covenant upon which they were merely grafted, and recognizing the miracle of our return to our homeland. Because there is suddenly such a thirst even among many rank-and-file Christians to study the texts and texture of the religion from which Jesus emerged, because we share a belief in the absolute morality of the Ten Commandments and in a God of love who wants and guarantees a world of peace (not *jihad*), and because we share a mutual acceptance of the Bible as the revealed and sacred word of God, Ohr Torah Stone (due to the generosity of beloved friends Susan and Roger Hertog) has established an Institute for Jewish-Christian Understanding and Cooperation.

But I'm getting ahead of my story. One of the major Evangelical Christian organizations, which has supported and visited Israel (and Efrat) during the worst periods of Intifada and suicide attacks, often calls upon me to speak before their various gatherings in Israel and Europe. In 2003, I was asked first to address an audience of five-thousand-plus students at Jerusalem's Convention Center and then to speak to some 250 leaders from throughout the world. That very morning (it was during the Festival of Sukkot), *HaAretz* newspaper had written a blistering editorial against them, emphasizing their right-wing political stance and claiming that the only reason for their friendship was to further their agenda of converting us.

The head of this particular group asked that I address the editorial in my talk to the leadership. I explained to them that before I could accept the bullet-proof bus they had so generously donated to us, I had carefully checked into their theology and practical agenda, by reading their brochures and studying their web-sites, to ascertain whether or not they were a missionary organization. If I understood them correctly, at the present time their goal was not to convert us (unless a particular Jew happens to approach them with the interest of converting); what was most important at that time was for every Jew in the world to become a good and committed Jew, and live in Israel. When that happens, they believe there will be a major world conflict, Armageddon – between

Christians and Jews on one side, Muslims on the other – over the control of Jerusalem. We will win that war jointly, after which the period of redemption will be upon us and all the righteous dead will be resurrected. Naturally, the founder of Christianity, Jesus, will be resurrected at that time, and he – the Messiah – will then convert all the Jews to Christianity. During my brief presentation of their theology of the end of the days, they listened with rapt attention, frequently interrupting my words with standing ovations, spirited applause, and "amen" exclamations of approval.

I continued my address, telling them that I had been in *kiruv* work for the entire period of my ministry, and that I reckoned it would take several hundred years to effectuate such a Jewish spiritual revival; to bring those good Jews to Israel would take another hundred years, and then the war, and then the resurrection. "In the meantime, I concluded, "we are being desperately threatened by extremist Islam today, and we must appreciate every hand of friendship offered us. I therefore accept with sincere gratitude your heart and your support." A standing ovation, fervent "ay-mens," and elongated applause were their spirited reaction to my words.

"But," I continued, "I must add one more point to be perfectly honest with you. I fundamentally agree with your eschatology, because we too have sources that insist that there will be no redemption without repentance, which means the Jewish return to God's Torah and to God's land. And of course we also have prophets who speak of an Armageddon, a Gog and Magog war over the stewardship of the holy city of Jerusalem; the prophecy includes a Jewish victory and then the beginning of the era of redemption and the resurrection of the dead. Moreover, I believe that Jesus will be resurrected, because my reading of the Gospels [greatly influenced by Professor David Flusser of the Hebrew University] teaches me that he was a good Jew.

"However, when he looks around at the world two thousand years later, and the adoring crowds who gather around him, he will express profound perplexity. 'What is this Sunday church?' he will ask. 'I went to the synagogue on Saturday. And bacon and eggs for breakfast? My Bible forbids pork products. And why celebrate Easter Sunday? The last supper was, after all, a Passover *seder*!' And so I believe that there will be a large and perhaps even mass conversion – but it will go in the other direction!"

Total silence enveloped the hall. No standing ovation, no spirited applause, no shouts of amen. Just silence.

And then the head of the group ran up to the podium, embraced me, and said into the microphone, "Brother Rabbi, let us agree to wait until the Messiah comes, and let him decide who will convert to whose religion."

"That's exactly what I said," I concluded. And with that, a burst of applause, a standing ovation and a chorus of amens. But in truth: we are not waiting for the Messiah – the Messiah is waiting for us, for us to come home, for us to begin to redeem.

Chapter Ninety-Five

The Berlin Memorial and Tractate *Pesaḥim*

This story begins in the 1970s, when I was visiting Israel – together with Moses Feuerstein, then President of the Orthodox Union of Jewish Congregations. He took me with him to call upon Rebbetzin Herzog, widow of Rav Yitzḥak HaLevi Herzog, the first chief rabbi of the newly-established State of Israel. She was a truly fascinating woman in her own right, very much involved in major projects of *ḥesed*. It was right before Yom HaShoah, Holocaust Memorial Day, and the rebbetzin recounted a fascinating incident that never made its way into the history books. She took out an old Vilna *Shas*, Tractate *Pesaḥim*, which she reverently kissed as she placed it gently on the table before us, and announced that that volume had been found among the personal effects of Adolf Hitler in the Berlin bunker where he had committed suicide with his mistress, Eva Braun. The allied forces discovered it, didn't know what to make of it, and apparently an important personage in the American State Department decided to present it to the chief rabbi of the new State of Israel.

Why did Hitler take a Talmudic tractate with him into the bunker? Clearly he was obsessed with the Jewish people, hell-bent on making

Europe *Judenrein,* on murdering the last Jew, on destroying Judaism. Did he know that *Pesaḥim* was the tractate dealing with the Festival of Jewish freedom from Egypt, of ultimate Jewish vindication and redemption? Did he believe in his twisted mind that he was burying the last Talmudic tractate? The answers to these questions are forever shrouded in mystery. But such is the fact of it: Tractate *Pesaḥim* was found in Hitler's bunker and given to Rav Herzog.

Fast forward to the week of Holocaust Remembrance Day 2006, when I was visiting Berlin because Ohr Torah Stone has eight rabbis and educators in Germany, and we were sponsoring two benefit cantorial concerts with Cantor Helfgot, one in Munich and the other in Berlin. The afternoon before the Berlin recital, I went to visit the Berlin Holocaust Memorial, designed by Peter Eisenmann. It is an outdoor memorial, resembling a sea of stones, memorial stones (*matzevot*), like those that one is used to seeing in a cemetery. These stones, however, are without any inscriptions: they are faceless, in various shapes and sizes; they are the monuments of *Klal Yisrael,* of the Jewish people entire, of Jewish lives not given a proper chance by Hitler to record their names in history, of charred remains without even a coffin for relatives to weep over. They are monuments of the dead and of the living, of all of us who still breathe and walk and speak, but who have also partially died in the Holocaust; and they are monuments of all of humanity, whose silence then, and whose anti-Semitism still today, mean that their souls and spirits were likewise destroyed by Hitler.

I walked through the maze of monuments, I lost my way, I felt as though I was living a nightmare in which the entire world had turned into a massive cemetery, I desperately sought an exit, I wanted to scream – and then I saw steps going down into a hellish netherworld. I tremblingly entered into a hall of pictures, individuals of varying ages and life poses, in the precise mode they were in when they had been taken to the death camps. And then I exited into the blessed light of a living street.

I picked up a brochure as I left; it said that there were 2,711 stones in the memorial. Why 2,711? Peter Eisenmann said it was arbitrary; it simply came out that way in the execution. But then I checked with Google. It turns out that there are precisely 2,711 pages of the Babylonian Talmud that we study in the *Daf Yomi* program. *Daf Yomi* is an international Talmud study program introduced in the early 1930s by Rav Meir Shapiro, dean of the famed Yeshivat Ḥakhmei Lublin (whose sacred books were publicly destroyed soon after Krystalnacht and whose building was turned into a medical seminary by the Nazis). There are now hundreds of thousands of adult students all over the globe studying the same page of Talmud each day and completing the entire Babylonian Talmud in seven years.

Hitler wanted to destroy the Jewish people; Hitler was destroyed in 1945 and a new Israel was reborn three years later with the establishment of the Jewish state. Hitler wanted to destroy Judaism, to bury the last Talmud tractate; *Daf Yomi,* the renaissance of the Jewish study of Talmud, the very *Shas* itself (2,711 pages), buried him. Those Hebrew letters missing from the memorial stones in Berlin are present on each page of the Talmud, testifying that those nameless souls did not live in vain. The letters that make up the Hebrew word for stone, *even,* also represent *av-ben,* the parent-child bond that links every generation to the last, in an eternal chain that proved stronger than the Egyptian pyramids and the Nazi crematoria.

Chapter Ninety-Six

From Lvov to Efrat: Journey of a *Parokhet*

In 1990, the former Soviet Union decided to reopen the last remaining synagogue in Lvov (generally known as Lemberg, in an area that had once been Poland).

Lvov was formerly a proud city filled with Jews, even great Jewish scholars like the Taz (the Turei Zahav, Rav David HaLevi Segal, 1586–1667), who wrote an important commentary on the *Shulḥan Arukh*. Then came the Soviet Communist regime, and synagogue after synagogue in Lvov was closed down. Now, on the heels of "perestroika," the dramatic disintegration of the Iron Curtain, and the recanting of Stalinist Communism, at least one synagogue was slated to be reopened for the High Holy Days.

I was contacted by the president of the Lvov Jewish community – who had recently come out of hiding and revealed himself as a Jew, with a request of the Ohr Torah Stone Institutions, specifically the Joseph Straus Rabbinical Seminary, for one hundred Hebrew-Russian *maḥzorim* (High Holy Day prayer books), and a rabbi for the Days of

Awe, Rosh HaShana and Yom Kippur. The rabbi had to be able to lead the prayers, read the Torah, blow the *shofar* and give sermons – preferably in Russian or Yiddish. At that time we had no Russian-speaking rabbinical students, and the only ones who were conversant in leading the prayers, reading the Torah and blowing the *shofar* were our Sepharadim. So we chose one student, Yedidya Cohen, taught him a few hundred basic Yiddish words and expressions, gave him one hundred *maḥzorim*, and sent him off to Lvov!

When he returned after Yom Kippur, he related an amazing story. The Jewish Agency representative with whom we had been dealing expected a maximum of fifty to sixty Jews to attend the services; after all, there had been no operational synagogue in Lvov for at least fifty years! He had suggested we send a hundred *maḥzorim* just in case – and to be ready for a larger group of the aged who might come for the *Yizkor* memorial prayer on Yom Kippur.

Well, about one thousand Jews converged upon the synagogue that first Rosh HaShana, shoving and fighting for seats. When the time for *shofar*-blowing arrived, the crowds inside and outside the synagogue were almost impossible to control.

The "rabbi" remembered a story I had told of a shepherd boy in the Ukraine who had been left at the doorstep of a kindly, childless Christian family when his Jewish parents were fleeing a pogrom. He knew he was Jewish, played with Jewish children, and went to the synagogue of the famed Ba'al Shem Tov (the founder of Hasidic Judaism) for Rosh HaShana. He shamefacedly told the great sage that he didn't know the prayers, but that he very much would like to join the congregation for this most sacred day of the Jewish calendar.

The Ba'al Shem Tov embraced him, and asked him if he knew the Hebrew alphabet, the *alef beit*. When the shepherd boy answered in the affirmative, for he had picked it up from his Jewish friends, the Ba'al Shem Tov explained that all he had to do was recite the *alef beit*. "Don't worry," he explained to the much-heartened youth. "God knows what is in your heart, and He will put the letters together to form the right words for you."

Our rabbi told the Russian crowd this story, in a broken but understandable Sepharadi Yiddish, and asked each of them to recite the *alef beit*, after which they would hear the sounds of the *shofar*.

An elderly Jewish woman cried out in Yiddish, "*Uber rebbe, vus tut men az mir veisin nit afilu der alef beis*?" "But Rebbe, what do we do if we don't even know the alphabet?"

Our rabbi told everyone to repeat each letter after him, *alef, beit, gimmel*, seven times, in perfect unison. Never, reported the rabbi, had he experienced a more meaningful *shofar*-blowing experience.

* * *

Ḥanokh Aḥiman, a resident of Efrat from its very beginnings, whose son Yinon served as Mayor of Efrat for fifteen years (and is today the Director-General of Ohr Torah Stone Institutions of Israel), served as the architectural designer of the *Rav Takhliti* (all-purpose) shul in Rimon, today the downstairs level of the main Rimon shul. Historically, it was precisely this space that hosted the very first Efrat *minyan* and now serves as the *beit midrash* in which *Daf Yomi* is taught to forty participants every morning.

Just before Ḥanokh had completed the finishing touches on the *Rav Takhliti* shul, he came to my home clutching a package very close to his heart.

He told me that right after World War II – he had spent the war years already living in "Palestine" – he was sent by the Bnei Akiva movement into the DP (displaced persons) camps in Europe to attempt to persuade as many young people as possible to come to Israel.

In one of these camps he met an elderly sick Jew, who was literally too weak to move. He had been the *gabbai* of the shul in Lvov, whose exceptional sanctity, according to legend, emanated from the fact that in the seventeenth century the Taz had been its rabbi. The curtained cover (*parokhet*) of the Holy Ark in that shul was considered very special; shul history had it that one particular Shabbat there had been a terrible pogrom in which both sons of the Taz had been murdered in sanctification of God's name, their blood spattered onto the *parokhet*. Many generations had cleaned the *parokhet*, but the blood spots could never be washed away.

The *gabbai* had miraculously saved the *parokhet*, guarding it with his life throughout the years of the Holocaust. He tearfully and lovingly presented it to Ḥanokh Aḥiman, to use it to cover a Holy Ark in the Holy Land of Israel.

Ḥanokh presented it to me, and it now graces the Holy Ark of the *Rav Takhliti* shul in Efrat every year on the High Holy Days.

Chapter Ninety-Seven

The Apostate and the Convert

One Friday afternoon, perhaps three hours before sunset, I was sitting in my garden studying the biblical portion of the week and preparing my Sabbath Torah lessons. A good-looking young man came up to me and said, (in English, but with a rather pronounced European accent), "I read your weekly column in the *Jerusalem Post*. That's why I came – and forgive me that I didn't make an appointment. I want to convert, and I want you to convert me." I explained to him that that was a heavy request for a few hours before the Sabbath; He told me that he was a great grandson of Rabbi Zolli of Rome. I immediately invited him for Shabbat.

Rabbi Israel Zolli was the chief rabbi of Rome who had converted to Christianity in 1944. The story of Rabbi Zolli's conversion had sent shock waves throughout the world Jewish community. In the midst of an internal controversy regarding his Chief Rabbinate, he claimed to have seen a divine vision and converted to Catholicism – joined by his wife and daughter. And here was his descendant who had been brought up as a Christian. I arranged for him to study with one of my students, and he was converted by a religious court in Jerusalem.

About a year later, he asked if he could visit for the Sabbath with his lovely fiancée, after which they both asked if I would perform their marriage ceremony. I agreed with alacrity, but he quickly added his one proviso: he wished to be married between Rosh HaShana and Yom Kippur, during the Ten Days of Repentance, in his great-grandfather's synagogue, the main synagogue in Rome. He wanted his wedding to be a *tikkun* (repair) for his grandfather's soul.

And so, in 1997, during the Ten Days of Repentance, I found myself, an expectant bride and groom, and no more than twenty other guests (including the cantor of the synagogue), in the rather immense, high-ceilinged and cavernous synagogue of Rome's ancient ghetto. Strangely enough, the synagogue didn't feel empty; I had the mystical and eerie sense that also present were the silent, stalwart, and stubborn souls of two thousand years of Italian Jewry, souls who had obstinately prayed in that synagogue of the ghetto despite the beckoning image of the founder of Christianity on the church painting outside, souls who had felt betrayed by the conversion of their former chief rabbi.

I began to intone the blessings of betrothal, the prayer shawl on my back feeling weighed down by the oppression of *galut* (exile), which felt more palpable here than in any other place I had ever been. When I came to the last of the seven nuptial blessings, however, that "Soon there will be heard in the cities of Judah and in the wide thoroughfares of Jerusalem, the sound of joy and the sound of gladness, the sound of grooms and the sound of brides," the bridegroom under the canopy suddenly shouted out in Hebrew, his eyes and his hands thrust upwards toward the vaulted ceiling and the heavens above:

"Do you hear, Grandfather, the promise of our prophets? You didn't believe it would happen, you thought the cross had conquered forever, and so you became a renegade. But the ancient promise is being fulfilled, every day and every night, in reborn Jerusalem. Listen to these words, Grandfather, and look down at our ancient land yielding new fruit, at our barren mother bearing laughing children, gaze with wonder at our nation reborn, – and wherever you may be, repent! Return,

Grandfather, return through me; allow me to be your *tikkun*, your repair, and may your tortured soul finally rest in peace…"

It was the most inspiring wedding ceremony I ever experienced.

Chapter Ninety-Eight

The *Ḥuppa* on the Tennis Court

Soon after his discharge from the IDF, Rafael became engaged to Ḥanni. Both were children of Efrat. Rafael was of Sepharadi origin and Ḥanni was Ashkenazi. They and their parents began to vigorously prepare for the wedding, planned for August 10 of that year.

And then the health of Rafael's father, who had undergone an operation for cancer several years earlier, began to deteriorate. One Thursday afternoon in mid-June, I received a tearful call from Rafael's mother. The doctor had just released her husband from the hospital, informing her that, from a medical perspective, he had days – not weeks – to live. She was filled with despair at the prospect of planning a wedding that her life's partner would in all likelihood not be attending. Rafael's mother begged me to inform the young couple of the precise medical report on Rafael's father's condition, and attempt to persuade them to make the wedding as soon as possible. She cried into the telephone, "I don't know myself whether it's fair to ask of the bride to agree to such a hurried wedding. I leave it in your hands, Rabbi: you know what's right."

I met the engaged couple at 11:00 P.M. that Thursday evening, after returning from a condolence call in Arad. I compassionately but honestly described the situation as I had heard it, suggesting the possibility of radically moving up the date of the wedding to Sunday (barely two-and-a-half days later), but admitting the inherent difficulties of such short notice and the concomitant compromise of the typical nuptial event so anticipated and longed for. Ḥanni immediately said, "The only important thing for me now is that Rafael's father be present at our wedding ceremony. The wedding must be on Sunday."

Both sets of parents were too overwhelmed by the family health situation and the shortness of notice to be involved in the preparations. So the close friends took over. Between Thursday evening at 11:30, when the couple left my home, and Sunday evening at 6:15 P.M. – with a Shabbat day in between during which no planning was possible – a magnificent wedding was designed and implemented. Three hundred and fifty people were called and invited, the Efrat tennis court was the designated venue, catering, tables, flowers, *ḥuppa*, lighting, band, and portable toilets were arranged, and everyone – including Rafael's father – was in attendance.

The sounds of music and dancing could be heard throughout Efrat until close to midnight – and Rafael's father lived until the following Thursday evening, when he surrendered his soul with a sense of peace and fulfillment. And I, the proudest rabbi in the world, felt a sense of unworthiness to represent a congregation of young people who could respond with such maturity, energy and expertise, to such a sensitive life-challenge.

Chapter Ninety-Nine

Love and Remembrance

It was August 10, 1983, and my family and I were just settling into our temporary apartment in Efrat. There were no telephones yet. The electricity tended to shut down every few hours and everything was rather primitive, though promising.

One day, a young Israeli woman whom I recognized as Naomi (not her real name) who had moved in shortly before us, appeared at our doorway. "Excuse me Rabbi, but I have a sensitive *shayla* [halakhic question] to ask you, and I hope it's all right to do so," she began, somewhat shyly and clearly ill at ease.

The question that unfolded was unique to the Israeli experience, one I had not encountered in my nineteen years at the Lincoln Square Synagogue pulpit. Naomi's first husband had been killed two years earlier in the Lebanon War. She was left with a baby girl, and had remarried several months before she came knocking at my door. "Tomorrow is the *azkara* [memorial service on the date of death] for my first husband at the cemetery where he is buried. We had a wonderful marriage and were blessed with a daughter. I'm now remarried and I love my present husband very much. Would it be disrespectful to him if I attended the memorial ceremony for my first husband?"

Certainly the issue was an extraordinarily complex one. Nevertheless, I explained to the woman that a new relationship, as good as it may be, did not obliterate the relationship that had been. This was especially true if her first marriage had borne the fruit of a daughter. I advised her to attend the *azkara*. Not an hour later, a young man whom I recognized as Naomi's present husband rang my doorbell. My heart immediately sank. Was he upset at my decision? Had I advised too quickly about a situation, which was not in the orbit of my personal experience, and about which there was no clear halakhic ruling?

When he began to ask his question, however, it became clear to me that he knew nothing of his wife's visit. As if I were totally oblivious of this previous history, he told me the story of the impending *azkara*. "I never really knew my wife's former husband. But he loved and nurtured a woman whom I now love; he gave his life for my country, and I have the privilege of rearing and loving his daughter. Rabbi, do you think it would be proper for me to honor him by attending the memorial service?"

After ascertaining that the deceased soldier's parents had attended their daughter-in-law's second wedding, and therefore would, most likely, be accepting of his presence, I confirmed that he could fulfill his desire to pay tribute to his wife's former husband and brushed aside my own tears of sadness and unworthiness before two individuals who were able to express such awesome sensitivity in the midst of tragedy and renewal.

Chapter One Hundred

Responsibility of Love

It was the wedding of Sivan Sagi to Elkana Harel. Both of them were "children" of the city of Efrat, one of the many second-generation couples who were *Efratim* marrying *Efratot*.

It was certainly a magnificent occasion – except for the fact that just a few years earlier, Sivan's father, Yair, had tragically died of cancer, a very young man at the height of his powers of intellect and *ḥesed*. He had been in charge of the student residences at the Hebrew University, where he had initiated and shepherded the PERAH program of Hebrew University, in which student volunteers helped underprivileged and troubled Jerusalem youngsters. His loss affected all of Efrat deeply, but especially his wife Raḥel, a very popular kindergarten teacher, and their young orphaned children.

I blessed Sivan at the *badeken* ceremony, in which the groom covers his bride's face with a veil and the father of the bride generally blesses his daughter. As I intoned the blessings, Raḥel burst out into uncontrollable weeping, which continued even as she walked her daughter to the nuptial canopy.

Suddenly and spontaneously, right before the ceremony was about to begin, Sivan's younger sister, barely a bat mitzva, took the microphone. She congratulated her sister and spoke of the great joy of the occasion of the wedding.

She then turned to her mother, urging her not to be sad but to be happy, insisting that her father was also joyous and participating in the wedding from his place in heaven.

Raḥel dried her eyes, took the microphone from her daughter, and without missing a beat, beautifully began to sing words from *Hallel*, psalms of praise to God:

> "You are my God and I shall praise You,
> My Lord and I shall exalt You.
> Give thanks to the Lord for He is good,
> His mercy endures forever."

The ceremony was ready to begin. Raḥel had taught her children the most profound message of love and life they could ever have learned.

Afterword

Open Your Eyes

It was 1980, and the summer of our daughter Elana's bat mitzva. We were still living in Manhattan, planning for our *aliya* to Efrat a few years hence, and I was serving as a scholar-in-residence at Kibbutz Ein Tzurim. We were going to have a Shabbat celebration for Elana at Lincoln Square Synagogue that fall – right after the High Holy Days – but on the day of the bat mitzva itself we had a party in the kibbutz. My parents-in-law came for the occasion. It was their first trip to Israel.

The kibbutz will never forget how my mother-in-law arrived with boxes and boxes of baked goods from New York, hardly realizing that she was bringing coals to Newcastle. We had a wonderful time showing off Israel – and what would in the future be Efrat – to "Poppi David and Poppi Charlotte" – who were with us almost every day in New York and were a most integral part of all of our lives. To my pleasant surprise, my in-laws seemed to react to this part of the tour with great excitement and even approval.

We arrived back in New York shortly before Rosh HaShana. My in-laws came home with us to help with our family's settling in, but immediately upon opening the door, my mother-in-law dived for the phone and called my mother. I remember the conversation by heart.

"Hello Rose – it's Charlotte. Yes, we're all home, safe and sound. But Rose, I should pay the travel agent double. It was the most worthwhile trip I ever made in my life. The highlight was what they call 'Efrat.' Rose, we have nothing to worry about. They took us to this empty mountaintop – at the end of the world, turn right – pretty enough in terms of scenic views, but with barely any vegetation and without a living soul. Your son and my daughter looked pleased as punch, as if they were showing off Switzerland, Paris, New York all rolled into one.

"Then your son starts the tour. He points to one empty hill, and he says, 'There is the synagogue'; to another barren peak, and he says, 'There is the school campus'; to another undeveloped flatland, 'Here are the first fifty cottages…'

"Rose, we have nothing to worry about. Not only won't there be an Efrat for them to move into in our lifetime, there won't be an Efrat for them to move into in *their* lifetime, or their children's lifetimes either. In the meantime, they're living in a Peter Pan, Alice in Wonderland dream world. I should pay my travel agent double his usual fee. It was the most worthwhile trip I ever took in my life…We have nothing to worry about; believe me, if they're banking on Efrat, they're staying in Manhattan!"

Nevertheless, on the tenth day of Menaḥem Av, 5743, we moved into Efrat, very much on schedule.

I had listened to my beloved mother-in-law with a smile in my heart. She now very happily and energetically lives with us in Efrat, where she helps my wife almost every day in their charity-thrift shop and is the most popular member of her large and constantly growing Senior Citizens Group (She calls it her *gan* – kindergarten).

In fact, at the beginning of the second intifada (when guns and not mere stones were used by the Palestinians) we sat down to our Friday evening Shabbat meal to the unmistakable sound of gunshots in the distance. We were about twenty people around the table, my wife and I sitting next to each other at its head. By this time, not only were we living in Efrat, but so were our parents and in-laws. My wife whispered to me not to make reference to the gunshots: "Perhaps my mother will think they're firecrackers," she said.

As if on cue, my mother-in-law rose from her place and looked directly at me accusingly: "Beloved son-in-law, is this your idea of a mother-in-law joke? You bring me to Israel to be shot by the Palestinians?"

She then turned to the assemblage – with a twinkle in her eyes. "Our children saved us, rescued us from a lonely old age. They packed us up and they brought us to Israel, to Efrat; they brought us home. And no matter the danger, this is the only place we ought to be; this is the only place we want to be!"

At the time of this writing, we have populated seven hills of Efrat with more than eleven thousand residents and twenty-eight synagogues – and we are still growing. Ohr Torah Stone Institutions numbers three thousand students in nine campuses with eleven educational institutions, ranging from junior and high schools, a rabbinic and teachers' seminary, a women's college, and graduate school, and specialized social service programs. Our hundreds of rabbinical and educational graduates spread Torah throughout the world.

My mother-in-law now walks the streets of Efrat, where she lives in a thriving city called home to her twenty-two grandchildren and great-grandchildren. My father-in-law and parents spent the happiest and most fulfilled period in their lives in Efrat, before they died, and their eternal resting place is the Gush Etzion cemetery.

The final message of these stories, the most important legacy I can leave to my beloved grandchildren, is: Never stop dreaming. But dream while you're awake, not only when you're sleeping. And make sure that your dream has a plan of action, which makes its realization a possibility. Most importantly, link your dream to the dream of "Yisrael Saba" – Grandfather Israel, to the dream of "Knesset Yisrael" – the eternal, historic House of Israel.

Let your dream be a ladder connecting heaven and earth, a connection between spirit and matter, which sanctifies every aspect of the physical world we inhabit.

Link your dream to God's dream, to God's goal for humanity. Work to perfect this world so that the Divinity will feel comfortable in every corner of creation. Don't pray to God to make your lives easy; pray rather that you gain the inner strength, courage and faith to be one of God's instruments to help further His plan of *tikkun olam*.

Make your ultimate vision the vision of the prophets, and use the laws of our Torah to guide your program of action for its realization.

Remember that you may not complete the process, but you must assume a share in its development. Not everyone who dreams sees their dream fulfilled, but if you do not have a dream, it surely will not be fulfilled. And, sometimes, if God truly wills it and you listen to His subtle messages, the fulfillment of the dream may be greater than the dream itself. I like to think that if you believe in a God who is invisible you will have the inner vision to dream the impossible; only those who dare dream the impossible have a chance at achieving the incredible…

I know that many say that seeing is believing; it seems to me that believing is seeing.

וְתֶחֱזֶינָה עֵינֵינוּ בְּשׁוּבְךָ לְצִיּוֹן

May God only open our eyes to see His return to Zion.

About the Author

Rabbi Shlomo Riskin resides in the city of Efrat, Israel, where he serves in the capacity of Chief Rabbi, and also as Chancellor of Ohr Torah Stone Colleges and Graduate Programs. He is the founding rabbi of Lincoln Square Synagogue in New York.

The institutions under his aegis include a broad network of high schools and university programs, a major rabbinical seminary, and a center for training women as Torah leaders.

His published works include: *Women and Jewish Divorce, A Haggadah Happening, Around the Family Table* and the *Torah Lights* series of biblical commentaries to *Bereshit, Shemot* and *Vayikra*.

Rabbi Riskin is a widely respected spokesman for the State of Israel and Modern Orthodoxy.

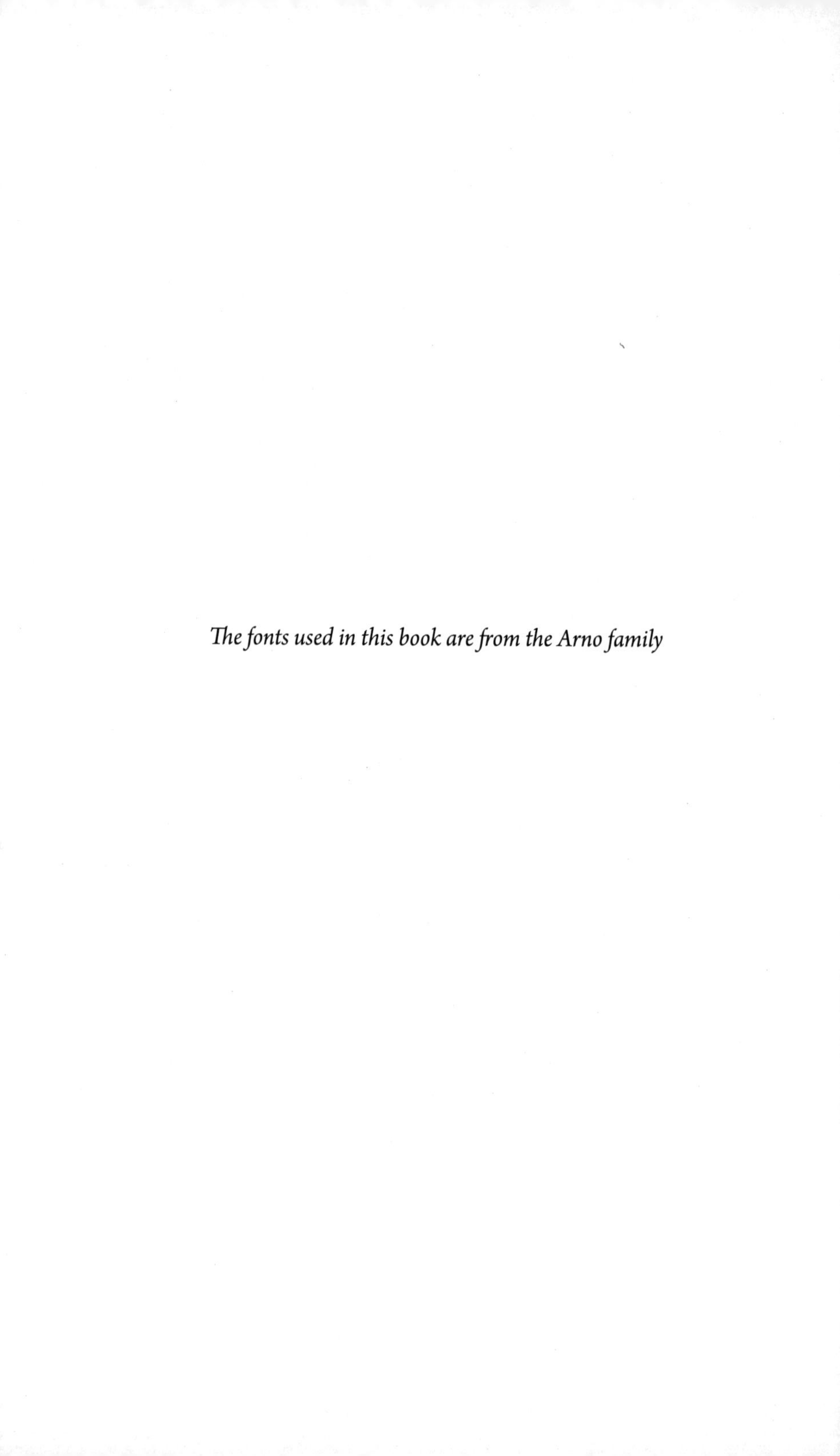

The fonts used in this book are from the Arno family

Other works by Shlomo Riskin
available from Maggid

The TORAH LIGHTS *Series – A Biblical Commentary*

Bereshit: Confronting Life, Love & Family

Shemot: Defining a Nation

Vayikra: Sacrifice, Sanctity & Silence

Yad L'Isha [*Hebrew*]

Siaḥ Shulḥan [*Hebrew*]

Maggid Books
The best of contemporary Jewish thought from
Koren Publishers Jerusalem